Silent Invaders

Pesticides, livelihoods and women's health

Edited by Miriam Jacobs and Barbara Dinham

ZED BOOKS
London & New York

in association with

PESTICIDE
ACTION
NETWORK *UK*

Silent Invaders was first published in 2003 by
Zed Books Ltd, 7 Cynthia Street, London N1 9JF, UK,
and Room 400, 175 Fifth Avenue, New York, NY 10010, USA
www.zedbooks.demon.co.uk

in association with

Pesticide Action Network, UK, Eurolink Centre,
49 Effra Road, London SW2 1BZ

Designed and typeset in Sabon by Illuminati, Grosmont
Cover designed by Andrew Corbett
Printed and bound in the United Kingdom by Biddles Ltd,
www.biddles.co.uk

Distributed in the USA exclusively by Palgrave, a division of
St Martin's Press, LLC, 175 Fifth Avenue, New York, NY 10010

A catalogue record for this book is available from the British Library

Library of Congress Cataloging-in-Publication Data available

ISBN 1 85649 995 2 (Hb)
ISBN 1 85649 996 0 (Pb)

Contents

Acknowledgements

Every book has a host of people standing behind the volume that stands on the shelf. This book is the result of their collaboration and support. We thank the authors of the papers in this volume and also all those who submitted papers. We would have liked to include more but that would have doubled the size of the book. We very much appreciated the guidance of all those who reviewed the papers. A few papers have appeared elsewhere, and we are grateful for the permission of the organizations and publishers to include them here. Andrew Chetley helped greatly with editorial assistance. Robert Molteno of Zed Books believed in the project from the start and was, as ever, patient and encouraging. We owe a special thanks to Novib, the Dutch member of the Oxfam family, whose funds helped us to establish the importance of seeing pesticide problems through 'gendered' eyes: the initiative would not have taken place without their input. There are many others – particularly the families and work colleagues of the editors – who have provided input and encouraged the project over the three years it has taken to bring this to press, and we thank you all.

Foreword

Rt. Hon. Clare Short MP
Secretary of State for International Development

We know that women in developing countries, and particularly those in rural areas, bear an immense workload, with responsibilities as earners and carers, and for bringing food to the table. Understanding the role of women in food and agriculture, and how environment and development strategies affect their lives and livelihoods, is central to progress in eliminating poverty.

We also know that over the last half-century, agriculture has been transformed through the intensive use of agrochemicals. The inputs have helped to increase food production, but the cost has been high – unacceptable health and environmental damage. The problem is particularly acute in developing countries, where poverty, meagre resources, lack of information and inadequate regulatory capacity make it near to impossible to use hazardous chemicals safely. In practice, unrestricted use of most pesticides has brought dangers to individual users, communities and their environment.

Development is a complex process and in trying to promote it governments face perhaps the greatest challenge of the twenty-first century – bridging the gap between rich and poor nations and enhancing the life opportunities of the poor in developing countries. In my first days in office I signalled the commitment of the British government to work with others systematically to reduce and then eliminate extreme poverty, and to ensure that the fight against hunger, conflict and disease receive the highest priority in our overseas development effort.

A thorough understanding of these realities on the ground is essential for policymakers if they are to establish the right development approaches and priorities. They need to be alert to policies that work and be willing to support innovative, effective strategies with the women and men whose lives they are seeking to improve.

Investment in agriculture has been neglected for decades. One consequence has been a growing gap between the rich and poor in both urban and rural areas. This is an important book because it is based on direct experience which demonstrates the need to promote well-targeted agricultural development, and to build capacity by giving high priority to information, knowledge and training.

The stories from all continents in *Silent Invaders* reveal the urgent need to support strategies for food and agriculture that take full account of the different roles and responsibilities of women and men. Policies need to address the difficult conditions in which poor rural communities live and work. By strengthening participation in developing the tools for improving agricultural production sustainably, development policies strengthen the organizational capacity of rural groups, and enable them to demand the support and services that are essential to improve their well-being.

The British government takes food safety and environmentally sustainable agriculture seriously. At home we have set up a combined department covering environment, food and rural affairs (DEFRA). My own ministry, the Department for International Development (DFID) has pioneered a vision of sustainable rural livelihoods. We are committed to increasing the focus on rural poverty and strategies for agriculture and trade in agricultural products that support this crucial development sector from a pro-poor perspective.

Happily, there have been some recent international initiatives to control the effects of hazardous chemicals, which will help all governments eliminate the most hazardous of them and help developing countries, in particular, to protect their own populations. The British government supported the development of the 1998 Rotterdam Convention on Prior Informed Consent in Trade in Hazardous Chemicals and the 2001 Stockholm Convention on Persistent Organic Pollutants. We are preparing to ratify both Conventions, and have provided financial support to help implement the treaties. We support other relevant international initiatives, such as the new International Treaty on Plant Genetic Resources for Food and Agriculture, and we are working for improved standards set by a new International Code of Conduct on the Distribution and Use of Pesticides.

These international processes may appear to be remote from experience on the ground, on which this book is based, but they play a key role in development and protecting the environment, and help to build important regulatory capacity and infrastructure in developing countries. The next step in their implementation is to make sure they support the field-level initiatives that have the greatest impact on the role of the rural poor, and of women in particular.

This book helps make women's part in agriculture visible. It reminds policymakers and researchers of the importance of documenting the experiences of both women and men. It also reminds us firmly that pesticides can act differently on women and men because of their physiological differences – an important reason for taking caution and supporting successful, safe and sustainable initiatives.

Silent Invaders provides important insights into the experience of poor rural communities. It will be valuable to governments, development agencies, and research and other institutions drawing up development initiatives which must take account of the realities of people's everyday lives and be firmly rooted in the direct experience of the poor. This book will help ensure that the development policies they promote are relevant, effective and on target.

1

Introduction:
the failure to protect women from pesticides

Marion Moses

> There is a crime here that goes beyond denunciation. There is a sorrow here that weeping cannot symbolize. There is a failure here that topples all our success.
>
> John Steinbeck, *The Grapes of Wrath*

> It has always seemed to me that those who are without power, who have to create their own in a makeshift way, know more about life than those who govern.
>
> John Berger, interview, 2002

Are attempts to 'do something about pesticides' inherently doomed? These legal toxic products continue to elude comprehensive labelling, and strict controls on human, wildlife and environmental contamination. How did we allow a toxic infrastructure of unsustainable farming practices that imperil the health of workers, consumers and the environment to become so ubiquitous, entrenched and resistant to change? Why are the voices of public health advocates and environmentalists muted in the cacophony of those who profit from the sale and use of these toxic products? Why does public perception of health impacts and environmental degradation from pesticides lag behind that of other toxics? Does the scientific community adequately address human health risks of pesticide exposure?

Silent Invaders addresses these questions by focusing on a population that is unheard, understudied and unlistened-to – women. *Vive la différence* may be fairly well understood in human social, psychological and behavioural terms. But the toxic impact of pesticides on women's health is only now emerging from decades of scientific and regulatory neglect. This book includes scientific studies of gender impacts of pesticides, and, importantly, voices of women themselves, and the demands of advocates for change. The challenges facing toxicology and epidemiology, the major disciplines in risk assessment, are a major focus, including the emerging field of endocrine disruptors.

Past failures to address low-level chronic exposures and potential additive and synergistic effects of multiple exposures is especially troubling in the case of pesticides. Billions of kilograms of these toxic chemicals are deliberately added to the global environment every year. Over 1,000 active ingredient chemicals and 1,200 other ingredients (inerts) are formulated into thousands of different pesticide products used throughout the world. Pesticide contamination is ubiquitous, affecting air, water, soil, food, domestic animals, wildlife, pets, humans, breast milk, even the developing fetus.

Most human pesticide exposures are involuntary, unknowing, and unwilling. Other legal toxic products, such as alcohol and tobacco, are voluntarily consumed. Their adverse health effects are well known, documented, acknowledged, and warned against. They are strongly regulated in many countries. Pesticides have a different history. There are several reasons for their special exemptions and exceptions, especially in the early days of lenient regulation and lax enforcement.

When DDT came onto the market in 1945, it was promoted as 'a boon to all mankind' (1946 advertisement in *Time* magazine). The World Health Organization was so impressed with DDT's effect on the anopheles mosquito that it even thought (incorrectly) that it could eliminate malaria by 1955. The first organophosphate (nerve gas type) insecticide, parathion, and the phenoxy herbicides 2,4-D and 2,4,5-T (constituents of Agent Orange), came onto the market in the 1940s. Farmers saw insects and weeds, pests that had been plagues for known human history, succumb to these miracle chemicals.

Chemical control supplanted biocontrol and other pest management methods in university studies in entomology and agronomy for decades to come. Research topics centred on what pesticide to use, in what amount, and for which pests. This is not surprising, since agricultural chemical companies were the major funders.

Two major problems were soon apparent – resistance and secondary outbreaks. Not all pests were killed by the potent biocides. A very small number of 'super-pest' survivors resistant to the chemicals passed their resistance on to future generations. Larger amounts and increasingly toxic combinations were needed to combat resistance. Over time many pests could no longer be controlled at all, and the search began for the next generation of pesticides.

Another problem was the broad spectrum of pesticide activity. They not only killed the 'bad' insects, but also their natural predators, the 'good' ones. Insects that had previously been kept under control by natural predators became major pests themselves, resulting in severe secondary outbreaks requiring even more pesticides to control. The more pesticides were used, the more were needed, and use skyrocketed. This led to what the late biocontrol expert Robert Van Den Bosch called *The Pesticide Treadmill* [1].

Concerns about the human health costs were countered by assertions that mass starvation and untold deaths from disease would result if practices were changed. The important value was agricultural production. In legislatures throughout the world, an essentially self-regulated agricultural chemical industry, in collusion with agribusiness and departments of agriculture, was dominant. The toxic infrastructure, and the unecological monoculture that both fed and resulted from it, continued to expand. Benefits were extolled, potential health and environmental costs ignored.

Then, in 1962, the pesticide industry was placed on the defensive for the first time. Rachel Carson's *Silent Spring* [2] challenged the conventional wisdom, with her description of the unseen, potentially devastating ecological effects of DDT and related persistent pesticides she called 'elixirs of death'. She raised public awareness of the interdependence of all life-systems, and was a birth mother of the environmental movement. Fallout from the book jolted legislators out of their torpor, and provided grist to the environmentalist mill that grinds to this day.

The 1970s saw the first attempts to fix the more egregious deficiencies in pesticide law. In the USA, where the Environmental Protection Agency was created in 1970, the use of all currently registered products (there were 70,000 at the time; there are now 20,000) was allowed pending future evaluation. Thousands of products in scientific limbo remained on the market while lengthy and litigious testing was done or redone.

As newly required animal testing data came in, evidence of carcinogenicity, teratogenicity, mutagenicity and other reproductive, neurological and chronic disease risks accrued. The rhetoric began to change. Environmentalists and public health advocates, proven correct in their alarm, demanded stricter controls based on potential human health impacts. They vigorously lobbied for major changes in pesticide laws. The pesticide industry countered with their usual practice of downplaying the hazards and trivializing the risks of exposure to their products.

A 'risk assessment' ritual language emerged with predictable and stereotypical views enshrined in such expressions as 'the dose makes the poison', 'sound science', 'safety factors', and 'the precautionary principle', among others. Differing views become flashpoints, reflecting the powerful defensive posture of industry to protect its products, and the efforts of public health and environmental advocates to restrict, control, or even ban them.

Pesticide medicine focused on educating health care providers to recognize and manage acute poisoning, considered to be the major health problem. The inherent toxicity of the more hazardous products was clearly contributory to most poisonings and fatalities. But the underlying cause was usually attributed to failure to follow label directions, or to use proper protective clothing or equipment (except for suicides). That many pesticides could not be used safely under usual conditions of agricultural practice was ignored or denied.

The conventional wisdom was that poisonings were preventable with training and proper use according to label directions; that mitigation of overexposure was attainable with protective clothing and equipment. Ignored were field conditions that would have caused heat stress/stroke if the workers actually wore the prescribed equipment. Also ignored were the conditions under which these toxic chemicals were stored, transported, used and disposed of. Most workers who mix and apply pesticides are illiterate, or have low reading skills. Even if they could read, labels are usually not in their native language.

For most workers, even a simple change of clothes is not available; masks and protective clothing are unheard-of, or unaffordable. Masks may be provided without filters, or one filter given out for an entire season of spraying (mask filters must be changed daily, or even more frequently, depending on conditions of use). The same pair of overalls may be worn all season and never washed. Electricity is not available in many areas; washing machines are unheard-of luxuries.

Acute poisoning, while devastating, is only one major pesticide-related health problem. As *Silent Invaders* documents, chronic effects is the other side of the equation. Long-term low-level exposures that do not cause acute illness are linked to chronic diseases, cancer in children and adults, adverse reproductive outcomes, Parkinson's and other neurological diseases, among others.

In some parts of the world, women make up 85 per cent or more of pesticide applicators on commercial farms and plantations. They work while pregnant and breastfeeding. Even when not directly handling pesticides, women in agricultural areas all over the world, live, work and raise their children in a toxic environment. We read their stories in this volume and realize that something is terribly wrong with the commerce in, and regulation of, pesticides.

References

1 Van Den Bosch, Robert. *The Pesticide Treadmill*, Berkeley, Calif.: University of California Press, 1977.
2 Carson, Rachel. *Silent Spring*, Boston, Mass.: Houghton Mifflin, 1962.

Part I

Pesticides versus people

2

Introduction to Part I

Barbara Dinham

Poverty is endemic in rural areas of developing countries. The income gap between urban and rural areas is increasing, and investment in agriculture has been stagnant for decades [1].[1] Women are often the poorest in rural societies. Against a background of poverty, many women and men farmers and agricultural workers use hazardous pesticides in risky and unsafe conditions. Chemicals are often promoted uncritically as essential for agricultural production, without consideration of more appropriate alternatives under the conditions of use, and without the advice, training and safety factors critical to protect health and the environment. More pesticides than ever are available in developing countries, and, with constraints on income, farmers will buy cheap products that are often older, more acutely toxic or adulterated.

The real effects of pesticides in these circumstances are not easily mapped. Acute effects are easier to observe, but even so may be confused with common illnesses. Limited access to medical care means that incidents are recorded mainly when a large number of deaths occur. Complex chronic effects – cancer, reproductive disorders, birth defects, effects on the immune system – are far more difficult to trace. There is some evidence that exposure to organophosphate pesticides damages the body's immune system. Environmental monitoring to identify water pollution, impacts on pollinators and beneficial predators, or effects on biodiversity is rare to nonexistent in most developing countries. Inappropriate pesticide use can lead to problems, such as insect pest resistance, that affect household income and local livelihoods and create the opposite effect to their intended purpose of increasing production.

The health, environmental and economic effects may impinge on women and men in different ways. Studies undertaken rarely look at the different pesticide impacts on the lives of both women and men, and almost no gender-disaggregated data are available to technicians, planners and policymakers in the field of agriculture and development, leaving policies and strategies to be formed on the basis of false or flimsy assumptions.

Women produce between 60 and 80 per cent of the food in developing countries [2]. In many African countries women undertake 90 per cent of hoeing and weeding and 60 per cent of harvesting and marketing activities. As a result of AIDS and migration (which draws more men than women to cities) there has been a rapid increase in women heads of household in rural areas; the proportion has reached 31 per cent in sub-Saharan Africa, 17 per cent in Latin America and the Caribbean, and 14 per cent in Asia. Income in women-headed households is lower than in those headed by men.

The exposure of women to pesticides is often grossly underestimated. Trainers, researchers and policymakers frequently assume that 'men spray pesticides', and women will be less exposed. Even in cultures where men are primarily responsible for spraying, women are exposed in many ways: through spray drift while working in the fields, harvesting crops within unsafe spray intervals, or by washing work clothes. As Margaret Reeves and Lucy Rosas here report, in California – which has a unique reporting system for pesticide use and pesticide-related illness – 3,991 pesticide poisonings were recorded between 1991 and 1996, of which 28 per cent were women. Official statistics often indicate relatively low numbers of women working in agriculture, but the figures ignore unpaid agricultural tasks on family farms, and women's employment in the informal agricultural sector. In Latin America, women are being recruited into non-traditional export crops such as flowers, melons, pineapple, vegetables, and into fruit packing.

Until the end of the 1980s, many governments subsidized pesticides, and their use was encouraged through agricultural extension services, often following the World Bank's training and visit (T&V) approach. This approach has been criticized for delivering messages to farmers, rather than working in a more participatory way to encourage experimentation through Farmer Field School-based integrated pest management (IPM) or other agro-ecological strategies (see Part IV below). Agricultural extension commonly encouraged inputs of improved seeds, fertilizer and pesticides, with credit to enable certain farmers to adopt the approach. Under structural adjustment policies, pesticide subsidies were discouraged, but at the same time economic liberalization encourages privatization of the service, which will favour advice on purchased inputs rather than information and training [3]. As a result poor farmers will inevitably seek out the cheapest pesticides available, often also the more hazardous compounds. Lack of training creates misunderstandings, and farmers often 'experiment' by mixing different pesticides, or using available products on a wide range of 'pests', including those for which the chemical is inappropriate.

If extension services encouraged a certain style of agricultural production, they also largely ignored the contribution of women farmers. Both women and men need access to information and appropriate advice on pest-management strategies to maximize their income, and minimize their dependence on hazardous chemicals. Only 5 per cent of extension services have been addressed to women, and only 15 per cent of the world's extension agents are women [4]. Failure to prioritize recruitment of women to agricultural extension systems makes it at worst impossible, as in Niger, and at best difficult, for women in many African communities to communicate their agricultural needs and their experience. In Senegal, rural services for women focus on stereotyped women's activities, such as health care or food processing, rather than socio-economic development.

Chapters in this section provide insight into the range of impacts of pesticides on women and men – whether small-scale farmers, tenant farmers, or those employed on larger farms and estates. Many in rural societies live with daily hazards and no real information or training to avoid the effects on their health or their local environment. Pesticides must be used with care, but in poor societies many factors make safety impossible. These include:

- lack of training in pesticide use, and ignorance about potential dangers to health and the environment;
- poor literacy, which makes it impossible to read or follow complex label instructions;
- inappropriate application methods and poor or faulty application equipment;
- poor regulation and easy availability of hazardous pesticides, including sales by untrained dealers;
- lack of personal protective equipment (boots, gloves, glasses), which are costly and not adapted to a tropical climate,

- lack of suitable washing facilities for humans, clothes and used containers;
- demand for containers, leading to reuse of poorly cleaned pesticide bottles, barrels or cans;
- poor household storage and disposal of unused mixtures and containers;
- lack of health centres, medical facilities, antidotes and poison treatment centres, as well as confusion of symptoms of pesticide poisoning with common illnesses.

These factors mean the risks from pesticides in developing countries are considerably higher than in industrialized countries; nevertheless, pesticide problems also occur in rich countries. In both parts of the world the rural voice is weak and lacks influence on government policy. Among the farm workers of California, 62 per cent live in poverty and the income for women is substantially lower than for men, some earning only half a man's wages. Many of the workers are migrants, and, in addition to language limitations, they are vulnerable to threats from their employers if they complain about working conditions.

Pesticides are tested in laboratories for carcinogenic and chronic effects before being placed on the market. But it is virtually impossible to link chronic effects to active ingredient exposure. Catharina Wesseling shows the methodological challenge of documenting health risks in developing countries, where exposure ranges from a single excessive dose to long-term repeated low doses, and exposure to multiple pesticides. Two of the chapers draw attention to the dangers: in the USA and Latin America studies have found increases in cancer among farmers and farm workers. But there is a lack of data to indicate differential impacts on women and men – most studies of infertility among agricultural workers, for example, focus on reduced sperm counts in men. It is important to increase awareness about gender-differentiated impacts: increased birth defects; elevated risks of spontaneous abortions and other reproductive problems; breast and cervical cancers, or penile cancer; and the potential gender-related effects of hormone-disrupting pesticides. Along with awareness, however, a precautionary approach and available alternatives are essential to reduce exposure at all levels.

The four studies from Africa – Zimbabwe, Niger, Benin and Senegal – demonstrate the many ways in which women are exposed to pesticides. Women are often fully involved in cash crop production either in their own fields, or – in a common sexual division of labour – through responsibility for weeding, plant health and harvesting. Women deliver household food security, but lack access to resources and training. With pesticide exposure in the field, responsibility for washing work clothes and cleaning pesticide containers for storage, women are both active and passive victims of pesticide use, and it is likely they are exposed to pesticides at least to the same extent as men.

The crushing effects of HIV/AIDS in Africa is graphically set out by Sam Page, who points to the devastating consequences of not acting immediately to support rural women. In Niger, women use pesticides on many crops, and in areas near the city there is little difference in the percentage of women and men using pesticides. In more remote areas, while more men than women use pesticides, women overwhelmingly buy cheaper products, which are more accessible through village traders. Women have significantly less information about the hazards than do men.

Women in Benin generally rely on husbands or male relatives for pesticide supplies – unless they can make purchases on the black market. But women have less time to spray pesticides, and poorer quality spray equipment or none at all, which means improvising with the use of straw tufts. Women must take babies and young children to the field, and babies are contaminated by spray drift or breastfeeding as their mother's skin retains pesticide residues.

The cotton sector in Benin, which accounts for 80 per cent of national pesticide use, has been racked with death and ill-health following a switch from pyrethroid pesticides to the more acutely toxic endosulfan. Children and young men were the main victims of fatalities, and women are left with increased responsibility as breadwinner, to run the farm and bring up children. This pattern reached tragic proportions with the enormous increase in suicides in the late 1990s in Andhra Pradesh, India, following insect resistance to pesticides, low cotton prices and escalating debt.

In Asia the almost universal staple food is rice, and in Southeast Asia women provide up to 90 per cent of labour for rice cultivation [5]. Women's contribution to agriculture is often ignored. Nasira Habib draws attention to the gender bias among policymakers in Pakistan, which leads to social and economic discrimination and ignores women's contribution to the agricultural economy. One quarter of all farms in Pakistan use pesticides, and women help mix highly toxic products – the time of maximum exposure – clear away after use, wash clothes, weed and thin crops and take food to men in the fields. Many are employed picking cotton. Women form the backbone of the rural economy in Pakistan, yet the National Agricultural Policy makes no mention of women in its goals. Women have no land rights, and no control over the family income.

In India, women's role in agriculture is acknowledged to a greater extent than in neighbouring Pakistan. Women work as labourers in their own and others' fields, but have no control over the products they use. Pesticide use is among the highest in the world; Daisy Dharmaraj and Sheila Jayaprakash characterize India's love affair with pesticides as an addiction. Women have almost no information about the extremely hazardous pesticides they use, and only around one-quarter of the women interviewed knew that pesticides were harmful. Yet three-quarters of the women suffered vomiting, respiratory problems, fatigue, skin and eye irritations and many had lost consciousness. Medical facilities are beyond reach, in terms of distance and money.

This section unpeels assumptions and shows how rural communities, which are often politically marginalized, need policies and practices that will reduce their exposure to hazards. Gender-aware strategies are needed that will increase agricultural productivity without undermining the health and strength of the women and men who struggle to keep rural economies afloat and provide basic food security for the poorest communities in the world. Vulnerable groups – children, poor women and men – are exposed to highly hazardous pesticides. These include not only acutely toxic pesticides but also those that may cause chronic effects or disrupt hormonal systems. Farmers need tools to sustain and increase productivity, but these must address long-term economic and environmental sustainability. The different and distinct impacts on, and needs of, women and men must be better understood and documented. The role of women in agriculture must be made more visible. Precautionary approaches need to be prioritized, which take seriously the health and environmental consequences to women, men and children of regular exposure to toxic substances.

References

1 'Better livelihoods for the poor: the role of agriculture', London: Department for International Development, 2002, p. 9.
2 Food and Agriculture Organization of the UN (FAO), Women and

Sustainable Food Security, Women and Sustainable Development Service, FAO, www.fao.org/FOCUS/E/Women/Sustin-e.htm

3 UN General Assembly, 'Improvement of the situation of women in rural areas', Report of the Secretary-General, Advancement of Women, A/56/268, 7 August 2001.

4 www.fao.org.

5 www.fao.org/gender/en/agrib4–e.htm; www.fao.org/sd/fsdirect/fbdirect/FSP001.htm.

3

'Nobody told me they were harmful': pesticide exposure and the health of women farm workers

Margaret Reeves and Lucy Rosas

Farm workers on the frontline of exposure to toxic pesticides

An estimated 2.5 million farm workers are employed in US agricultural fields in one of the most hazardous occupations [1]. In addition to long work days and physical injuries, farm workers are directly exposed to toxic pesticides – by mixing or applying pesticides during planting, weeding, thinning and harvesting crops; and during post harvest processing and packaging. Pesticide-related illnesses can occur even when pesticides are legally applied using regulated application methods with presumably adequate protection and washing facilities [2]. Farm workers may unknowingly enter fields in which toxic residues remain on the crops and soil. Airborne drift of pesticides away from the application site exposes thousands to toxic poisons every day, often without their knowledge.

Within the economically and politically marginalized farm worker population, poverty and poor housing, diet and working conditions magnify the problems created when working with pesticides. About 79 per cent of the migrant and seasonal farm worker population in the US are Hispanic – the vast majority of Mexican origin. At least 800,000 farm workers lack adequate shelter and washing facilities. Many live in their cars; others live in groups of 10 to 12 in trailers, garages, tool sheds, converted barns, caves, tents or hotel rooms [3,4]; and 62 per cent live in poverty. The situation is substantially worse for women. The median annual income for women is $2,500 to $5,000, whereas for men the figure is $5,000 to $7,500 [5].

These factors make safe handling of even moderately hazardous chemicals difficult if not impossible. Although most farm workers are regularly exposed to toxic pesticides, few studies have assessed the impacts of pesticides on farm worker men. Even fewer have looked at women, despite the fact that farm worker women make up at least 19 per cent of the US workforce [6]. In crops such as cut flowers, women may account for 50 per cent of the workforce, and up to 80 per cent of workers tipping (thinning) grapes.

Health effects of pesticide exposure in women and men may be different in important ways. Women on average have lower body weight and a higher proportion of body fat than men. Women's breast tissue has been associated with significant accumulation of fat-associated pesticides such as DDT. When women breastfeed, these pesticides (or their breakdown products) may be passed on to nursing infants. In addition, effects of certain pesticides on human hormones may affect women and men differently and can have negative impacts on developing fetuses.

The Organización en California de Líderes Campesinas (Farm Worker Women's Leadership Network) and Pesticide Action Network (PAN) North America have reviewed data on pesticide-related illnesses and compiled personal stories to document related health

---

Box 3.1 Large-scale pesticide poisonings are common

Despite federal and state laws aimed at protecting farm workers, they continue to be victims of pesticide poisoning. In July 1998, 30 farm workers near Firebaugh, California, were rushed to a nearby clinic following exposure to the toxic pesticide carbofuran used on cotton [7, 8]. They had entered a field only two hours after pesticide application, in violation of the required 48-hour restricted entry interval. Their employer had failed to provide required field posting and oral notification of the application.

In November 1999 mist from a sprinkler application of the carcinogenic soil fumigant metam sodium blew into the town of Earlimart, California, forcing 150 people, nearly all farm workers, to evacuate their homes and sending 29 people to hospitals. Victims complained of nausea, vomiting, headaches, burning eyes and shortness of breath [9]. Josefina Murgia, 38 and the mother of three, received a $6,000 bill for her trip to the hospital. 'I don't have that type of money', she said. 'Paying the bill would mean my family would go hungry.' County agriculture officials said it appeared the company followed county regulations in applying the pesticide [10].

problems faced by farm worker women. For acute poisonings the project relies heavily on California data since it is the only US state with a fully financed, mandatory full reporting system for occupational pesticide-related illnesses. Armed with information about the day-to-day dangers of pesticide exposure, farm worker women and their advocates will be better equipped to demand appropriate responses from employers, health care practitioners, and government regulators.

Agricultural pesticides and women's poisonings in California

Since 1990, California Environmental Protection Agency's Department of Pesticide Regulation (DPR) has managed the state's unique reporting systems for both pesticide use and pesticide-related illnesses. These two reporting systems, which have been discussed in detail elsewhere [11], are key elements of the state's regulatory programme, considered the most extensive in the world. The purpose is to protect workers by tracking use and identifying problem areas in order to guide development and implementation of appropriate regulations for pesticide use and worker safety. Despite these efforts, both pesticide use and pesticide-related illnesses continue unabated in California.

Table 3.1 Reported use of toxic pesticides in California, 1991–95

Pesticide category	Change 1991–95 (million kg/year)	Increase (%)
Restricted-use pesticides	21.8	33
Acute systemic toxins[a]	13.6	–
Carcinogens	10.6	129
Reproductive toxins	8.2	–
Endocrine disruptors	6.9	17
Nerve toxins[b]	3.0	21
Total reported pesticide use[c]	94.7	30

[a] Defined by the US EPA as Category I acute systemic toxins.
[b] Defined by the US EPA as Category II nerve toxins.
[c] Uses include: production agriculture, post-harvest treatment, structural pest control, and landscape.

Source: Reference 12.

Pesticide use is on the rise

Contrary to popular opinion, pesticide use in production agriculture in California increased 30 per cent to more than 94 million kg of active ingredient from 1991 to 1995. During this period, use of the most toxic pesticides increased as well. This category includes cancer-causing pesticides, restricted-use pesticides, nerve toxins and endocrine disruptors, which increased by 129 per cent, 33 per cent, 21 per cent and 17 per cent, respectively (Table 3.1).

Women exposed to toxic pesticides in the field

Each year the DPR reports about 2,000 possible poisoning cases. From 1991 to 1996 this included 3,991 cases related to pesticide use in agriculture, of which 1,113 (28 per cent) were poisonings of women (Table 3.2). Among a total of 68 different crops listed, cotton, grapes and broccoli were associated with the greatest numbers of poisoning cases (Table 3.3), although 30 per cent of cases gave no associated crop. Some crops may therefore represent even greater risks than the data suggest. DPR data were also incomplete with respect to the pesticides responsible for poisonings. Cases frequently listed more than one possible poisoning agent. Of 246 compounds listed as possible poisoning agents during this period, 71 (29 per cent) appear on the PAN North America list of *most toxic* pesticides used in California – carcinogens, restricted-use pesticides, EPA's Category I acute nerve toxins, endocrine disruptors, developmental and reproductive toxins, and extremely toxic systemic poisons [12].

Table 3.2 Number of California cases of pesticide illness reported for women, 1991–96

Year	Total no. of agricultural cases	No. of agriculture cases for women	Women as % of total
1991	724	211	29
1992	725	186	26
1993	503	116	23
1994	557	161	29
1995	721	185	26
1996	761	254	33

Source: California Department of Pesticide Regulation 1999.

Table 3.3 Top ten crops for women's poisoning cases in California, 1991–96

Crop	No. of cases	Pesticide use, 1995 (million lb)
Grapes (all)	138	58.7
Cotton	125	17.7
Broccoli	114	1.3
Ornamentals	43	0.8[a]
Tomatoes	38	14.2
Oranges	36	9.9
Alfalfa	24	7.2[b]
Lettuce	21	3.9
Strawberries	21	7.1
Almonds	12	12.0

Notes
[a] Illness data were listed for 'ornamentals'. Pesticide use was reported for nursery and greenhouse products combined, but not separately for ornamentals.
[b] Illness data were listed for 'alfalfa'. Pesticide use was reported for 'hay', of which alfalfa is a subset.
Sources: Pesticide illness data from California Department of Pesticide Regulation 1999; Pesticide use data from reference 12.

Most pesticide poisonings occur when farm workers are doing field work, such as picking, field packing, weeding and irrigating. From 1991 to 1996 men's poisoning cases were mostly associated with drift (53.6 per cent) and field residues (22.4 per cent), while sources of women's exposure were more evenly distributed: drift (30.0 per cent), residues (23.8 per cent), ground application (11.2 per cent) and hand application (10.6 per cent). In almonds and strawberries, where ground application was an important source of pesticide poisoning, women accounted for 13 per cent and 37 per cent of reported poisonings respectively. In ornamental plants, women made up 63 per cent of the reported poisonings.

The tip of the iceberg: under-reporting is common

A US EPA estimate of 10,000–20,000 acute pesticide-related illnesses among agricultural workers each year in the United States is based on extrapolation of physician-reported cases in California [13]. It is likely that this is a serious underestimate however, since reporting requires that workers identify the problem and seek treatment; that physicians correctly diagnose and report the poisonings; and that the cases are properly investigated and reported by state authorities. According to a government report, US EPA has 'no capability to accurately determine national incidence or prevalence of pesticide illnesses that occur in the farm sector' [14,15]. Chronic, long-term effects are rarely documented [16].

There are several reasons for under-reporting of pesticide-related occupational illness. In mild or moderate cases, the symptoms are non-specific and may be confused with common illnesses including gastrointestinal problems, upper respiratory disease and other flu-like illnesses. Physicians are often not trained to recognize symptoms of pesticide poisoning and fail to consider possible occupational exposure when treating agricultural workers [17]. Physicians may also fail to test farm workers for pesticide exposure because they are unfamiliar with the few tests available. Other cases go unreported for lack of access to health care, since many farm workers work in areas chronically short of physicians and hospitals [18]. Even when services are available, employers do not provide most farm workers with health insurance benefits. Unionized farms offer their workers health insurance, but some only provide this during the cropping season.

Workers' Compensation is the system through which most on-farm illness reporting in the USA occurs (except on small family farms, where it may not be required) [19]. Unfortunately, most farm workers are unfamiliar with the system and do not understand that if they are injured or become ill on the job their employer is required, under section 170 of the Federal Insecticide, Fungicide and Rodenticide Act of 1947, to assure and pay for their transportation to a medical facility. Many farm workers speak only Spanish, which greatly limits their ability to navigate US laws and regulations. Employers may discourage reporting as a way to avoid increases in insurance premiums, medical fees or fines for violation of worker safety laws [20]. The threat of retaliation by an employer is very real, and farm workers may 'choose' to endure job-related illnesses rather than report them for fear of termination [21,22]. In decades of work with farm workers, we have heard repeatedly that complaints about work conditions will likely lead to the response, 'If you don't like it, leave. There are plenty of other workers waiting to take your job.' This threat is particularly real for undocumented workers who fear deportation.

Box 3.2 Carmen's Story

'Nobody told me what they were, nobody told me they were harmful.' Carmen had recently emigrated from Mexico to California's Salinas Valley. On an early August morning in 1997, Carmen and a crew of workers were cutting lettuce. In response to a plane spraying pesticides two fields away, the foreman told workers to leave the field immediately. About fifteen or twenty minutes later, they were told it was safe to return to work. Shortly thereafter Carmen began to feel sick, 'My lips, tongue and throat were numb. I felt very weak, dizzy and nauseated.' A female co-worker also began to feel sick. 'We both thought the sickness would pass, so we waited a while. But when the symptoms seemed to get worse, we went to the foreman and told him that we were feeling sick.' He took the women to the company's personnel office where they were examined by a nurse. The nurse treated the incident as a pesticide poisoning, requiring them to take a shower and to wash their hands and face thoroughly. Carmen was never given the name of the pesticide to which she was exposed. After the initial examination, she was taken to a doctor, who conducted various tests, but concluded that there was nothing wrong with her; she just needed rest.

But Carmen's symptoms persisted; 'I kept going to see doctors and they all said that I was fine. One doctor told me that it was just my nerves, nothing else, and he gave me pills.' She saw approximately five doctors between August and October 1997, yet none was willing to say that her illness was directly related to her work. The lettuce season ended, and Carmen had not recovered.

The following spring Carmen again reported for work in the lettuce fields. On her first day, she felt sick. The next day she felt even worse, experiencing weakness, chills and a sense of disorientation. She visited a doctor, who gave her vitamins and told her to return to work in five days. However, she was unable to find a doctor, including the one who had prescribed the vitamins, willing to sign a form to give her the medical release required by the company.

Health hazards of pesticide exposure

Women exposed at work and home

Although the acute hazards of pesticide exposure are similar for all adults, women and men can have different types of exposure. At home, women often have primary responsibility for house cleaning and as a result may be exposed to pesticide residues in household dust [23] home disinfectants and pest control products [24,25] and when laundering pesticide-contaminated clothes [26]. A study of Iowa farm families found that even when farmers' wives had not handled pesticides, they still had measurable herbicide and insecticide residues on their hands [27]. In farm worker housing, risk of additional exposure may be even greater since homes are frequently located near agricultural fields. Some pesticide residues may also persist longer indoors than outdoors since organisms, light, moisture and heat influence how quickly they break down [28]. In a Washington study, researchers compared pesticides in household dust in farm worker homes near orchards and other homes at least a quarter of a mile away. Concentrations of all the organophosphate pesticides tested were significantly higher in the farm worker homes [29].

Exposure to organophosphate pesticides

While farm workers are routinely exposed to a large variety of agricultural chemicals, the organophosphate pesticides (such as parathion, mevinphos, phosalone and methamidophos) are those responsible for most of the occupational deaths and poisonings in the USA and throughout the world [30,31,32,33,34]. Organophosphate pesticides exert their toxic effects by blocking the body's production of an enzyme essential to the proper functioning of the nervous system: acetylcholinesterase (cholinesterase). Symptoms of organophosphate or carbamate poisoning include blurred vision, salivation, diarrhoea, nausea, vomiting, wheezing, and sometimes seizures, coma and death. Not surprisingly, mild to moderate pesticide poisoning may easily be misdiagnosed as gastric flu, bronchitis or asthma, and even severe pesticide poisoning is often misdiagnosed.

A California study of 535 pregnant women showed that those who worked with pesticides or lived near agricultural fields had significantly lower cholinesterase levels than those only exposed to household pesticides, indicating potential organophosphate poisoning even in the absence of other symptoms [35].

Cancer

Studies have shown increases of some types of cancers among farmers, farm workers and non-farm residents of agricultural regions [36]. Farmers and farm workers experience similar increases in multiple myeloma and cancers of the stomach, prostate and testis, while farm workers show unique increases in cancers of the mouth, pharynx, lung and liver [37]. In the few existing studies of cancer in agricultural women, ovarian cancer was possibly linked to atrazine [38], breast cancer with organochlorine insecticides [39], and soft tissue sarcoma [40], multiple myeloma and non-Hodgkin's lymphoma [41] with phenoxy herbicides. Another study reported elevated risks of cancer among children of farm workers or residents of agricultural areas [42].

Box 3.3   Childhood cancers in California

In 1984 the small town of McFarland, California, gained national attention when a cancer cluster was discovered among children of farm worker parents. Eight children were diagnosed with various types of cancer. Their parents worked in the fields and had direct contact with pesticides. Some were pesticide applicators that had worked in the fields for eight to ten years. Some of the mothers worked while pregnant. Nora Gonzales gave birth to a child born without his left hand. By the age of three, her son José Luis had already undergone eight operations on his hand. Nora had worked in vineyards near McFarland during the first six months of her pregnancy.

Maria's Story

'I didn't know that they [pesticides] were harmful to the child I was expecting. Nobody told me they were harmful so I continued to work.' Maria Robles had been a farm worker for several years in California's Central Valley. She worked in the fields while pregnant. During her pregnancy, she would often eat grapes from the bunches that she was tipping (thinning fruit bunches). She had no idea that the pesticide residues were harmful to her and her baby's health. Her daughter Miriam Robles was diagnosed with leukaemia at the age of 8. Both Mrs Robles and her husband had been directly exposed to pesticides. Miriam never recovered from her illness; she died in 1992 at the age of 11. Thousands of farm workers who continue to toil the fields of California and throughout the nation have no knowledge of the health effects of pesticide exposure.

Sources: One of the several McFarland cases recorded by Marion Moses of the Pesticide Education Centre, San Francisco. *Harvest of Sorrow/Cosecha Dolorosa*, Part I (Video), Pesticide Education Center, San Francisco, 1992.

Sterility or reproductive damage

A large number of pesticides are known to cause reproductive damage. Although reduced fertility has been reported among agricultural workers [43], almost all studies of pesticide-related changes in fertility focus on reduced sperm counts or sperm motility in men. One recent University of Iowa study, however, compared 281 women treated for infertility with 216 who had given birth. It showed a two- to twentyfold increased risk of infertility for women who had worked in agriculture-related jobs [44]. After accounting for tobacco use and other confounding factors, the study reported significantly higher rates of ovulatory dysfunction, tubal problems and endometriosis (which can cause infertility in women). Although the connection to pesticide use was not definitive, the results strongly suggest such a connection and warrant serious attention.

Birth defects

Birth defects are the major cause of infant mortality and illness in the USA. They occur in 3 to 7 per cent of all births [45]. Although increased numbers of birth defects have been recorded among farm area residents [46], few studies have looked at farm workers. Patterns among other pesticide-exposed groups strongly suggest exposure-related effects. A Minnesota study of births to state-licensed, private pesticide applicators was compared to the state registry of live births from 1989 to 1992 [47]. Rates for all birth abnormalities for applicators and non-applicators were higher in crop-growing regions of the state, where the heaviest use of phenoxy herbicides and fungicides also occurred. Increases in birth defects were most pronounced for infants conceived in the spring, when phenoxy herbicides are routinely applied. Similar studies show associations between pesticide exposure and birth defects in Iowa (with the herbicide atrazine), Nebraska (with atrazine), and Colorado (with several pesticides) [48].

One California study showed that limb reduction defects among offspring of agricultural workers occurred three to fourteen times more frequently than among the general US population [49]. A follow-up study showed 1.6 times greater risk for limb reduction defect when parents were involved in agriculture [50]. The risk was greater when mothers lived in counties with high agricultural productivity (2.4 times) and high pesticide use (3.1 times).

Spontaneous abortion

Farm worker women are typically exposed to organochlorine and organophosphate pesticides that have been linked to elevated risks of reproductive problems [51]. A study of grape workers in India reported that exposure to pesticides (including lindane and parathion) resulted in almost six times the spontaneous abortion rate of non-exposed couples, as well as significantly greater chromosomal damage [52]. A Washington state study of maternal occupation and fetal death found that farm worker women experienced significantly greater risk of spontaneous abortion compared to the unexposed control group [53]. Mothers who were exposed to pesticides in their work in the flower industry in Colombia experienced both higher risk of spontaneous abortion (2.2 times) and premature birth (1.9 times) compared to unexposed women [54]. In a rural California study, stillbirths and miscarriages in women exposed to pesticides during their first and second trimesters were 5.5 and 4.8 times more likely, respectively, than in unexposed women [55].

Developmental effects

Many pesticides are known to disrupt the human endocrine system, a complex array of glands, organs and tissues that secrete hormones into the bloodstream. Hormones are transported throughout the body and function to control virtually every bodily process and to maintain balance among different body systems. Too little or too much hormone can cause a wide range of physiological or neurological problems. Maternal exposure to endocrine-disrupting chemicals appears to pose an elevated risk of developmental abnormalities in the reproductive organs of both female and male fetuses. In both sexes the external genitalia, brain, skeleton, thyroid, liver, kidney and immune system are also potential targets for endocrine-disrupting chemicals [56]. Endocrine-disruptors may exert their negative effects indirectly as well if they impair the immune or nervous systems or cause cancer in endocrine glands [57,58]. Since some endocrine-disrupting chemicals persist in body fat, they may also exert their effects long after exposure. Women generally have proportionately more body fat than men, increasing their potential to accumulate more endocrine-disrupting chemicals and/or face greater exposures related to changes in body fat levels.

A call for greater precaution

Difficulties of pesticide-health studies

Despite the fact that millions of farm workers are routinely exposed to multiple pesticides over extended periods of time, few studies have addressed the relationship between farm worker exposure and subsequent illness. Women in particular have been under-studied. Prior to 1989 epidemiological studies of occupational mortality and cancers related to pesticide exposure did not examine diagnoses specific to women. The eight major occupational mortality studies from this period excluded women, and only four studies looked at breast cancer and cancers of female reproductive organs, despite strong evidence suggesting the need for such research [59].

When pesticide effects are investigated it is often impossible to determine conclusively which pesticides are responsible for a suspected pesticide-related illness. Even with apparently clear cases of acute poisoning, more than one pesticide may be used at a time or, even if applied singly, may contain 'inert' ingredients or contaminants that may be responsible for some or all of the observed symptoms. In addition, pesticide active ingredients are often quickly metabolized once absorbed by the body, and their metabolites may be as toxic or even more toxic than the parent compound. Pesticide-health studies are further complicated by variation in individuals' susceptibilities to pesticides, which are affected by many factors including diet, age, gender, occupation, use of alcohol, tobacco or drugs, family disease history, genetics, climate and other factors [60]. Such studies must also include measures of pesticide exposure. True exposure data are rarely available and are often estimated using largely inadequate surrogate information such as occupation or job title.

Making the definitive link to pesticide exposure is even more difficult with delayed-onset or chronic diseases, since multiple exposures may occur over extended periods of time and since effects may not show up for up to fifteen to thirty years. This is exacerbated in migrant farm worker populations that routinely move among states or even countries, making it difficult to track.

Farm workers and their advocates respond

In order to protect farm workers, grassroots organizations, environmental organizations and farm worker unions have adopted multifaceted and complementary strategies. Around the country a number of groups have developed outreach and education programmes on the dangers of pesticides and appropriate responses in the event of suspected exposure. Simultaneously, other efforts are directed at banning the worst pesticides, improving protective regulations, demanding compliance with existing laws, improving farm worker access to medical care, and increasing our knowledge of the relationship between pesticide exposure and illness.

Precaution should be the standard

Whether it is a lack of information, the inadequacy of the regulations or poor enforcement of laws and regulations, we must recognize that current US regulatory processes, even in the most regulated state of California, fail to protect farm worker women and their families adequately [61].

Government regulators face powerful lobbying efforts by the chemical industry demanding scientific certainty in demonstrating the dangers of pesticides. In order to ban, restrict, or otherwise regulate a pesticide, the chemical must be shown to pose an unacceptable risk. However, since it is almost impossible to determine the true risk of illness among farm workers from exposure to a single chemical, manufacturers and non-industry scientists often estimate risk by extrapolation from animal studies. Farm workers and others on the frontline of pesticide exposure are not offered the opportunity to participate in subsequent decision-making about what level of estimated risk they are willing to accept for the benefit of industry profits. On behalf of farm workers, rural residents, consumers and the environment, we should replace the current system with a precautionary principle approach in which pesticides are assumed dangerous until proven safe – a standard difficult to meet but one that does not put hundreds of thousands of farm worker women and their families at risk of pesticide-related injury, illness or death.

References

1 *Accident Facts*, Itasca, Ill.: National Safety Council, 1996.
2 US General Accounting Office (GAO), *Pesticide on Farms: Limited Capability Exists to Monitor Occupational Illnesses and Injury*, GAO/PEMD-94–6, December 1993.
3 Ciesielski, S., Loomis, D.P., Mims, S.R., Auer, A. In *American Journal of Public Health*, 84 (3), 1994: 446–51.
4 Greenhouse, S. 'As economy booms, migrant workers' housing worsens',

New York Times, 31 May 1998.

5 Mines, R., Gabbard, S., Steirman, A., *A Profile of US Farm Workers*, US Dept of Labor, Office of the Assistant Secretary for Policy, Office of Programme Economics Research Report 6, 1997.

6 Mines *et al.*, *op. cit.*

7 Centers for Disease Control (CDC). 'Farm worker illness following exposure to carbofuran and other pesticides – Fresno County, California, 1998', *Morbidity and Mortality Weekly Report (MMWR)*, 48(6): 113–16, 1999.

8 Rodriguez, R. 'Pesticide control deadly issue', *The Fresno Bee*, 10 August 1998.

9 'Pesticide mist forces evacuations', *Associated Press*, 15 November 1999.

10 Hanley, C. 'Earlimart residents present county leaders with 183 sickness complaints', *Associated Press*, 9 December 1999.

11 Maddy, K.T., Edmiston, S., Richmond, D. In Ware, G.W. (ed.) *Reviews of Environmental Contamination and Toxicology*, 114, 1990.

12 Liebman, J. *Rising Toxic Tide: Pesticide Use in California, 1991–1995*, San Francisco: Pesticide Action Network, 1997.

13 Blondell, J. In *Occupational Medicine: State of the Art Reviews*, 12(2), 1997: 209–20.

14 US GAO. *Pesticide on Farms*, GAO/PEMD-94-6, December 1993.

15 US GAO. *Hired Farmworkers*, GAO/HRD-92-46, February, 1992.

16 Pease, W.S., Morello-Frosch R.A., *et al.*, *Preventing Pesticide-related Illness in California Agriculture: Strategies and Priorities*. California Policy Seminar, 1993.

17 Moses, M. 'Pesticides'. In Last, J.M. and Wallace, R.B. (eds) *Maxcy–Rosenau–Last Public Health and Preventive Medicine*, Stamford, Conn.: Appleton & Lange, 1992, pp. 479–89.

18 Slesinger, D.P. In *Journal of Rural Health, Research Reviews*, 8(3), 1992: 227–34.

19 Becker, W.J., Wood, T.A. *An Analysis of Agricultural Accidents in Florida for 1991*. Special Series Report SS-AGE-31, Florida Cooperative Extension Service, 1992.

20 Maddy *et al.*, *op. cit.*, 1990.

21 Lantz, P.M., Dupuis, L., Reding, D., Krauska, M., Lappe, K. In *Public Health Reports*, 109(4), 1994: 512–20.

22 Moses, *op. cit.*, 1992: 479–89.

23 Simcox, N., Fenske R.A., *et al.* In *Environmental Health Perspectives*, 103(12), 1995: 1126–34.

24 Moses, M. 'Pesticides'. In Wallace, R.B. (ed.) *Maxcy–Rosenau–Last Public Health and Preventive Medicine*. 14th edn, Stamford, Conn.: Appleton & Lange, 1998.

25 Zahm, S.H., Ward, M.H., Blair A. In *Occupational Medicine: State of the Art Reviews*, 12(2), 1997: 269–89.

26 Easley, C., Laughlin, J., Gold, R, Schmidt, K. In *Bulletin of Environmental Contaminants and Toxicology*, 28, 1982: 239–44.

27 Camann, H., Harding, H.J., Clothier, J.M. In *Air & Waste Management*

Association, VIP-50, 1995: 548–54.

28 Bradman, M.A., Harnly, M.E., *et al.* In *Journal of Exposure Analysis and Environmental Epidemiology*, 7(2), 1997: 217–34.

29 Simcox, *op. cit.*, 1995.

30 Blondell, J., Dobozy V.A. *Review of Chlorpyrifos Poisoning Data*, Office of Prevention, Pesticides and Toxic Substances, Washington: US EPA, 1997.

31 Keifer, M.C., Mahurin, R.K. In *Occupational Medicine: State of the Art Reviews*, 12(2), 1997: 291–304.

32 Moses, M., Johnson E.S., *et al.* In *Toxicolology of Industrial Health*, 9(5), 1993: 913–59.

33 Savage, E.P., Keefe, T.J., Mounce, L.M. In *Archives of Environmental Health*, 43, 1988: 38–45.

34 Weinbaum, Z, Schenker M.B., *et al.* In *American Journal of Industrial Medicine*, 28, 1995: 257–74.

35 De Peyster, A., Willis, W.O., *et al.* In *Archives of Environmental Health*, 48(5), 1993: 348–52.

36 Moses, M. 'Occupational exposure to pesticides and cancer in humans: Summary of selected studies', Paper presented at the Rachel Carson Council Conference, Chevy Chase, Md., 26 October 1996.

37 Zahm, S.H., Blair, A. In *American Journal of Industrial Medicine*, 24(6), 1993: 753–66.

38 Donna, A., Crosignani, P.F. *et al.*, *Scandinavian Journal of Work, Environment and Health*, 15, 1989: 47–53.

39 Falck, F., River, A., Wolff, M.S., Gobolds, S. In *Archives of Environmental Health*, 47, 1992: 143–6.

40 Vineis, P., Terracini, B., *et al.* In *Scandinavian Journal of Work, Environment and Health*, 13, 1986: 9–17.

41 Zahm *et al.*, *op. cit.*, 1993.

42 Holly, E.A., Aston, D.A., Ahn, D.K., Kristiansen, J.J. In *American Journal of Epidemiology*, 135(2), 1992: 122–9.

43 Fourtes, L., Clark, M.K., Kirchner, H.L., Smith, E.M. In *American Journal of Industrial Medicine*, 31, 1997: 445–51.

44 Voss, M. 'U of I study links female infertility, farm-related jobs: suspicion focuses on chemicals', *The Des Moines Register*, 14 July 1997.

45 Moses, *op. cit.*, 1992

46 Garry, V.G., Schreinemachers, D., Harkins, M.E., Grifith, J. In *Environmental Health Perspectives*, 104(4), 1996: 394–9.

47 Garry *et al.*, *op. cit.*, 1996.

48 Garry *et al.*, *op. cit.*, 1996.

49 Schwartz, D.A., Newsum, L.A. Markowitz-Heifetz, R. In *Scandinavian Journal of Work, Environment and Health*, 12, 1986: 51–4.

50 Schwartz, D.A., LoGerfo, J.P. In *American Journal of Public Health*, 78, 1988: 654–7.

51 Sever, L.E., Arbuckle, T.E., Sweeney, A. In *Occupational Medicine: State of the Art Reviews*, 12(2), 1997: 305–25.

52 Rita, P., Reddy, P.P., Reddy, S.V. In *Environmental Research*, 44, 1987: 1–5.
53 Vaughn, T.L., Daling, J.R., Starzyk, P.M. In *Journal of Occupational Medicine*, 26, 1984: 676–8.
54 Restrepo, M., Munoz N., Day N.E. *et al.* In *Scandinavian Journal of Work, Environment and Health*, 16, 1990: 232–8.
55 Pastore, L, Hertz-Picciotto, I., Beaumont, J. In *American Journal of Epidemiology*, 141, 1995: 573.
56 Colborn, T., von Saal, F.S., Soto, A.M. In *Environmental Health Perspectives*, 101(5), 1993: 378–84.
57 Benbrook, C. *A Primer on Pesticides Identified as Endocrine Disruptors and/or Reproductive Toxicants*. Washington, D.C.: National Campaign for Pesticide Policy Reform/The Tides Center, 1996.
58 Zahm *et al.*, *op. cit.*, 1997.
59 Levine, R.S., Hersh, C.B., Hodder, R.A. In *Epidemiology*, 1(2), 1990: 181–4.
60 Sever *et al.*, *op. cit.*, 1997.
61 Reeves, M., Schafer, K., Hallward, K., Katten, A. *Fields of Poison: California Farmworkers and Pesticides*. San Francisco: Pesticide Action Network, 1999.

4

Multiple health problems in Latin America

Catharina Wesseling

Agrochemical markets in developing countries have been rapidly expanding, in particular in Latin America [1]. The use of pesticides is one of the most burdensome occupational and environmental health hazards in developing countries because this intrinsically dangerous technology is promoted in settings that lack resources to control it.

Over 700 active ingredients are in use worldwide, each with distinct chemical and toxicological properties. A variety of health effects may occur [2], including systemic poisonings; topical lesions of skin and eyes; respiratory, immunological, neurological and developmental disorders; reproductive dysfunction; and cancer. Health effects arising from pesticide exposures remain uncertain or unknown because of gaps in scientific knowledge, lack of records, or incorrect diagnoses. This chapter illustrates the development of new approaches and research on pesticides and human health in Latin America, especially in Costa Rica. It highlights exposure and health problems among women.

Exposure to pesticides

Pesticide exposures occur in occupational and non-occupational settings. Pesticides are primarily used in agriculture, the main economic sector of most developing countries, and in vector control and control of domestic and industrial pests. Rural agricultural populations are usually at highest risk.

Women's role in the agricultural workforce

In Latin America, agriculture provides economic support for some 112 million people. In Central America, the living of almost half the population depends on farming; at the turn of the millennium, 4.3 million people or 41 per cent of the economically active population were agricultural workers [3]. Agriculture in Latin America – in particular the production of ornamental plants, tropical fruits and vegetables – relies heavily on chemical inputs.

From the mid-1980s, job opportunities opened for women in non-traditional export crops such as flowers, melon, pineapple, or vegetables in most Central American countries [4], but the number of women employed remains low. In 1999, women made up less than 6 per cent of the formal agricultural workforce of Costa Rica [5]. However, unpaid agricultural tasks on family farms are common, but not counted in the statistics. Rural women play an important role in the informal agricultural sector, for example in the coffee harvest. In Chile, the employment of agricultural workers in the fruit industry has seasonal variations and relies heavily on the female workforce. Estimates of the Chilean *temporeras*, temporary women workers with unstable labour contracts, vary between 200,000 and 400,000 [6].

Farmers and employed agricultural workers are the group at highest risk of pesticide exposure and consequent health effects. Hazardous work practices continue despite increased awareness. Direct handling of pesticides (spraying and mixing) is most often by men. Women experience indirect exposures on re-entry to recently sprayed fields, through working close to fields being sprayed, or when selecting and packing freshly sprayed fruits and vegetables, or directly when applying pesticides in the packing plants of banana plantations in Central America.

Contact with pesticides outside the work site

Pesticide exposures extend to all sectors of the population through contact with contaminated environments in intensive pesticide use areas, through consumption of contaminated food and water, and through spraying for vector control or control of domestic pests. Pesticide application in and around the home is often a woman's task. Vector control programmes, primarily based on chemical pest control methods, are facing a resurgence of the vector-transmitted diseases of malaria and dengue due to resistance to pesticides. DDT was the only persistent organic pollutant (POP) to be exempted from a global ban and will continue to be used indoors in some twenty-five endemic developing countries for malaria control. Depressed cholinesterase activity and symptoms have been reported in Nicaragua among children living close to a fumigation airport and residents exposed to aerial applications [7, 8].

Gender differences in health effects

Acute poisonings

Poisoning surveys have identified dangerous pesticide agents widely used in Central America, in particular paraquat, carbofuran, terbufos, methomyl, methamidophos, methyl-parathion, and aluminium phosphide [9,10,11]. Surveillance systems of acute health effects from pesticides are being set up in all Central American countries; in 1998, almost 6,000 pesticide poisonings were reported in five of the seven Central American countries [12]. An estimate, corrected for underreporting, arrived at 30,000 pesticide poisonings annually in the entire region [13].

Women are less likely to handle highly toxic insecticides and usually have lower incidence rates for systemic poisonings than men. Acute poisoning outbreaks have occurred when women work in recently sprayed fields, but these have often remained undocumented. In Viña del Mar, Chile, two poisoning epidemics were detected among women who had performed tasks in recently sprayed areas. In 1996, 58 of 64 reported poisonings concerned women; of 120 poisoning cases in 1997, 108 of the 110 women were temporary workers, nearly all employed in the flower industry [14]. In a survey of 300 temporary women workers in the fruit industry in Chile, 15 per cent of the orchard and 17 per cent of the packing plant workers considered pesticides the most disturbing factor at work. Of the 134 women who had been exposed to pesticides, almost half had experienced symptoms of systemic poisoning; 23 per cent reported dermal injuries, 19 per cent eye irritation, and 10 per cent respiratory problems that they attributed to pesticides, including spray drift from fumigation chambers to the packing plant [15].

Suicides

Non-occupational accidental and suicidal pesticide poisonings are much more frequent among agricultural workers than among the general population, due to easy availability of pesticides. In Surinam, the incidence of paraquat suicides correlated closely with amounts of paraquat imported and distributed for agricultural use [16]. On the other hand, a hypothesis has emerged that exposure to organophosphate pesticides may cause depression leading to increased risk of suicide among farming populations. In Serra Gaucha, Brazil, a high proportion of farm workers presented minor psychiatric disorders, which strongly associated with pesticide exposures [17]. In Ecuador, suicide rates with pesticides were extremely high in a potato farming population [18].

Topical injuries: high rates among women

Acute or chronic dermal and eye injuries from irritating, caustic and sensitizing pesticides are usually not captured by surveillance systems, although such injuries are probably more widespread than systemic poisonings. High and increasing rates of dermal lesions have been found particularly among female agricultural workers [19], with rates as high as 7.5 injuries a year per 100 women employed in the banana and ornamental plant industries in Costa Rica. Although few systemic poisonings occur among women in Central America, the upward trend of dermal lesions indicates increasing contact with pesticides, which may not have high acute toxicity but which are often suspected of causing mutagenic, carcinogenic or reproductive effects.

The annual incidence of pesticide illness among the mainly women workers of packing plants of banana plantations in Costa Rica decreased from 3.4 to 1.1 per 100 workers between 1993 and 1996. This may be partially due to improvement in working conditions, but increased underreporting and treatment by company doctors are also likely [20]. In addition, injuries related to cleaning of the packing plants and water basins, a women's job identified as one of the five most risky tasks on banana plantations, did not decline (4.0 and 4.5 per 100 workers in 1993 and 1996, respectively).

Among men, the herbicide paraquat is the most frequently reported pesticide associated with skin and eye injuries in Costa Rica [21,22]. In 1996, 25 per 100 herbicide sprayers on banana plantations filed a claim for an occupational pesticide-related accident requiring medical attention, the majority because of paraquat. The fungicide chlorothalonil has been identified as a risk factor for ashy dermatitis among banana plantation workers in Panama [23], and the fungicide maneb as an occupational risk factor for dermatitis among potato growers in Ecuador [24].

Genotoxic effects and genetic susceptibility markers

Cytogenetic changes (chromosomal aberrations, sister chromatid exchanges, micronuclei, and changes in chromosome number) may be viewed as an early biological effect from a chemical insult, which at the same time is a risk indicator for the future development of diseases such as cancer and congenital malformations. A series of recent studies in Brazil, Mexico and Costa Rica have reported increased genetic damage among pesticide-exposed workers [25,26,27], while no such increase was found in Chile and Colombia. In Costa Rica, among banana workers exposed to the nematicide dibromochloropropane (DBCP) in the 1970s, genotoxic effects were more evident in genetically susceptible workers – that is, those with 'unfavourable' inherited polymorphisms of critical genes involved in the metabolism of toxic substances [28]. Few studies have addressed risks specifically for women. Among female workers of packing plants of banana plantations with exposure to the fungicides thiabendazole and imazalil, an increased prevalence of genotoxic changes was observed [29]. The increase of genotoxic effects among greenhouse workers in a Mexican study with non-specified pesticide exposures also concerned primarily women [30].

Cancer

Studies on cancer and various pesticide exposures are slowly increasing in Latin America, among both women and men. In Colombia exposure to organochlorine insecticides was detected as a risk factor for female breast cancer [31]. Studies in Rio de Janeiro and Mexico City failed to confirm this result. However, a recent Mexican report related high levels of exposure to DDE, the major metabolite of the insecticide DDT, with increased breast cancer risk, particularly for post-menopausal women [32]. Cancer risk in populations of rural counties of Costa Rica with high pesticide use tends to be higher than in rural counties with low pesticide use. This is evident for both overall cancer risk and the risk for specific cancer sites, in particular female hormone-related cancers and lung cancer in men and women [33]. Male banana workers have excess risk of penile cancer, melanoma and lung cancer; and female banana workers for cervical cancer and leukaemia [34]. Excess cancer risk for children of parents exposed to pesticides is increasingly documented. In Brazil, elevated risks of Wilm's Tumour, a childhood malignancy of the kidney, were reported where the father and mother both used pesticides frequently [35].

Reproductive effects

The most striking evidence of reproductive effects is the sterility in thousands of male banana workers exposed to DBCP during the 1970s. The case of Costa Rican workers is best known [36], but victims are spread throughout Central America and other Latin American countries, such as Ecuador. In Costa Rica, the wives of the DBCP victims have also claimed reproductive effects such as sterility and malformations, but no formal studies have been carried out. One study on congenital malformations in Colombia among female workers in the cultivation of flowers found an increased risk only of haemangioma [37], whereas in Chile a high prevalence of malformations in the region of Rancagua was attributed to pesticide exposures among temporary women workers in the fruit industry [38]. In Colombia, women exposed to pesticides in the flower industry had increased rates of abortions and premature children in pregnancies that occurred after they started working in floriculture [39].

Respiratory effects

An association between long-term paraquat exposure and respiratory symptoms was observed in Nicaragua, but no alterations were found in tests of pulmonary function [40]. However, a recent study in South African workers exposed to paraquat demonstrated a decrease in oxygen uptake during exercise [41], which may be the explanation for the contradictory findings in Nicaragua. This is a good example of how research in developing countries can answer questions that may be harder to address in industrialized countries.

Neurotoxic effects

The toxic action of many pesticides is directed to the nervous system. An increasing body of evidence is emerging of deleterious effects of different pesticides on the central nervous system, peripheral nervous system and the developing brain before birth or in the newborn. Populations in developing countries are at very high risk, particularly babies and young children. In Mexico, inferior developmental skills, neuro-muscular deficits, and memory and drawing deficits were observed in pesticide-exposed children in agricultural communities compared to similar children without pesticide exposures [42]. Persistent damage in the central and peripheral nervous systems has been demonstrated in workers previously poisoned with cholinesterase-inhibiting pesticides in Nicaragua and Costa Rica [43,44,45]. A recent study demonstrated important neurobehavioural deficits among male vector control sprayers in Costa Rica who had been previously exposed to DDT [46].

Endocrine disrupting effects

Endocrine disrupting, immunological, and other effects have not been studied in Latin America. An exception is the study among Mexican agricultural workers exposed to EBDC (ethylene bis-dithiocarbamate) fungicides, which detected abnormal levels of thyroid stimulating hormones [47].

Documenting pesticide-related health risks in developing countries

The risk of ill health from pesticides is primarily determined by exposure and toxicity. Health risks in developing countries differ considerably from those in industrialized countries: exposures are in general much higher due to excessive applications and inadequate use conditions; and more dangerous pesticides are used. In addition, exposed populations are susceptible because of poor health status, malnutrition, endemic infectious diseases, illiteracy and young age. In view of the unfortunate reality of frequent and severe exposure, pesticide research in developing countries can answer open questions of health effects from pesticides, and contribute to policymaking in developing countries and beyond. Health research should include assessment of intensities and time patterns of exposures; assessment of both acute and chronic health effects; interaction between pesticides; evaluation of the impact of interventions; and assessment of gender differences and other susceptibilities. Documenting health risks in developing countries is a methodological challenge [48,49].

Multiple exposures and multiple health effects

Exposures vary greatly in potency, frequency, intensity and duration, whereas other factors such as types of pesticide formulation, routes

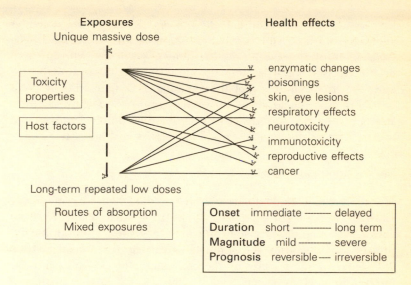

Figure 4.1 Schematic illustration of the complex relationships between a range of possible exposures and potential health effects

of absorption (oral, dermal or respiratory) or climatic conditions also influence the amount of toxic compound that reaches the target organ(s) to produce the toxic effect(s). Many pesticides produce multiple health effects in relation to different types of exposures – and populations are exposed to multiple pesticides simultaneously or in succession. We do not know the full range of health effects of the hundreds of toxic pesticides surrounding us. The entanglement of exposure and toxicity patterns (Figure 4.1) complicates the study of health effects among pesticide-exposed populations. This is true for any research setting, but particularly so in developing countries where exposures are complex, and human and technical resources are insufficient.

Epidemiology studies

Epidemiological research on environmental and occupational health in a developing country setting is constrained by poor infrastructure, poor disease and population registries, and lack of expertise in occupational and environmental epidemiology. Government sectors often have strong ties with economically influential sectors, which creates additional obstacles for researchers. Nonetheless, there have been valuable research experiences on human pesticide exposure and health effects in many developing countries. Reviews are available for Latin America and on a global scale [50,51]. Despite an early focus on safety aspects and acute poisonings, evidence of chronic health effects of pesticide hazards is steadily building up, as demonstrated in Part II of this volume, on pesticide-related health research.

Hazard identification

Health research could focus merely on the identification of the hazards – populations exposed to which pesticides and to what extent. Knowing the precise health impact is not a precondition for prevention and control measures. It is feasible to build on existing knowledge of the toxicity of the compounds in use and prioritize interventions. However, epidemiological research linking quantified health effects with exposure data is the most powerful tool to achieve action because policymakers have difficulties in acknowledging potential health effects. Local evidence is a strong incentive.

Pesticide import and use data combined with data on toxicity can guide hazard identification. Breaking down data by regions and/or crops identifies populations at high risk. By 1999, preliminary import data indicated an overall use of 57,000 tonnes in the Central American region [52], which is roughly equivalent to 1.5 kg of active ingredient per inhabitant and 13 kg per agricultural worker. In Costa Rica, it had been estimated that 64 kg of active ingredients were used per worker on banana plantations. Other high-risk areas include melon in Central America, and non-traditional export vegetables in Guatemala, with an even higher pesticide consumption than on the Costa Rica banana plantations [53].

A crude analysis of import data in Costa Rica in terms of toxicity illustrates hazard identification as an uncomplicated procedure, which can, nonetheless, be used for adjustments of agricultural policies. Of the 16,400 tonnes of imported pesticide formulations during 1998, 3,100 tonnes (19 per cent) were WHO class Ia and Ib pesticides (extremely and highly hazardous). These included 600 tonnes of terbufos, a compound with a recorded death toll of five young Costa Rican workers in a decade [54] and occupational fatalities in Nicaragua; and 160 tonnes of methamidophos, a recognized peripheral neurotoxicant [55]. In addition, large amounts of other

Table 4.1 Selected pesticides of special toxicological concern which are among the ten most imported pesticides in one or more Central American countries

Pesticide	No. of countries	Toxicological concern
Paraquat	7	Fatal occupational and accidental poisonings Chemical burns in skin and eyes Suicides
Mancozeb	7	Cancer
Terbufos	5	Fatal occupational poisonings (WHO Ia)
Methamidophos	4	Acute poisonings (WHO Ib) Delayed peripheral neurotoxicity
Methyl bromide	3	Acute poisonings (WHO Ib)
Aluminium phosphide	3	Acute poisonings Suicides
Carbofuran	3	Acute poisonings (WHO Ib)
Methyl parathion	2	Acute poisonings (WHO Ia)
Copper arsenate	2	Cancer
Aldicarb	1	Acute poisonings (WHO Ia), including food Groundwater pollution Immunotoxicity

Source: Database, Central American Institute for Studies on Toxic Substances, Universidad Nacional, Costa Rica.

pesticides entered the country which are severely restricted or banned in a number of industrialized countries, such as 2500 tonnes of mancozeb, a carcinogen and endocrine disruptor [56]; 900 tonnes of the neurotoxic and ozone depleting methyl bromide, a fumigant to be phased out worldwide by the year 2015 [57]; 520 tonnes of the fumigant aluminium phosphide, the cause of major suicide epidemics in Central America [58] and other developing countries such as India; and 400 tonnes of the herbicide paraquat, as noted above the most frequent agent in pesticide-related occupational accidents in Costa Rica since the mid-1980s. The situation is no better in other Central American countries (Table 4.1).

Qualitative and quantitative exposure assessment

Qualitative methods to evaluate exposures provide useful insight. Simple field observations or group discussions with applicators or other exposed workers can characterize risks. In Nicaragua, a research programme is addressing risk perception of farmers and reasons underlying risky behaviour. Quantitative measurements of exposures can refine this approach. Exposure assessments among small producers and plantation workers in Nicaragua and Costa Rica have detected serious deficiencies in the handling of pesticides [59, 60]. It has been observed by measuring residues on the skin and in urine and evaluations using fluorescent tracer that personal protective equipment does not provide adequate protection in tropical conditions [61]. Women's skin exposures have been addressed in two studies in Costa Rica, in a nursery growing flowers for export [62] and in the packing plant of a banana plantation [63]. Although in both studies it was difficult to interpret the levels of residues in terms of potential health effects, many of these women claimed pesticide-related symptoms. All exposure studies evidence that the obstacles to reducing risks from pesticides to levels considered acceptable in industrialized countries are difficult or impossible to overcome in developing countries.

Research on non-occupational pesticide exposures in Central America is almost non-existent. Episodes of mortality of large quantities of fish and other aquatic organisms and chemical pollution of rivers and other waterways by pesticides have been repeatedly documented in Central America, frequently in connection with banana and cotton cultivation. It is not known what this pollution means in terms of human exposures through, for example, contact with contaminated waters during recreation or consumption of contaminated fish. One study attempted to measure environmental exposures due to the drift of pesticides applied on a banana plantation towards a nearby community, but the banana company, aware of the study, changed aerial application practices and schedules during the sampling period [64]. Nonetheless, the study provided evidence of continuous environmental pesticide exposure of the community. Pesticide residues of the insecticide chlorpyriphos were detected in the air, and of the fungicide propiconazole in surface water and soil in the school and a residential house in the centre of the village. This supports findings of studies on pesticide health effects and low cholinesterase levels in children and communities of the Nicaraguan cotton fields. Monitoring programmes to control pesticide residues on locally consumed food are incipient at best. In Costa Rica, the sampling methods and analytical residue results of locally consumed food are not routinely revealed to the public, except for assurances that levels exceeding FAO tolerances are only infrequently detected. However, each pesticide is considered separately and the total load of pesticides in food is not evaluated.

Where we stand today

Women are more involved in agriculture and more frequently exposed to toxic pesticides than official statistics show. Women have special reproductive and other gender-related risks, which need to be specifically assessed. Despite the difficulties of undertaking environmental and occupational health research, this review evidences that studies undertaken with sound methods succeed in testing their hypotheses in developing countries. It is noteworthy that so many studies are positive, since most methodological difficulties would obscure any real effect rather than showing false effects. Evidence is clear not only for acute poisonings and dermatosis, the most easily detectable health problems, but also for genotoxic effects, alterations to organs and systems (respiratory, nervous and reproductive systems), and excesses of cancers later in life. There are many dangerous substances in use. This situation is not acknowledged by international and national regulators and policymakers. We need to use this knowledge urgently. Risk assessment and risk management based on local data and results from studies conducted in other developing countries with similar exposure conditions are a big step forward in preventing adverse health effects from pesticides in developing countries.

One limitation is the difficulty of unravelling the complex exposures and of pinpointing specific pesticides. Finding the guilty substance(s) makes it possible to set priorities for prevention and control and facilitates regulatory decisions. However, focusing on specific pesticides may not be the best way to achieve more sustainable policies. Questioning certain health effects can be prolonged for decades without action [65]. Furthermore, blaming a single substance for a specific health effect may obscure the outrageously complex exposure and toxicity patterns that make people ill, and that indeed define the unsustainability of agricultural and vector control policies. We must move away from this toxic culture, and lobby for sustainable agriculture policies such as full support for organic agriculture.

We need to go beyond local risk assessment and apply the precautionary approach, using proactive policymaking to solve pesticide problems.

Note

Thanks to Timo Partanen for comments on the manuscript.

References

1 Akhabuhaya, J., Castillo, L., Dinham, B., Ekström, G., Huan, N.H., Hurst, P., Pettersson, S.E., Wesseling, C. 'Multistakeholder collaboration for reduced exposure to pesticides in developing countries'. Recommendations to Sida with particular reference to Costa Rica, Tanzania and Vietnam, 2000. www.pan-uk.org/Pub31.htm.
2 Keifer M. (ed). 'Human health effects of pesticides', *Occupational Medicine: State of the Art Review*, 12, 1997: 203–41.
3 Wesseling C. In *International Conference on Occupational Safety and Health*. Washington, D.C.: Inter-American Development Bank, 19–20 June 2000.
4 Mendizábal, Weller (ed.). *Exportaciones agrícolas no tradicionales del Istmo Centroamericano. ¿Promesa o espejismo?* Panama: ILO, 1992.
5 Instituto Nacional de Estadísticos y Censos, Costa Rica www.meic.go.cr/inec.
6 Wesseling, C., Parra, M., Elgstrand, K. 'Fruit production, pesticides and the health of women workers'. International Development Cooperation Internal Report 4, Stockholm: National Institute for Working Life, 1998.
7 McConnell, R., et al. In *Environmental Research*, 81(2), 1999: 87–91.
8 Keifer M., Rivas, F., Moon, J.D., Ceckoway, H. In *Occupational Environmental Medicine*, 53, 1996: 726–9.
9 McConnell, R., Hruska, A. In *American Journal of Public Health* 83, 1993: 1559–62.
10 Wesseling, C., Castillo, L. In *Memorias del Primer Taller Centroamericano en Ecología y Salud*, ECOSAL. 1–3 September 1992. El Salvador: Pan American Health Organization (PAHO), 1992, pp. 83–112.
11 Wesseling, C., Hogstedt, C., et al. In *International Journal of Occupational Environmental Health*, 7, 2001: 1–6.
12 Henao, S. 'Plaguicidas en Centroamérica. Seminario sobre Legislación de Plaguicidas en el Istmo Centroamericano', Guatemala, 18–20 May 1999.
13 Murray, D., consultant PLAGSALUD, personal communication, 1999.
14 Wesseling et al., op. cit., 1998.
15 Medel, J., Riquelme, V. *La salud ignorada. Temporeras de la fruticultura*. Santiago, Chile: Ediciones CEM, 1994.
16 Perriens, J., Van Der Stuyft, P., et al. In *Tropical and Geographical Medicine*, 41, 1989: 266–9.

17 Faria, N.M., Facchini, L.A., *et al.* In *Rev. Saude Publica*, 33, 1999: 391–400.

18 Cole, D.C., Carpio, F., Leon, N., *Rev. Panam. Salud Publica*, 8, 2000: 196–201.

19 Vergara, A., Fuortes, L. In *International Journal of Occupational and Environmental Health*, 4, 1998: 199–201.

20 Wesseling, C., van Wendel de Joode, B., Monge, P. In *International Journal of Occupational and Envrionmental Health*, 7, 2001: 1–6.

21 Wesseling, *op. cit.*, June 2000; Wesseling *et al.*, *op. cit.*, 1992; Wesseling, Hogstedt, *et al.*, *op. cit.*, 2001; Wesseling, Van Wendel de Joode, Monge, *op. cit.*, 2001.

22 Wesseling, C., Castillo, L., Elinder, C.G. In *Scandinavian Journal of Work, Environment and Health*, 19, 1993: 227–35.

23 Penagos, H., Jiménez, V., Fallas, V., O'Malley, M., Maybach, H.I. In *Contact Dermatitis*, 35, 1996: 214–8.

24 Cole, D.C., Carpio, F., Math, J.J., Leon, N. In *Contact Dermatitis*, 37, 1997: 1–8.

25 Antonucci, G.A., de Syllos Colus, I.M. In *Teratogenicity Carcinogenicity Mutagenicity*, 20, 2000: 265–72.

26 Gomez-Arroyo, S., Diaz-Sanchez, Y., Meneses-Perez, M.A. *et al.* In *Mutagen Research*, 466, 2000: 117–24.

27 Steenland, K., *et al.* In *Environmental Health Perspectives*, 105, 1997: 1126–30.

28 Au, W.W., *et al.* In *Environmental Health Perspectives*, 107, 1999: 501–5.

29 Ramirez, V., Cuenca, P. Castro, R.. In *Environ. Mol. Mutag.* 31 (Supplement 29), 1998: 71.

30 Gomez-Arroyo *et al.*, *op. cit.*, 2000.

31 Olaya-Contreras, P., Rodriguez-Villamil, J., *et al.* In *Cad Saude Publica*, 14 Supplement 3, 1998: 125–32.

32 Romieu, I., Hernandez-Avila, M., Lazcano-Ponce, E., Weber, J.P., Dewailly, E. In *American Journal of Epidemiology*, 152, 2000: 363–70.

33 Wesseling, C., Antich, D., *et al.* In *International Journal of Epidemiology*, 28, 1999: 365–74.

34 Wesseling, C., Ahlbom, A., Antich, D., *et al.* In *International Journal of Epidemiology*, 1996: 1125–31.

35 Sharpe, C.R., Franco, E.L., de Camargo, B., *et al.* In *American Journal of Epidemiology*, 141, 1995: 210–7.

36 Thrupp, L.A. In *International Journal of Health Services*, 21, 1991: 731–57.

37 Restrepo, M., Munoz, N., Day, N.E., *et al.* In *Scandinavian Journal of Work, Environment and Health*, 16, 1990: 239–46.

38 Rojas, A., Ojeda, M.E., Barraza, X. In *Rev Med Chil*, 128, 2000: 399–404.

39 Restrepo *et al.*, *op. cit.*, 1990.

40 Castro-Gutiérrez, N., McConnell, R., *et al.* In *Scandinavian Journal of Work, Environment and Health*, 23, 1997: 421–7.

41 Dalvie, M.A., White, R., *et al.* In *Occupational Environmental*

Medicine, 56, 1999: 391–6.
42 Guillette, E.A. In *Central European Journal of Public Health*, 8 Supplement, 2000: 58–9.
43 Rosenstock, L., Keifer, M., *et al.* In *The Lancet*, 338, 1991: 223–6.
44 Wesseling, C., Keifer, M., Ahlbom, A., *et al.* In Wesseling, C. 'Health effects from pesticide use in Costa Rica: an epidemiologic approach' [dissertation], Stockholm: National Institute for Working Life, 1997.
45 McConnell, R., Keifer, M., Rosenstock, L. In *American Journal of Industrial Medicine*, 25, 1994: 325–34.
46 van Wendel de Joode, B., Wesseling, C., *et al.* In *The Lancet*, 357, 2001: 1014–16.
47 Steenland *et al.*, *op. cit.*, 105, 1997: 1126–30.
48 WHO/UNEP. *Public Health Impact of Pesticides Used in Agriculture*, Geneva: WHO, 1990.
49 Wesseling, C., McConnell, R., *et al.* In *International Journal of Health Services*, 27, 1997: 273–308.
50 McConnell, R., Corey, G., Henao, S., *et al.* In Finkelman, J., Corey, G., Calderón, R. (eds) *Environmental Epidemiology: A Project for Latin America and the Caribbean*, Metepec, Mexico: Pan American Center for Human Ecology and Health, EPA, IPCS, Global Environmental Epidemiology Network, 1993, pp. 147–201.
51 Wesseling, McConnell, *et al.*, *op. cit.*, 1997.
52 Database of pesticide imports at the Central American Institute for Studies on Toxic Substances (IRET), 2000.
53 Murray, D., Hoppin, P. In *World Development*, 20, 1991: 597–608.
54 Database, IRET, *op. cit.*, 2000.
55 McConnell *et al.*, *op. cit.*, 1994, McConnell *et al.*, *op. cit.*, 1999.
56 Steenland *et al.*, *op. cit.*, 1997.
57 UNEP, 'Methyl bromide getting ready for the phase out' *Ozone Action Special*, 1998.
58 Wesseling *et al.*, *op. cit.*, 1992.
59 Aragón, A., Aragón, C., Thörn, Å. In *International Journal of Occupational and Environmental Health*, 7, 2001: 295–302.
60 van Wendel de Joode, B.N., de Graaf, I.A., *et al.* In *International Journal of Occupational and Environmental Health*, 2, 1996: 294–304.
61 Spruit, O., van Puyvelde, M. 'Evaluation of the protective equipment used during herbicide application on banana plantations', Internal report No. 304, Wageningen Agricultural University, Environmental and Occupational Health Group, 1998.
62 Dijkstra, E., Timmermans, H. 'Occupational exposure to pesticides in a chrysanthemum nursery in Costa Rica. Dermal exposure to chlorothalonil and methomyl of applicators and cutters', Wageningen Agricultural University, Department of Air Quality, 1993.
63 Vaquerano, B.D. 'Characterization of occupational dermal pesticide exposure on a banana plantation in Costa Rica', MSc, University of Costa Rica, 1995.

64 Smits, N., Snippe, R., de Vries, J. 'Exposure to pesticides due to living next to a banana plantation. A pilot study', Internal report No 312, Wageningen Agricultural University, Environmental and Occupational Health Group, 1999.
65 Smith, C. In *International Journal of Occupational and Environmental Health*, 6, 2000: 2635.

5

Rural mothers with HIV: eliminating pesticide exposure

Sam L. Page

Governments and the international community should prohibit the use of immuno-suppressing pesticides for use by smallholder farmers in AIDS affected areas. Efforts should be made to encourage safer methods of pest control.

Recommendation 18, 'The HIV/AIDS pandemic and its gender implications', Report of the expert group meeting, 13–17 November 2000, Windhoek, Namibia

More than 12 million women and 10 million men were living with HIV in sub-Saharan Africa by the end of 1999 [1]. That HIV-infected women outnumber HIV-infected men is a pattern not seen on other continents. The vast majority live in rural areas, where they subsist on various forms of agriculture. Southern Africa has been hardest hit by the crisis, partly because of the mobility of the male workforce. In Zimbabwe the estimated antenatal HIV prevalence is currently around 25 per cent. Men usually acquire infection first and subsequently pass it on to their wives based in their rural homes. Many local traditions have made women particularly vulnerable.

For a woman living in the rural areas, the first time she realizes that she may have HIV is when her husband or baby dies of an AIDS-related disease. As a smallholder farmer widowed by AIDS, her prospects for survival with HIV are grim, and she can expect to begin developing AIDS-related infections within about two years.

HIV/AIDS has six stages of development [2]. The initial infection is followed by an asymptomatic period during which time viral activity can be regulated to some degree by conserving the immune system. In developed countries, some HIV-positive people live healthy lives for fifteen years or more without anti-retroviral drug therapy:

the average is about ten or eleven years before serious symptoms develop. In Africa this period lasts, on average, seven years and may be far shorter for HIV-positive people living in extreme poverty [3]. This huge difference in life expectancy is attributed to the differences in lifestyle, access to health care, and diet between affluent Westerners and impoverished people in Africa. Rural African women are particularly at risk as they are constantly exposed to a range of agents that actually suppress immune function.

Potential causes of immune suppression in rural women

Likely causes of immune-suppression in rural African women, which hasten the conversion to full-blown AIDS, are fundamentally due to poverty, traditionally based inequality and the drudgery of farming. These can be summarized as follows:

- poor diet;
- exposure to organophosphate pesticides;
- fatigue due to hard labour;
- exposure to other infections;
- successive pregnancies;
- re-infection with sexually transmitted infections (STIs) and HIV;
- anxiety due to poverty and family rejection.

Poor diet

A healthy diet is the primary defence against rapid degeneration of the immune system. Various food crops indigenous to Africa, such as finger millet, bulrush millet, pumpkin, cowpea, bambara and groundnut are rich in many essential vitamins and minerals and could contribute to a diet that would promote good health in HIV-positive people. Unfortunately, these crops have been marginalized in countries such as Zimbabwe, where smallholder agriculture has been commercialized. Low input-requiring food crops that cannot be propagated by seed, including cassava, sweet potato and taro, are of low priority with local research and extension, while Zimbabwe's agrochemical industry, especially the major seed companies, has influenced government policy to promote hybrid maize as the main food staple. As a result, many people in both the rural and urban areas now subsist on a monotonous diet of refined maize-meal sadza and rape: a diet lacking in all the major nutrients [4].

Box 5.1   **The threat to food security in Zimbabwe**

Zimbabwe is at particular risk from famine as a result of the HIV/AIDS epidemic because of colonial policies and laws, which are still enforced today. In pre-colonial times Shona women were skilled in the production, storage and processing of a wide range of nutritious indigenous food crops. With the coming of the extension service in the 1930s, plough cultivation was introduced and promoted as a male occupation, excluding women from what became a key farming activity. Ploughing, together with the ban on intercropping, created a new task of weeding, which inevitably became 'women's work'. Ploughing loosens the soil and encourages the germination of weeds, whereas underplanting cereals with spreading crops, such as cowpea and pumpkin, smothers weeds, can enrich the soil, and allows much higher food production from the same area of land.

The following research and extension policies, instigated by the agrochemical industry, have had a serious negative impact on local food security in Zimbabwe:

- The ban on the use of open-pollinated maize varieties, unique to Zimbabwe, forces smallholders to buy hybrid maize seed every year. The production of hybrid maize requires costly external inputs, such as fertilizer and pesticides. Hybrid maize has been bred with a soft kernel to improve its milling qualities, but to the detriment of its storage qualities. This means that rural women are obliged to use large amounts of organophosphate pesticides in order to preserve their maize grain from one harvest to the next. These women risk contamination not only when they apply the pesticide in the granary but also during their task of winnowing, before it is pounded or ground into mealie-meal [5].
- The strict enforcement of monocropping has led to the demise of important food crops, such as cowpea, pigeon pea, pumpkin and melon, traditionally grown in mixed cropping systems.
- The ban on dambo cultivation, according to legislation passed in 1927 and in 1952, has restricted the production of rice, taro and Livingstone potato.
- Government research focused on the 'improvement' of seed-propagated crops has led to the demise of non-seed crops such as sweet cassava, sweet potato, taro and Livingstone potato.
- The introduction of exotic vegetable crops, such as tomato, rape and cabbage has increased pest problems and replaced the more nutritious, less pest-susceptible, indigenous, green leafy vegetables.

> - The commoditization of maize has led to the demise of small grain crops, such as sorghum and millet.
>
> Rural families impoverished by AIDS require zero-input, labour-preserving, survival strategies for food and cash crop production. This means food crop varieties that are nutritious; tolerant to drought, pests and diseases; able to be stored using traditional methods; grown using a farming system which discourages weeds and promotes soil fertility.

To absorb the recommended daily dose of the nutrients for HIV-positive adults, massive amounts must be consumed every day; for example, one kilogram of fresh guavas for vitamin C, and one kilogram of bambara for vitamin B complex [6]. Vitamin and mineral supplements must be bought in private pharmacies as they are currently unavailable in most government clinics and hospitals. This costs approximately US$15 per month – out of the reach of many, especially rural women.

Exposure to organophosphate and carbamate pesticides

Organophosphate and carbamate pesticides can act as immuno-suppressants [7,8]. Experiments have shown that pesticide exposure can reduce T-cell proliferative response and cell mediated immunity in a range of mammals, including humans. In host resistance tests, pesticide-induced immunotoxicity reduces resistance to bacterial, viral and parasitic infections and promotes tumour growth in a number of animal species. Previous or concurrent sickness is known to make pesticides more toxic. In humans exposed to pesticides, T- and B-cell deficiencies are more noticeable among people with pre-existing disease [9].

Extremely toxic pesticides are applied by women and children in many African countries. While male smallholder farmers may be afforded some degree of protection through wearing overalls and gumboots, in the communal areas women and children are not usually protected at all. Children are too small to wear protective clothing, and women cannot wear overalls for cultural reasons. Small-holder farmers at most risk from pesticide poisoning are those who produce cash crops such as cotton and horticultural produce. In Zimbabwe, malathion, dimethoate and monocrotophos are the most

Table 5.1 Division of farm and household tasks between women and men in a cotton-growing area of Zimbabwe

Task	% women	% men
Farm planning and decision-making	20	80
Sourcing small grain seed (for food crops)	25	75
Herding livestock	75	25
Planting cotton and maize*	25	75
Planting food crops*	40	60
Thinning cotton*	20	80
Weeding*	50	50
Conventional scouting in cotton*	25	75
Buying pesticides*	25	75
Fetching water for mixing with pesticides*	75	25
Spraying cotton with pesticides*	15	85
Guarding fields against wild animals and livestock	25	75
Picking cotton*	10	90
Pre-grading cotton*	50	50
Baling cotton*	50	50
Transporting bales to depot and receiving payment*	5	95
Harvesting maize*	75	25
Shelling maize*	80	20
Harvesting traditional food crops	100	0
Storing food crops*	75	25
Repairing granary	25	75
Smearing cow dung over granary walls	100	0
Applying chemicals to stored grain*	85	15
Winnowing of grains*	100	0
Grinding of grains*	85	15
Cutting down old cotton stalks*	80	20
Labouring off-farm for cash	0	100
Labouring off-farm for food	100	0
Cooking food	90	10
Carrying firewood	40	60
Carrying water	100	0
Washing dishes and family clothes	80	20
Repairing huts	98	2
Childcare	95	5
Taking children to the clinic	90	10
Caring for the sick	100	0

* Activity involves direct contact with organophosphates and carbamate pesticides.

commonly used organophosphates in these farming systems. For women there is an additional risk from their task of winnowing grains that have been stored with the organophosphate grain protectant pirimiphos methyl. The consumption of vegetables that harbour pesticide residues is also common in rural areas.

Extreme tiredness and fatigue will, over time, put extra stress on the immune system. Table 5.1 lists the common farm and household tasks and how these are shared between women and men in a cotton growing area, showing where these involve exposure to organophosphate pesticides. Such demanding physical activity is likely to be a contributing cause of immuno-suppression in women with HIV.

Other factors

Evidence that exposure to other infections depresses immunity directly is complex and sometimes paradoxical [10], but clearly long-term and severe debilitation from recurrent infections will lead to severe nutritional and therefore immune deficiency states. Parasitic diseases such as malaria and bilharzia are on the increase. Intestinal infections are common from poor hygiene and contaminated water. Many diseases go untreated in rural women. There is a great deal of pressure on women to produce many children, but rapidly repeated childbearing can suppress the immune system [11,12]. Rural women are at risk of multiple infections with sexually transmitted diseases if their husbands continue to be unfaithful.

Stress can be a major factor in immuno-suppression [13]. Women in Africa bear responsibility for childcare, care of the sick and the provision of household food security. Many rural women are living in extreme poverty; once their husbands die of AIDS they may become destitute as a result of paying medical expenses and funeral costs [14]. Women are constantly worried about having sufficient food and money for their children's school fees [15]. AIDS widows may be ostracized by neighbours and family.

The consequences of premature death of HIV-infected women

The number of orphans in Africa is increasing at an alarming rate. By the end of 2000, it was expected that 13 million children had lost a mother or both parents to AIDS: more than 10 million are under fifteen. In southern Africa the number of orphans is approaching 10 per cent of the population [16]. Many households are headed by children, some as young as ten years [17]. Orphaned children often drop out of school and may suffer from illness and wasting due to malnutrition. They will also be suffering from trauma at the loss of their parents [18]. In the absence of their parents, children may lack the cultural values and behaviour necessary for integration into society [19]. They become alienated and may be a threat to peace and security.

One of the most agonizing worries for people with AIDS is the fate of their children [20]. Rural women deserve the chance for longer life whether or not they have dependent children. In the case of mothers, the imperative to help is increased because of the impact on child survival and the development and human rights costs of ignoring their needs.

Recommendations to increase longevity in HIV-positive mothers

Information, support, food supplements

Given the scale of impoverishment caused by so-called 'structural adjustment' programmes, and low levels of government action, recommendations for HIV-positive mothers must be based on low-cost activities that can be implemented by non-government organizations. Information on HIV/AIDS must be made accessible to illiterate and semi-literate people living in rural areas to help them understand the causes of disease and the structure and function of the immune system. They need information on diet, the need for clean water and recommended food supplements.

It is crucial that women know their status regarding HIV/AIDS. The earlier the infection is confirmed the sooner women can attempt to reduce the risks of immune-suppression. However, women will only be motivated to find out their status when they have access to resources to improve their life expectancy. Access to voluntary counselling, testing and support must be greatly increased, and linked with tangible benefits. Nutritional supplements should be heavily subsidized in Africa and made widely available in shops and community centres at affordable prices, before people are dying of AIDS.

Indigenous food crops that have a low external input and labour requirements, such as cassava, sweet potato, sorghum, millet, bambara and fruits, should be encouraged. Community support groups offer the best hope for women who are seeking to protect themselves from infection or to live positively with HIV. The many churches scattered throughout rural areas are already doing a great deal of work on HIV prevention and care of the dying. Other community-based organizations such as schools and NGO project offices can foster support groups. Farmer Field Schools have been shown to provide information and support to vulnerable people in Cambodia and widows in the Zambezi Valley [21].

Production of pesticide-free food and cash crops

International agreements regarding the safe use of pesticides should be observed and the use of immuno-suppressing pesticides, notably organophosphates and carbamates, should be banned globally, but as a priority in high HIV-prevalent areas. Alternative methods of pest control such as the use of tolerant and resistant crop varieties, crop rotation, mixed cropping, conservation of natural enemies, biological control and the use of natural repellents and herbal insecticides should be mainstreamed within national research and extension programmes.

AfFOResT is a local NGO in Zimbabwe which has developed systems for the production of organic vegetables and cotton without any significant drop in yield by smallholder farmers who had previously been heavily dependent on conventional pesticides. These Farmer Field Schools have attracted many AIDS widows keen to reduce their expensive inputs. Many other NGOs throughout Africa support low-input, sustainable agriculture; these practices should be documented and more widely promoted by international agencies. Local government research and extension should reorientate their policy towards farmers living with HIV and AIDS [22].

Rural women need training and support to process cash crops to a standard acceptable in both local and overseas markets. Processing of nutritious food crops into fortified biscuits and juices for people living with HIV should be developed. To improve their economic position, African women farmers must be well organized and able to negotiate with buyers, skills that can be learnt through 'training for transformation' [23]. Micro-credit can enable groups of self-reliant women to build up small-scale, community-based business enterprises.

Conclusion

African women, as mothers and farmers, have been responsible for household food security and family survival. A serious, integrated effort by the international community, can help the millions of HIV-positive women achieve a life expectancy comparable to those living with HIV in Western countries. This sound development investment will enhance the quality and longevity of a crucial sector of the population who ensure child survival and community stability in the majority rural population. Eliminating exposure to hazardous organophosphate pesticides and fostering sustainable agriculture are key components. Such a strategy is far more cost-effective, sustainable and feasible than making anti-retroviral therapy widely available in rural areas. It would require greatly scaled up international and national resource commitment, but would be money extremely well spent.

Note

This is an abridged version of a paper that first appeared in Southern Africa AIDS Information Dissemination Service, *SAfAIDS News*, 9(1), March 2001, which we thank for permission to reproduce. www.safaids.org.

References

1 United Nations. 'The HIV/AIDS pandemic and its gender implications'. Division for the Advancement of Women, Report of the Expert Group Meeting, Windhoek, 13–17 November 2000.

2 Chaitow, L. *HIV and AIDS the Natural Way*, Shaftesbury: Element, 1999.

3 Iliff, E. Harare, *pers. comm.*, 2001.

4 Page, S.L.J., Page, H. In *Journal of Agriculture and Human Values*, VII(4), 1991: 3–19.

5 Page, Page, *op. cit.*, 1991.

6 Gooch, J. Nutritionist, University of Zimbabwe, Harare, *pers. comm.*, 2001.

7 Sharma, R.P., Tomar, R.S. In Ballantyne, Marrs (eds) *Clinical and Experimental Toxicology of Organophosphates and Carbamates*, Oxford: Butterworth Heinemann, 1992, pp. 203–10.

8 Rodgers, K.E., Devens, B.H., Imamura, T. In Ballantyne, Marrs (eds) *op. cit.*, 1992, pp. 211–22.

9 Repetto, R., Baliga, S.S. *Pesticides and the Immune System: The Public Health Risks*, Washington: World Resources Institute, 1996.

10 Le Souef, P.N., Goldblatt, J., Lynch, N.R. In *Lancet* 356, 2000: 242–4.

11 Berer, M. In Berer, M. Ravindram, S. (eds) *Reproductive Health Matters*,

London: Blackwell Science, 1999, pp. 198–207.

12 Cauchi, M.N., Gilbert, G.L., Brown, J.B. *The Clinical Pathology of Pregnancy and the Newborn Infant*, London: Edward Arnold, 1984.

13 Fellen, D. In Moyers, B. (ed) *Healing the Mind*. New York: Doubleday, 1993.

14 Page, S.L.J. In Topouzis, D., du Gerny, J. *Sustainable Agriculture/Rural Development and Vulnerability to the AIDS Epidemic*, FAO and UNAIDS Best Practice Collection, 1999.

15 Page, S.L.J. Presented at AIDS, Livelihood and Social Change in Africa, Wageningen, 15–16 April 1999.

16 UNAIDS/UNICEF. Children orphaned by AIDS: Frontline responses from eastern and southern Africa, 1999.

17 Foster, G. In *AIDS Care 7*, 1995: 3–17.

18 Mukoyogo, C., Williams, G. In *Strategies for Hope*, Series No. 5. Oxford: Action Aid, AMREF and World in Need, 1991.

19 Mupedziswa, R. In *Journal of Social Development in Africa*, Harare: School of Social Work, 1998, pp. 98–105.

20 Hampton, J. In *Strategies for Hope*, Series No. 2. Oxford: Action Aid, AMREF and World in Need, 1990.

21 Topouzis, D., du Guerny, J. *op. cit.*, 1999.

22 Page, *op. cit.*, 1999.

23 Freire, P. *The Pedagogy of the Oppressed*, Harmondsworth: Penguin, 1972.

6

Women, pesticide use and access to information: experiences from Niger

Marian J.H. Hulshof and Sankung B. Sagnia

Women's role in agriculture in southwest Niger

Women play an important role in the agriculturally based economy of Niger. Agriculture is the main activity of 88 per cent of the population. Women make up 47 per cent of the total labour force, and 92 per cent are involved in agriculture [1]. Most agricultural production is destined for family consumption. Compared to men, women have limited access to pesticides and information on pesticide risks. Women, young children and babies are more at risk when exposed to pesticides. Crop protection programmes need actively to involve women to ensure that their agricultural production benefits from new developments in crop protection. The failure to address women will have a negative effect on total food production and food security, as well as on the health of women and future generations.

Millet (*Pennisetum typhoides*), sorghum (*Sorghum bicolor*), cowpea (*Vigna unguiculata*) and groundnut (*Arachis hypogaea*) are the dominant crops in the country. Millet, sorghum and cowpea are usually grown as food crops, while groundnut is generally grown as a cash crop. In the study area, the region around Niamey in the southwest of Niger, other important crops are rice (*Oryza sativa*), grown on the banks of the river Niger in irrigated perimeters or as a flooded crop, and vegetables, grown under irrigation in the dry season in the River Niger valley or near ponds.

The largest ethnic group in southwest Niger is the Zarma. Among the Zarma, as in many rural societies in the country, a rather strict labour division exists in agricultural production [2,3]. Men grow staple crops, such as millet, sorghum and cowpea, while women cultivate groundnut, Bambara groundnut (*Voandzeia subterranea*), okra (*Hibiscus esculentus*) and vegetables. Older men who are no longer capable of growing millet may grow groundnuts 'to keep themselves busy'. Irrigated crops like rice and vegetables are often grown in relatively new peri-urban areas of production and destined for the market. Here the division of labour is not so strict, but more men than women are seen.

The male head of a Zarma household should traditionally supply all basic needs of the family and is therefore responsible for staple food production. He and his male family members execute a large part of the field work in the staple crops. He takes all decisions and controls the harvest. Part of the staple food production is stored for family consumption, part of it may be sold in order to buy clothes, soap and other basic needs, and fulfil some social obligations. Women may be asked to help on the family plot, especially with sowing of millet and harvesting of cowpea. They are also responsible for certain post-harvest activities.

In addition to their many labour-consuming domestic tasks, and obligations on the family plot, almost all women cultivate fields of their own and grow some vegetables in home gardens. The women are entirely responsible for their personal fields and carry out all activities themselves (or pay somebody to do part of the work, such as ploughing). Women can spend the income from these personal fields as they like, although they are supposed to supply the family with vegetables and spices.

However, this traditional task division is under pressure as a result of increasing population, declining soil fertility, shortage of arable lands and temporary migration of male household members. Agricultural production on family plots no longer satisfies food requirements in many households. Non-farm activities account for nearly half the income in rural households in the western part of Niger. The major part of this income is spent on food to fill harvest shortfalls [4]. Men and women of all age groups mentioned shortage of food as their most important problem. Rural women implied that in practice they may contribute considerably to the provision of basic family needs, even though this is traditionally a men's task. They often use the revenues from their personal fields and other economic activities for expenses that were traditionally the men's responsibility – such as buying clothes and school supplies – and also to contribute to family food security.

Use of pesticides in crop protection

Declining soil fertility, low and unreliable rainfall, and pests and diseases all contribute significantly to low yields. In 1983, the Niger government started a crop protection programme by introducing 'Village Crop Protection Brigades' (Programme Brigades Village-oises). In each village volunteers were trained in monitoring and controlling pest problems. This crop protection programme was based on the use of pesticides, which were supplied free. From 1990 onwards the government stopped pesticide subsidies, and the activities of the village crop protection brigades diminished. The Village Crop Protection Programme was exclusively for men. Only male volunteers were trained; the treated crops were mostly millet and cowpea, for which the men are responsible [5,6].

Most farmers, women or men, in southwest Niger growing rain-fed crops in traditional cropping systems no longer use pesticides because of the high costs compared to the limited economic benefits, and because, with the exception of some pesticides for seed treatment, they are not available in the villages. The situation is different for farmers growing irrigated rice and vegetables, which are often produced for the market in areas close to larger cities where pesticides are more easily available. These farmers generally have cash to buy pesticides, and the economic benefits of pesticide use are more evident. Although farmers growing rainfed crops know and use many traditional crop protection methods, nearly all farmers, whether they grow rainfed crops, vegetables or rice, see pesticides as the best remedy against pests and diseases. Almost all would use pesticides 'if they were not so expensive', or 'if they were available when you need them'. These findings have been confirmed by other studies [7,8].

The national Crop Protection Service (Direction de la Protection des Végétaux – DPV) plays a major role, by organizing spraying campaigns on food crops in areas where important crop losses due to pest outbreaks are forecast. Most of the campaigns target grass-hoppers, other migratory insect pests and bird pests, in millet, sorghum and cowpea, but other pests and crops may be treated. The DPV applies pesticides by hand sprayers, trucks or airplanes.

When farmers use pesticides, they generally have no idea what they are applying. The pesticides for sale on markets in Niger, where most farmers buy their pesticides, are often poorly packed and labelled; they may be outdated and security measures are not taken. Dusting powders may be sold right next to vegetables. In a study that analysed market samples of pesticides, it appeared that the contents of a package often did not correspond with the label and that unlabelled packages sold as 'poison' or 'pesticide' contained a wide variety of active ingredients (or sometimes no active ingredients) The study found that highly persistent and banned pesticides, such as aldrin, were being sold illegally [9].

Gender differences in use of pesticides

Regardless of the crop or the kind of pest, women use less pesticide than men (Tables 6.1 and 6.2). For traditional crops gender differences in pesticide use are difficult to compare. While more men than women use pesticides (Table 6.3), this may be a crop rather than a gender effect. As explained, women do not grow millet and cowpea, and men rarely grow groundnut. If groundnuts are attacked less by pests and diseases than millet and cowpea, it would be logical to use less pesticide. The necessity of applying pesticides in the field is debatable for all three crops, and depends very much on the situation. Nevertheless, using pesticides for seed treatment is strongly recommended for all three crops in southwest Niger. A gender effect would be indicated if fewer women than men use pesticides for seed treatment.

Although gender differences in pesticide use were not statistically significant, the percentage of women using pesticides is consistently lower than men. This corroborates other studies in the Sahel. For example, a large-scale study in five Sahelian countries found that only 23 per cent of the women use pesticides, against 85 per cent of the men, although both sexes are equally involved in agriculture [10].

Table 6.1 Women and men farmers using pesticides on tomato and cabbage (municipality of Niamey, 1998 survey)

Crop	% of men	% of women
cabbage	100 (n = 30)	82.3 (n = 17)
tomato*	96 (n = 28)	94.4 (n = 18)

* Differences were not significant in tomatoes.

Table 6.2 Women and men farmers using pesticides on rice against different pests (more than one pest possible, southwest Niger, 1998 survey)

Pest	% of men (n = 41)	% of women (n = 19)
Insects	31.7	21.0
Diseases	22.0	5.3
Weeds	7.3	0
Rodents	19.5	10.5
Birds	5.0	5.0

Women seem to use pesticides less often than men, and appear to be either less informed about the kind of pesticides they use, or to use different pesticides to men – or both, as appeared in one of our surveys (Table 6.4). We found in the vegetable survey (mostly tomato and cabbage, grown by both men and women) that the most popular pesticides among the women were the dust formulation of Super-Homaï (active ingredients diazinon + thiram + methyl thiophanate) and 'DDT' (the name 'DDT' seems to be given to almost any liquid pesticide). More than half the vegetable growers, both men and women, used at least one pesticide of which they did not know the name. Use of a more expensive pesticide, Karate (active ingredient

Table 6.3 Women and men farmers using pesticides in rainfed field crops (two villages south of Niamey, 1998 survey)

Crop	Using pesticides for seed treatment		Applying pesticides in the field	
	% of men	% of women	% of men	% of women
millet	45 (n = 40)	n.a.	7.5 (n = 40)	n.a.
cowpea	34.5 (n = 40)	n.a.	5.7 (n = 35)	n.a.
groundnut	n.a.	15 (n = 40)	n.a.	0 (n = 40)

n.a = not available.

Table 6.4 Men and women farmers using different kinds of pesticides in vegetables (more than one pesticide possible, municipality of Niamey, 1995 survey)

Trade name	Active ingredient	% of men (n = 53)	% of women (n = 22)
Baygon	propoxur	2	0
Decis	deltamethrin	8	0
Dimethoate	dimethoate	13	0
Karate	lambda-cyhalothrin	30	5
Lindane	lindane	2	0
Super-Homaï	methyl-thiophanate + thiram + diazinon	8	32
'DDT'[1]	unknown	51	55
Unknown[2]	unknown	58	18

[1] DDT' is not officially sold in Niger, although it cannot be ruled out that there is some illegal trade. Farmers seem to use this name for any liquid pesticide.

[2] Answers included: 'wettable powder', 'liquid pesticide', 'powder', 'red pesticide', 'white pesticide'.

lambda-cyhalothrin), is very popular among the male vegetable growers, but rare among the women, or they may use it without knowing its name.

With the exception of one woman rice grower who claimed to have sprayed pesticides using a ULV sprayer, we did not find any women using spraying equipment. All women farmers applied pesticides using watering cans (on vegetables) or manually, for instance in case of dust formulations such as Super-Homaï. Applications with ULV sprayers is done by male labourers or male family members.

Women appear not only to use fewer pesticides but also to have less access to information on pesticide risks. During a survey of sixty rice growers, ten statements were made to both women and men farmers concerning the benefits and the risks of pesticides, and farmers were asked to say if they agreed or disagreed. Men had on average six right answers, while women had on average five right answers. In another study among forty female farmers, we found that only one-third knew that they had to take precautions when using pesticides.

Explaining gender differences in access to pesticide use and information

Differences between women and men in this area of Niger may be due, among other things, to the following [11]:

• Women are less mobile than men, especially in rural areas, and often do not have the opportunity to visit local markets because of distance and time constraints. Moreover, they are less able to visit pesticide stores, which are only found in the larger cities. In one of our survey villages we found that if women used pesticides at all, they bought Super-Homaï, one of the cheapest and most available pesticides in village markets in the region. The only exception was a woman using a liquid pesticide that her husband had bought in town.

• Women lack the financial means to buy pesticides, or have other priorities.

• The real importance of women's crops for family food security may be underestimated, not only by the farmers themselves but also by crop protection officials, policymakers and extension workers. Thus any development programme involving the use of pesticides is more likely to address male farmers.

• The large majority of agricultural extension workers in Niger are men. Although a male extension worker may train or hold meetings with groups of women farmers, such contact is much easier for female extension workers.

Although women use less pesticide on their personal fields than men, this does not mean that they do not handle pesticides:

• Their domestic tasks may involve manipulation of pesticides or pesticide containers: empty pesticide containers are sometimes used for collecting water or storing cooking oil and seeds. In some rural societies, also including southwest Niger, women play a major role in seed selection and treatment just before the onset of the rainy season (e.g. decortication of groundnuts and cowpeas, dehusking of maize cobs). Given the fact that this produce may be treated with dust formulations of organophosphorus and organochlorine insecticides before storage to protect against storage pests (as we found frequently), any person preparing the seeds for storage faces risks of contamination. Pesticides may be stored in the house and may be used by women for other purposes, for example controlling head lice, body lice and bedbugs.

Box 6.1 Gender barriers in information exchange and transfer

The ease with which information is transferred and received depends to a large extent on who is delivering and who is receiving the message. The fact that most extension staff in Niger and in other sub-Saharan African countries are men means that a large portion of the farming populace is marginalized. Tradition and other social barriers add to this already difficult situation. In most African societies, extension messages targeting women are better delivered through women extension agents. Moreover, contact between men and women, particularly when they are not familiar with each other, is limited. This point is illustrated by an experience that the second author had in northern Nigeria, similar in many respects to most of Niger, during a survey in 1991 on cowpea storage systems at village level. In the area of food storage and preservation, there is a lot to be learnt from women, who are responsible for a large part of the storage of the family foodstuff and seed stock. This underlines the important role they play in household food security. Whereas his female partner was allowed to interview the women and enter their stores to observe how the cowpeas were stored and protected from pest infestations, and collect samples for laboratory analyses, this was not the case for the second author. This 'gender barrier' seriously affects information exchange and transfer in both directions. Women are guardians of much traditional knowledge but are denied access to valuable extension information, including safe pesticide use.

- Women use certain pesticides, mostly for seed treatment, on their own fields.
- Some government crop protection campaigns involve large-scale pesticide applications by trucks or planes, during which large areas near villages may be sprayed with pesticides.

Risks of pesticide use for women, babies and young children

Women, babies and young children are more at risk in contact with pesticides because of:

- Illiteracy: only 8 per cent of adult women in Niger can read and write, against 24 per cent of adult men [12]. Most women cannot

Box 6.2 A precious but risky food commodity

The Sahel region is prone to locust outbreaks and endemic grasshopper infestations. In Niger, thousands of hectares of crops and rangelands are infested and sprayed annually against these pests. In the 1999 cropping season 183,963 hectares were infested, of which 54 per cent (99,781 hectares) were sprayed with insecticides [13]. Interestingly, the markets in urban centres in Niger are flooded with dry grasshoppers sold as a snack. A bag of dried grasshoppers costs from 2 to 2.5 times more than that of millet just after harvest – so, despite their pest status, grasshoppers are a lucrative commodity. Nevertheless, most people are ignorant of the health risks they run in eating these creatures, which have sometimes been harvested using pesticides. In 1999, a local newspaper in the capital Niamey reported cases of poisoning in those eating the dry insects. The symptoms included stomach pains, diarrhoea and vomiting. Women are particularly prone to pesticide poisoning, through absorption via body fat and milk due to the liposolubility of some compounds, and the poisoning incidents included nursing babies, indicating that these poisonous compounds can easily find their way into the mother's milk.

read labels or messages on pesticides. This situation can be exploited by unscrupulous pesticide vendors who sell poorly packaged and labelled pesticides, as well as pesticides from dubious sources. It is very common to find pesticides being sold which are not in their original packaging.

- Possible ill effects of pesticides on babies through pregnancy or breastfeeding: women in Niger have on average seven pregnancies during their lifetime, and almost all women breastfeed their babies, 61 per cent of them for almost two years [14]. (Note also the positive, protective effects of breastfeeding.)
- Possible ill effects of pesticides on babies and young children that accompany their mothers to the field. Child health care is women's responsibility. The toxicity of pesticides depends on body weight. As such, babies and young children are more vulnerable than adults to pesticide exposure.
- Women are not usually invited to extension meetings or training sessions that deal with pesticide use, precautionary measures or health risks, and they do not feel that such invitations, when

addressed to the village or a group of farmers in general, concern them. If extension messages do reach them, no special attention is paid to the gender dimension, e.g. risks for unborn babies or nursing children.

Lessons for the future

It can be concluded that women in southwest Niger have less access to pesticides, and less access to information on pesticide use and its risks to health and the environment, than men. This may not only lead to serious health problems in women and children caused by pesticides, but may also have serious economic consequences. Pesticide use in southwest Niger is still mainly seen as a matter for men, with no attention paid to women's needs. If this continues, women's agricultural production will not benefit from new developments in crop protection; an increasing gap between men's and women's agricultural production could affect, for instance, family food security and the economic independence of women.

To develop a crop protection programme that takes the gender dimension into account, data collection should stress the economic importance of women's agricultural production and show differences in access to information on, and alternatives to, pesticide use. Research and extension programmes should consider specific women's needs, paying special attention to women's crops and access to information on crop protection and crop protection methods and materials for women. Women need to be recruited into the extension service and trained in crop protection to help achieve these targets.

Note

We would like to thank Oumarou Saïdou, Mounkeïla Guirmey, Aline Ouedraogo née Rouamba, Gilbert Silva, Idé Dodo, assistants and students of the Extension Division of DFPV for their invaluable assistance in collecting the data.

References

1 UN Statistics Division, *The World's Women 2000: Trends and Statistics*. Women in Development Network http://www.focusintl.com/statr1f4. htm.

2 Olivier de Sardan, J.P. *Les Sociétés Songhay-Zarma (Niger–Mali), chefs, guerriers, esclaves, paysans*, Paris: Editions Karthala, 1984.

3 Hopkins, J., Levin, C., Haddad, L. In *American Journal of Agricultural Economics*, 76, 1994: 1219–25.

4 Hopkins, J., *et al.*, *op. cit.*, 1994.

5 Yaye, H., Danga, I., Haag, J. *Résultats de l'évaluation du Programme Brigades Villageoises (ULV)*, Cellule de Suivi et Evaluation, Niamey, Niger: DPV, 1989.

6 De Groot, A. In *International Journal of Pest Management*, 41(4), 1995: 243–8.

7 De Groot, *op. cit.*, 1995.

8 De Groot, A., Djibo, H. 'Possibilités de lutte intégrée en cultures maraîchères au Niger', *Sahel PV Info*, 54, 1993: 12–20.

9 Knirsch, J. *Pestizid-lebenszyklus-analyse dreier pestizide in Niger.* Eschborn: GTZ, 1993.

10 ILO. 'Analyse de la place des femmes, une expérience au Sahel', *Genre et développement,* Dakar: Programme BIT-ACOPAM, 1996.

11 Malena, C. *Gender Issues in IPM in African Agriculture,* NRI Socio-economic series 5, Chatham: Natural Resources Institute, 1994.

12 UNDP, Human Development Reports, *Human Development Indicators 2002.* http://hdr.undp.org/reports/global/2002/en/.

13 'Bilan provisoire campagne 1999', *Bulletin Phytosanitaire*, 15/99, DPV, Niger: DPV, 1999.

14 Republic of Niger and UNICEF, *Enquête à indicateurs multiples de la fin de la décenie*, MICS2, November 2000. www.childinfo.org/MICS2/ newreports/niger/niger.pdf.

7

Caught in the cotton trap: women's exposure and dependence in Benin

Simplice Davo Vodouhe

Pesticides became important in agriculture in Benin with the promotion of cotton, which provides significant revenue for the country and a cash income for the farmers involved in production. Cotton accounts for about 80 per cent of pesticides imported to Benin. Although the quantity of pesticides used is low compared to other countries, there are many cases of poisoning, including at least 70 deaths in the 2000 cotton-growing season [1], and 24 in the 2001 season [2]. Poisoning incidents occur mainly because of the context in which pesticides are used, and because farmers are not aware of the need to take precautions. The situation is aggravated by illiteracy, which makes it impossible to follow label instructions. This is a more serious problem for women, the large majority of whom are illiterate. The lack of relevant and accessible alternatives compounds the problem.

Contrary to common belief, women are stakeholders in cotton production. Women became involved in cotton production and in spraying synthetic pesticides when the price of cotton seed in Benin increased. To earn more money farmers increased their land planted to cotton, and consequently the time allocated to spraying. Men have no time to spray women's farms; they must do it themselves and bear the consequences.

This chapter reports on a study in the cotton-growing areas of Aklampa and Lonkly, which looked at how women acquire chemical pesticides, the routes of their exposure, and the effects on their health and livelihoods. It reports on cases illustrating incidents where women are the main actors, and focused on women because they are a vulnerable group. All the women interviewed use or have some problems with pesticides, and the conclusion focuses on the need to consider women as both active and passive victims of pesticide use.

About the study and the area

The author has worked with these villagers for many years, and has spent time in Lonkly and Aklampa discussing production problems with farmers. He was involved in the production of conventional cotton in a neighbouring district of the village Lonkly, but abandoned this approach because of the negative effects of chemical pesticides on health and the environment, and because farmers receive little financial return from growing conventional cotton. He now promotes organic agriculture in the village of Aklampa. The study was conducted in Fon and Adja, the farmers' languages. Discussions with farmers were open and women participated fully. Information included in this report was confirmed by at least three sources, in addition to direct observation and visits to the interviewees' fields. This allowed observation of the position of farms relative to rivers where pesticides are a source of drinking water contamination for part of the population.

The study took place in Aklampa and Lonkly, which have similar characteristics with respect to climate and soil fertility, but different cultural backgrounds. The population of Aklampa is about 14,000 and the main language is Fon, while the population of Lonkly is about 16,000. Men head most households and the families are mostly polygamous. In both villages women outnumber the men.

In addition to cotton, both regions produce cassava, maize, peanuts and cowpeas, with cashew nut trees being the main difference between the farming systems. Pesticides are extensively used on cotton, and its pesticide distribution system is the main way farmers obtain chemical pesticides. Once acquired, pesticides are very often diverted for use on food crops, particularly for spraying on cowpea and grain storage. Women are involved in these activities.

Women's access to pesticides

To understand the extent of women farmers' access to agricultural inputs in general and chemical pesticides in particular, it is important to be aware of the perceptions of extension agents on the role of women in rural development and the division of labour between women and men. In general, women farmers fall into two groups: heads of household and married women.

Women heads of households

The proportion of women-led households is smaller than those headed by men. These women are widows, divorced, single or became heads when their husbands migrated to town for job opportunities. They have charge of most of the family expenses.

Married women

Married women work on their husbands' farms, and most also manage a small plot given to them by their husband or his relatives. They can work on these plots only when they have finished work in their husband's field. There are some differences between monogamous and polygamous families. In the former, wives work mainly on their husband's farm, while in the latter some wives manage a larger farm to enable them to feed their children. Husbands assist on their wives' farms for the most difficult activities. Women sow, weed and harvest in addition to managing the home. In fact there is a clear labour division between men and women.

Although women are among the main stakeholders of agricultural production they do not have easy access to farm inputs. This is as true for a woman head of household as for a married woman. In general neither group has direct access to the facilities offered by the extension services. This situation arises partly because men dominate the extension service, and the few women employed usually play a minor role – even fewer are in positions of influence.

In Benin, the national extension service is in charge of all agricultural products. It is dominated by the government extension service, which is organized according to the subdivisions in the country, and well represented in all regions. Different agricultural services give advice to farmers on the use of agricultural inputs and other technologies. Private companies are in charge of the distribution of pesticides and other agricultural inputs.

Only a few shops sell pesticides in Benin, and this limits product choice. Farmers have access to cotton pesticides, and will use these products on other crops – for example in grain storage and on food crops, including tomatoes and vegetables. Most women farmers are involved in food crop production, but the official structure for supplying pesticides in rural areas limits their availability to women.

Officially, intervention institutions deal with farmers through their organizations. Farmers are organized into Groupements Villageois (GV) at the village level. The GVs gather to form a Union at District level, called Union Sous-Préfectorales des Producteurs (USPP), which is in charge of the supply of input and credit to farmers, and acts as an intermediary body between farmers and external institutions. This is the first line of contact between pesticide suppliers and farming organizations: the USPPs supply GVs with the inputs requested, mainly for cotton production. The Unions come together to form six Departmental Unions of Producteurs (UDP). Women are very poorly represented in these organizations, and do not play any important role in the management committees.

Women usually apply for agricultural inputs, including chemical pesticides, through their husbands or male relatives. They very often sell cotton through the same person. In spite of this, their important role in the cotton production sector is not acknowledged. Because they are denied pesticides from what is often the sole source of supply, and because pesticides are difficult to buy, women use the pesticides they obtain not only on cotton but also on vegetables.

Men and women also buy chemical pesticides on the black market. These pesticides rarely include instructions for use. The two main sources of black-market pesticides are Togo and Nigeria. There are few border controls and Togolese farmers earn a better price by selling pesticides to farmers in their neighbouring country rather than using them on their own farms. Generally these products still carry labels on the containers. Pesticides originating from the eastern neighbour, Nigeria, are rarely labelled, but have a reputation for effective action and are usually less expensive than pesticides sold through official channels in Benin.

A gender division of labour

Most activities requiring strength are carried out by men or by hiring labour. Before the cotton-boom period, men used to spray pesticides in women's fields. But as men's farm size increased, the spraying period lengthened and the men managing these large farms do not have time to work on women's fields. As a result women producers gradually began to apply pesticides themselves. The change in the division of labour has had some effect on women's exposure to pesticides. Generally women farmers cannot spray a farm the same size as a man's in the same time.

Women's exposure to pesticides in the cotton sector

Women are exposed to pesticides actively, through their own use of chemicals, and passively. The data quoted here are based on studies carried out in the villages of Lonkly and Aklampa, in the regions of Couffo and Collines respectively. In the former 34 women were interviewed, and in the latter 30 women. All of the women interviewed have grown cotton and cowpea and used chemical pesticides on both crops.

Women's exposure derives from the lack of personal protective equipment, the poor quality of spray equipment, pesticide storage, recycling of pesticide containers, and practices during spraying. Women have responsibility for washing their husbands' clothes, including those used for spraying. No special precautions are taken, and this leads to another route of exposure.

Protective equipment

Women interviewed said that those promoting pesticide use told men in the village that personal protective equipment must be worn during spraying, but none of the women had seen the required clothes, and they wear clothes they have available (see Table 7.1).

Only 15 per cent of the women interviewed in Lonkly village wear some form of mask to minimize inhalation during spraying. Some 21

Table 7.1 Clothes worn by women in Aklampa and Lonkly while spraying

	No.	%
Trousers	15	23
Skirt	18	29
Cloth	28	44
Shirt	51	79
Scarf	34	53
Hat	10	15
Nose/mouth mask	10	15
Total interviewed	64	

per cent of women sprayed with their breasts uncovered, exposing their bodies to the pesticide. Usually women would not take their babies to the farm when spraying. But for one-third of the women interviewed the scarcity of equipment forced them to spray in one session, and being at the farm for a longer period they had to take their babies and leave them at the edge of the field. Women must feed their babies at the field without any specific precautions, even those who have sprayed with their breasts uncovered. Breastfeeding babies are exposed to spray drift and skin residues. Sadly, women are contaminating both themselves and their babies.

Quality of the equipment

Women use the spray equipment available. Of the 64 women interviewed 38 (60 per cent) used a battery-operated sprayer; 26 used press sprays (40 per cent); and six (10 per cent) applied pesticides to cowpea and cotton with straw tufts (some women use more than one method). The clump-of-straw method usually involves immersing the straw tuft in a basin containing the chemical products. The basin may be on their heads or carried in their hands. Inevitably, some of the liquid leaks onto their head or bodies. This is common when spraying cowpea. To protect cowpeas, farmers will use the pesticides available in the village or sold on the black market by itinerant traders – generally cotton pesticides. This raises two problems: pesticide misuse and inadequacy of application methods. Women are the main victims of this situation as their room for manoeuvre is very limited.

Storage

Farmers commonly store pesticides in their bedrooms (49 per cent), a storehouse (31 per cent) or in the field (20 per cent). Families are in constant contact with the pesticides stored in the bedroom. Pesticides can contaminate other goods as women carry them to the field together in a basin. The usual way for a woman to carry food and drinking water – and pesticides – from home to the field is on her head. This is another source of contamination.

Pesticides containers

Asked what they did with the empty containers of endosulfan, women indicated that: 8 per cent keep them for home use; 63 per cent throw them in the bush; 19 per cent bury them; and 10 per cent burn them. Only 8 per cent of the interviewed women reuse the endosulfan containers – a hazardous pesticide now being recommended for use on cotton in Benin – because of the small capacity (1 litre). In fact, the number of women who reuse larger containers is much greater, reaching 26 per cent in Lonkly. In some other areas in the country, people use all the containers with a capacity around 4 litres. Before use, they clean them with water collected after preparing sodabi, a local drink. This water is said to be effective in removing pesticides. Once the containers are cleaned, they are used for keeping oil, drinking water and sodabi and sometimes porridge for the baby, fetching water from a well, and other normal container uses. It is not unusual to see these containers on sale in the village market.

Unsafe activities while spraying

Although women usually eat before spraying, 23 per cent of those interviewed indicated that they would eat in the field. Because spraying is physically demanding, farmers need to consume high-energy food. One woman recounted how she was affected as a result of spraying on an empty stomach: Mrs Assiba went to spray without eating, and felt dizzy. After some time she could not continue and fell down. Having called for help, neighbours brought food and she recovered. Although women know they should not eat and drink during spraying, it is difficult to obtain the application equipment and it is slow and clumsy to operate. Women need to break for a rest: during this pause some will take food and drink without washing their hands.

Pregnancy and breastfeeding

The survey found that 35 per cent of women spray while still breast-feeding, and 3 per cent of those interviewed were pregnant. This is particularly hazardous because of the need to bring babies to the field. Many women suspect a link between spraying and aborting, and some women farmers joined the organic cotton programme because they had suffered an abortion after spraying, or after assisting their husband spraying.

Health impacts of spraying

Because of the shortage of spray equipment, women have access to it for only a limited time. As a result 32 per cent of women said they

Table 7.2 Common health effects on women in Lonkly and Aklampa

	Lonkly (%) (n = 34)	Aklampa (%) (n = 30)
Headache	82	22
Skin irritation	79	41
Dizziness	79	9
Nausea	18	2
Vomiting	12	
Cough		33
Convulsion		19
Eye problems		19
No effects noted	17	24

had to spray their cotton field while ill, particularly when their husband had no time to help, or when they had no funds to hire labour. Women indicated that under these circumstances their illness was compounded, and some had been forced to go to hospital for treatment.

Women have a duty to harvest cotton and to pick vegetables. During the study, one woman reported that she went to her husband's cowpea field to help, unaware that the field had been sprayed two days previously. She became ill and had to go to hospital. Women were asked to describe health problems they experienced during and following spraying (Table 7.2).

Headaches, skin irritation and dizziness are the most common symptoms in Lonkly, followed by nausea and vomiting. In Aklampa, skin irritation and coughs are the most common complaints, followed by convulsions, eye problems, dizziness and nausea. More women noted health effects in Lonkly, although some more severe effects (convulsion) were noted in Aklampa.

Concluding remarks

Poor practices and pesticide-related ill health stem from a lack of information, limited choices, illiteracy (particularly among women), and lack of known alternatives to chemical pesticides. There is a lack of sound decision-making at a political level, recognising the need to protect farmers from pesticides, and the distinct need to target information to women to protect them. No information or statistics are available at national, regional and local levels which take account of women and men's different uses of and exposure to pesticides.

References

1 Ton, P., Tovignan, S., Vodouhe, S.D., 'Endosulfan deaths and poisonings in Benin', *Pesticides News*, 47, March 2000: 12–14.
2 Tovignan, S., Vodouhe, S.D., Dinham, B., 'Cotton pesticides cause more deaths in Benin', *Pesticides News*, 52, June 2001: 12–13.

8

A woman's work is never done: agriculture in Senegal

Abou Thiam with Seynabou Sissoko

In the agricultural sector in Senegal, women make up nearly 60 per cent of the active population, and play many roles as farmers in their own fields and as workers in their husband's fields. As in other countries in Africa south of the Sahara, Senegalese women are responsible for numerous activities in cultivation. The division of labour between women and men means that women have responsibility for preparing the seed bed, planting, hoeing, weeding, harvesting, winnowing, sorting and storing the crop, and its sale. This is in addition to their daily tasks such as collecting water, pounding grain, collecting wood for the fire and feeding their family. Women must equally earn money and produce food for the family. In domestic agriculture, they cultivate vegetables, market garden crops and rice.

The falling productive potential of the land, exacerbated by desertification (see Box 8.1) has significant implications for the work of rural women. In effect, the agricultural tasks of women are heavy; the reduction in yields and the increasing practice of growing crops for cash require additional work in order to produce more.

Pesticide usage in Senegal

Chemical pesticides and fertilizers are increasingly used on crops grown commercially (cotton, sugar cane, vegetables) [2] as a result of monoculture, soil exhaustion, resistance of certain pests to pesticides, low price of the basic crops on the international market and the messages conveyed in training. The tendency is exacerbated by the inhospitable climate, population growth and new regulations over access to land. Cereal crops, such as millet and sorghum, receive very little pesticide, contrasting with rice, especially in the valley of the

> **Box 8.1 Agriculture in Senegal**
>
> Lying on the west coast of Africa, with plains and plateaux covering the bulk of the country, Senegal contends with a low and disrupted annual rainfall and creeping desertification. Nearly half the soils are poor [1], and only 20 per cent of the land is arable. Nevertheless, diverse agricultural systems support cash crops of groundnuts and cotton and subsistence crops of millet, rice, sorghum, maize and cowpeas. Market gardening is an important activity, and is concentrated along the coast between the capital of Dakar and St. Louis in the north. Fishing contributes significantly to the economy. Agriculture is an engine of the economy, but has been in profound crisis a result of physical, ecological, socio-economic and political factors. Of an estimated population of 10 million, nearly 40 per cent live in cities – the highest rate in the Sahel region – while about 60 per cent of the agricultural sector is made up of young women and men farmers.

Senegal River [3], which uses a great deal. A recent report revealed that around 2,500 tonnes of pesticides are imported annually with a value of 11 million CFA (US$20 million) [4]. Pesticide use is dominated by insecticides, many of which are hazardous organophosphates, which are difficult to use without affecting the health of poor farmers [5]. In the 1997–98 season pesticide use amounted to 138,931 kg of powder formulations, 5,988 litres of emulsifiable concentrates, and 90,625 litres of ULV (ultra low volume) formulations [6].

The massive use of chemical pesticides is often justified by invasions of desert locusts [7]. During the locust plagues of 1974, pesticides were sprayed over an area of 1.5 million hectares, almost entirely (80 per cent) by air. In the desert locust swarm that invaded over 2 million hectares in the 1988–89 cropping season, 72 per cent of pesticides were applied aerially [8]. The periodic invasions of locusts add to other attacks on cereals by beetles, caterpillars, weeds and insects. While figures are available for the spraying against migratory pest outbreaks, the market for other pesticide use is poorly recorded and not at all transparent. There is little control over the quality and quantity of the products used, and a significant part disappears into an informal market after entering the country illegally.

Pesticides often arrive in large containers in the villages in regions where demand is high, for example in the market gardening zone of the regions of Dakar and St Louis. The sellers of food and household goods are often also distributors of pesticides, and they repackage pesticides in cans, bottles, buckets, plastic sachets or other unmarked containers for sale to farmers. Unsafe practices have brought about numerous poisonings and fatal accidents in rural Senegal [9,10]. Among the factors responsible for pesticide problems in the rural areas are:

- ignorance about the products and their danger to health and the environment;
- users are ill-informed and often cannot read the labels, so cannot respect instructions given by the manufacturer;
- non-use of personal protective equipment (boots, gloves, glasses, etc.) during the application of pesticides, as these are costly and not adapted to a tropical climate;
- conditions of storage and faulty conservation of pesticides;
- inappropriate application methods, or poor and faulty application equipment;
- demand for the containers – bottles, barrels, metal or plastic cans (often made attractive by the manufacturer) – to store water, milk or cooking oil. Residues of pesticides in poorly cleaned containers have been fatal;
- lack of regulated sales and inappropriate storage accentuates the dangers;
- use of pesticides for other and inappropriate purposes, such as killing fish, treating body lice, or applying to the wrong pests/crops;
- disposal contrary to regulations intended to protect health and the environment;
- presence in the country of banned, severely restricted, or inappropriate pesticides.

Analyses have found residues of pesticides in fruits and vegetables sold on the markets in Dakar. The organochlorine pesticides most frequently found are HCB, heptachlor, lindane and aldrin. Dieldrin, endosulfan, DDE (a breakdown product of DDT) and chlordane have been found in cherry tomatoes. The traces found are higher than the maximum residue levels allowed in France [11].

Women and children exposed

Problems linked to the use of chemical pesticides and fertilizers particularly affect rural women. They carry out many activities of production associated with the use of chemical pesticides, and are prominent in the market gardening sector. They are responsible for many of the aspects of rain-fed cultivation, the processing of fish and other seafoods, and are the main producers of rice, the main staple food, in the southern region of Casamance.

Women and children are especially exposed to the negative effects of chemical pesticides used in vegetable, rice and cotton fields [12]. In most societies in Senegal the decision-making power and access to the means of production are in the hands of men. The husband buys the pesticides at the market or in the village shop. He does not pass on information to his wife about the product, and often does not know much himself. As soon as pest damage appears, whatever product is readily available in the house is used: a fungicide could be used rather than an insecticide, or vice versa. Farmers practising subsistence agriculture on poor land have hardly had recourse to pesticides, but suffer the consequences of pesticide use by their neighbours.

In Senegal, some efforts have been made to increase the literacy of the rural population, and of women in particular. However, even when a farmer can read in her own language, she may not be able to read the label instructions, which are complicated and often in French or English. Many accidents are caused by a lack of knowledge [13].

In certain regions of Africa 100 per cent of the fields are managed by women, and many women are custodians of traditional agricultural techniques – such as mixed cropping and crop rotation – which play a key role in the battle against pests.

The activities supporting women suffer too often from a charitable approach, or may focus on 'women's areas', such as health care and grain milling, at the expense of promoting socio-economic development and restoration of the environment. In order to be heard, women in Senegal have understood the pressing necessity to form their own modern organizations: women's groups, associations or co-operatives, and projects.

A dangerous practice: pesticides used to conserve seafoods

Women on the Atlantic coast south of Dakar (the region of Thies) dry and sell fish. They are organized in co-operatives; for example, that of Mbour consists of around 700 women. Problems face the women and commercial intermediaries in preserving the fish, protecting them against insects, transporting and selling to various internal markets and in Mali, Guinea and other nearby countries.

Table 8.1 Results of analyses of pesticides found in processed sea foods and diverse powders

Sample	Analysis	Product identified	Commercial name	Results (ppm)	Results (%)	Acceptable daily intake (mg/kg)	Maximum residue limit (mg/kg)
Guédj séché (dried fish)	quantitative	Pirimiphos methyl	Actellic	213		0.01	0.5
Guédj	quantitative	Malathion	powder	30.32		0.02	0.5–3
		Fenitrothion	Gaïndé™	108		0.03	0.5
Powder	qualitative	Malathion	powder		1.98	0.02	0.5–3
		Fenitrothion	Gaïndé™		2.12	0.03	0.5
Guédj	qualitative	Malathion	powder	107		0.02	0.5–3
		Fenitrothion	Gaïndé™	2.41		0.03	0.5
Salt		None					
Guédj		Malathion	powder	82		0.02	0.5–3
		Fenitrothion	Gaïndé™	82.23		0.03	0.5
Salt		Deltamethrin	K'Othrine™	692		0.01	0.05
Powder		Pirimiphos	Actellic		2	0.01	0.5

Source: Reference 14.

During the rainy season fish dry poorly, and may be stored for some time before selling. The fish are vulnerable to pest attacks which can cause losses of 10–45 per cent. To prevent these problems, the women fish dryers and the commercial intermediaries douse their dried fish with a mixture of salt and powdered insecticide which they call 'DDT' – analyses carried out in 1982 showed that it was a formulation of fenitrothion [15]. In 1991, the Institute of Food Technology (ITA) carried out a study on the quality of processed fish and other seafoods at the point of sale. It appeared that the processors mix pesticides with salt or brine, or they sprinkle them directly on the baskets packed with the produce. Pirimiphos methyl, malathion, fenitrothion, deltamethrin, lindane, DDT are often used for the treatment of other stored foodstuffs such as grains.

Analyses of samples of salt, powder, and processed products taken from fishing centres (Thiaroye, Kayar, M'Bour, Joal) have shown that the levels of pesticide residue have risen and are largely above the admissible standards (see Table 8.1). This activity presents risks for consumers, but even greater risks for the processors who apply the products with unprotected hands. Energetic measures need to be taken to stop such practices.

Conclusion

Women's work in agriculture in Africa is essential to the production and processing of agricultural products. Very little attention has been paid to the effects of pesticides on women and children in spite of their major role in agricultural production, and their direct or indirect use of chemical pesticides. In many regions, women are still excluded from the means of production in farming: agricultural information, access to credit and training, and the majority of activities and projects do not consider women essentially as agricultural producers. Experience shows that in programmes to improve agricultural production, it is essential to introduce strategies to give women access to land and credit, and technical assistance to appropriate technologies. Senegalese women (in both urban and rural areas) are often exposed to pesticides at work in the fields and in preparing food for the family. In order to avoid accidents, of which they are the main victims, it is imperative to reinforce their access to information regarding the risks associated with pesticide use and training in the area of plant protection. Significant efforts must be made to recognize and provide greater support to the multidimensional role of women in agriculture.

References

1 Ministère de l'environnement, *Programme d'action national de lutte contre la desertification*, Dakar, 1998.

2 Thiam, A., *Protection des cultures au Sénégal: pesticides et lutte intégrée*. Report for the Pesticides Trust, PAN Africa, March 1998.

3 Thiam, A. 'Les produits phytosanitaires dans l'écosystème du Delta du Fleuve Sénégal'. In *Cahiers Agriculture*, 5, 1996: 112–17.

4 Direction de l'environnement, *Etude de cas sur les Polluants Organiques Persistants (POPs)*, Rapport Ministère de l'Environnement et de la Protection de la Nature et UNEP Chemicals, Dakar, May 1999.

5 Kawalec, M., Bhatnagar, V.S. *Etude sur la gestion phytosanitaire des cultures dans la région du Sahel*. Mission FAO, Ministère du Développement Rural et de l'Hydraulique, Dakar: DPV, 1992.

6 Ministry of Agriculture, Plant Protection Department, 1998.

7 Ndiaye, R. *Réglementation des pesticides dangereux au Sénégal*, Série Monitoring & Briefing No. 4. Dakar: PAN Africa, October 1999.

8 UNITAR/MEPN, National Profile. *Evaluation des capacités nationales de gestion des produits chimique. Ministère de l'Environnement et de la Protection de la Nature*, Dakar: Direction de l'Environnement, 1997.

9 Germain P., Thiam A. *Les pesticides au Sénégal: une menace?*, Série Etudes et Recherches, No. 83–83, Dakar: ENDA, June 1983.

10 Thiam, A. In *La lutte anti-acridienne*, Paris: John Libbey Eurotext, 1991, pp. 193–206.

11 Diop Y., Niane, B., Diouf, A., Ciss, M., Ba, D. *Dosage des pesticides organochlorés dans les fruits et légumes vendus sur les marchés de Dakar*, Quinzièmes journées médicales et pharmaceutiques de Dakar, 17–20 February 1997.

12 Germain and Thiam, *op. cit.*, 1983.

13 Germain and Thiam, *op. cit.*, 1983; Thiam, *op. cit.*, 1996.

14 Gning, R.D., 'Un exemple d'utilisation des pesticides au Sénégal: les produits halieutiques transformés'. From seminar 'Les produits chimiques et notre santé', Rodale Sénégal, Thiès, February 1997.

15 Germain and Thiam, *op. cit.*, 1983.

9

Invisible farmers: rural roles in Pakistan

Nasira Habib

Women play a key role in the rural economy in Pakistan, and their agricultural labour leads to direct exposure to pesticides. As in many societies, there is a gender bias not only among policymakers but also in society, which reinforces the problems facing rural women. This chapter is based on interviews with women and in-depth surveys conducted between 1993 and 1996 in seven villages near Liaqatpur in the Punjab, and five villages in the districts of Khairpur and Hyderabad in the Sindh.

Women face social and economic discrimination compounded by new hazards in rural areas as pesticide use increases. About 25 per cent of farms in Pakistan now use pesticides; while women bear a major responsibility for farm work, their contribution to the agricultural economy is not recognized. Any short stay in a rural area is sufficient to observe women active in many jobs in the fields. At a meeting of twenty women in a village in Sindh, they listed at least twenty-five agriculture-related activities in which they are actively involved with their men. One woman said, 'I get up early in the morning and run either to the fields or to the animal shed. Who has the time to wash one's face? We do not even have the time to say our prayers, the workload is so much.'

The National Agriculture Policy makes no mention of women in the statement of its objectives, and only four minor references to women in the overall document. It provides no clear policy for the development of rural women, who form the backbone of the rural economy. This discrimination is reflected in the official documents and reports and as a consequence encourages officials to overlook and marginalize women's work.

The Census of Agriculture does acknowledge the work of women in agriculture. It indicated a drop in their contribution from 42.6 per cent of all family workers in agricultural households in 1980 to 36.2 per cent in 1990. In 1980, women constituted about 25 per cent of all full-time and 75 per cent of part-time workers. In 1990, the Census registered 25.87 per cent and 61.25 per cent, respectively. As the whole process of assessing the contribution of women is flawed, the validity of the figures is highly questionable. These figures do not correspond to the reality because the smaller the size of the landholding, the more intense, active and efficient the role of the women becomes. It is not cost effective for smallholders to hire paid labour.

The decade from 1980 to 1990 saw a further fragmentation of land holdings. Fragmentation means that women's work has to be even more intensive in order to make agriculture economically affordable. Women have to work more, longer and harder. They are economically active and substantially contribute to many activities, including:

- crop farming and livestock keeping;
- post harvest activities;
- household management;
- off-farm and non-farm economic activities;
- bearing and rearing children and looking after the sick.

While some of these activities are recognized as important, the visibility of women is selective and their invisibility is rooted both in economic and in social factors. Rural women of Pakistan are economically active but are also economically dependent. Women have neither ownership nor control over resources and are expected to surrender their rights in favour of brothers or husbands.

Women work and produce on land they do not own. With the introduction of market economics the situation has further deteriorated. The harvest is sold by and through men, and men control income. Land is owned by men and the fruits of the land are enjoyed by men. Thus men automatically become visible and women become invisible. Who actually worked in what way to produce the crops is not taken into account.

Other factors, like lack of access to credit facilities, gender bias in transfer of new technologies and required training, education and extension, further compound the matter and force women to remain behind the scenes.

The pervasive patriarchal ideology reinforces the economic subordination further. Gender discrimination starts from the early days of a female child. She is taught not to value herself when it comes to equality with males in the family. This applies even to small matters such as eating food of the same quality. The systematic unjust socialization takes root in the conscious and unconscious minds of women. A woman has no power to make decisions on how to behave or dress, whether or not to get an education, whom to marry, whether to have children and how many, whether to plan a family, whether to maintain ties with her parents' family, marriage or divorce, contact with the outside world, her health and so forth. All powers are vested with the males of the family.

Such circumstances make the woman unaware of the complexities of the outside world and foster an ignorance of the laws of the country that govern her life. She does not know how she is made a featherless bird. But she knows full well that individually it is not easy to fight for her rights, even if she wishes to. She is caught in a complex web and thus succumbs to male authority and dominion.

Women's encounter with pesticides

Women have always played a key role in disease and pest management, which takes the form of various activities of soil improvement and fertility management as well as direct measures to eradicate diseases in crops and animals. But with the advent of new pest management techniques and technologies women have been bypassed. As only men are recognized as farmers, they have become the focus of extension. In order to comprehend fully women's encounters with pesticides, and the impact of these chemicals, it is necessary to look at their total farming workload.

In the area studied in Liaqatpur, over sixty farm working activities carried out by women have been identified, in the course of which they frequently encounter toxic chemicals. The survey notes that, generally, women are not directly involved in spraying pesticides, but are exposed to them in the following activities:

- helping mix pesticides;
- washing tanks;
- disposal of empty containers;
- washing pesticide-soaked clothes;
- storage of pesticides;
- weeding and thinning;
- picking cotton;

- storing the harvested cotton;
- collecting sticks and using them for fuel;
- taking food to men in the fields.

Generally, women wash clothes in water courses which are near or run through the fields. In most cases, houses are surrounded by the fields that are sprayed, exposing all the inhabitants to deadly poisons. During weeding – a task which falls to women five to six times a season – pesticides are inhaled and absorbed. Cotton crops are sprayed at least six or seven times in a season, and in sugar-cane fields the exposure is even greater.

Taking food to men in the fields brings women to freshly sprayed fields, and can prove extremely dangerous. Jobs like taking animals to the fields, cutting fodder for animals, taking care of vegetable plots, collecting material for fuel, bathing animals in the water courses, are all activities where women could be affected by the poisons, in addition to direct involvement in agriculture or related activities that expose them to the hazards of pesticides.

Major hazards arise from cotton production

Cotton picking is one of the main areas of women's exposure to pesticides. Exposure begins when women treat the seeds with sulphuric acid and carries on through to storage of the picked cotton. Seed treating is carried out using a large vessel, where acid is mixed thoroughly with the seeds in a ratio of 2 grams of acid to 1 kilogram of cotton seeds. After a few minutes, the seeds are washed off with water and dried. Then the seeds are ready to be sown. The same vessel is used for other purposes in the house such as washing clothes.

Women are engaged in cotton picking for a period of two and a half to three months. This constant and prolonged exposure to toxic chemicals poses in many ways greater health problems than spraying itself. While picking, the women are vulnerable to cuts and skin rashes that further expose them to the hazards of pesticides. Studies quoted in the report of this survey have shown that 'out of a total of 88 female cotton pickers only 1 per cent could be termed out of danger. 74 per cent had blood acetylcholinesterase (AChE) inhibition between 12.5–50 per cent. 25 per cent were in dangerous conditions where blood AChE inhibition was between 50–87.5 per cent.' After picking, women are not in the habit of changing clothes that may have had contact with pesticides.

Box 9.1 A history of pesticide use in Pakistan

In the 1950s chemical pesticides were used for the first time in Pakistan to combat locust attacks. In 1954, formulated pesticides amounting to 254 tonnes were imported. That was the beginning of the pesticide business in the country. Until 1980, the government controlled the import and subsidized the distribution of pesticides.

In 1995 pesticide sales were worth 9 billion rupees (US$222 million), excluding the relatively large quantities smuggled across the border. About 145 pesticide formulations have been registered. Pyrethroids make up 45 per cent of the market by value, followed by organophosphates at 39 per cent, organochlorines at 9 per cent and carbamates at 4 per cent. Approximately 90 per cent of insecticides are used on cotton – which is grown on an area of 6.62 million acres.

According to the Agriculture Census, in 1980 some 4 per cent of total farms used chemical plant protection measures; this rose to around 25 per cent in the 1990s – that is, 1.28 million farms, or up to 16 per cent of the total cropped area.

Free aerial spraying was previously provided to control pest attacks on major crops. The Plant Protection Department has a fleet of twenty-two aircraft, which sprayed about 351,000 hectares of crop area in 1995–96.

Influenced by international campaigns, 21 pesticides have been de-registered, including four of the Dirty Dozen pesticides, and their import banned. However, the overall situation regarding overuse, and strict enforcement of regulations, seems bleak. The policy and regulatory focus are on 'quality standards' and adulterated pesticides, rather than on quantities of usage.

All the respondents pick cotton during pregnancy as well, which poses additional problems: 'I go for picking even to the last day during pregnancy', said one woman. Women feed children in the fields, without first washing, posing serious health hazards for the mother and child. During the survey, it was noted that some of the women carry their small children while picking cotton. Many children were found in the fields either helping their mothers or just following them. All the young pickers were girls.

During cotton picking, pesticide poisoning has increased and symptoms reported include sneezing, muscular pain, dizziness, nausea, burning skin, itching, coughing, headache, blisters on body and suffocation.

Vulnerability and health care

The women interviewed found it ridiculous to be asked how they treat symptoms of poisoning and laughed at the researcher for suggesting they consult a doctor. It is not possible to acquire medicine for small ailments. One of them remarked, 'Unless we are unable to move, we do not think of going to a doctor or of taking medicine.' Some local remedies are used; for example, in cases of skin burning, mustard oil or butter oil is applied. 'Where can we get that much money to spend on treatment for burns?' remarked a woman. This is a reflection of the low status assigned to women and how they have internalized it. They cannot 'afford the luxury of medicines' when there are so many other needs to be attended to in the family. The needs, problems and interests of women come last.

One woman who did spray pesticides, Perveen, has been adversely affected. Her most painful complaint is that she cannot hold food in her stomach; she vomits as soon as she consumes any. Other symptoms include sneezing, watery discharge from her nose, and pain in the ribs. She has taken medicines but to no avail. She feels better for three or four days and then the complaints recur.

Generally speaking, farmers feel that there are many new diseases which were unheard of in the past. Although there is no laboratory-tested evidence, they tend to attribute the introduction of diseases like recurrent fever, blurred eyesight, diabetes, blood pressure and cancer to the use of chemical pesticides and chemical fertilizers.

The examples reveal rural women's vulnerability to chemical pesticides. Unfortunately, in the absence of proper diagnostic procedures, it is difficult to pinpoint the cause of any illness as arising from exposure to pesticides. An exception is the case of acute poisonings. However, treatment is far from straightforward. As a doctor from Liaqatur commented, 'doctors are not trained to find the cause of a particular ailment where farmers are exposed to pesticides. Thus they are unable to diagnose the illnesses properly. Generally, painkillers are given in such cases.' As women's access to health care, even during times of visible discomfort, is minimal there is no monitoring of the absorption of pesticides, of the impact on blood, reproductive organs, size of infants, and so on.

While the pesticides law has been amended several times, the amendments have focused on the issue of the quality of the chemicals; no mention has been made of the threat facing human health.

Towards a just and equitable society

A number of reforms are essential to ensure better visibility for women's work and to recognize their role in the mainstream of agriculture. It is of paramount importance that land reforms be initiated that guarantee joint ownership of agricultural land by men and women. Training and appropriate technology oriented towards women must urgently be introduced, especially where they are already key actors. Effective measures are needed to encourage participation of women in market processes. A rapid policy shift would be helped by studies which highlight women's roles in various areas, including:

- the socio-cultural life of rural Pakistan with a focus on gender relationships;
- women's role in securing food and fibre;
- the relationship between economic dependence and access to nutritious food;
- women's qualitative and quantitative contribution to agriculture in all ecological zones;
- the role of women in natural resource management;
- documenting women's knowledge on agriculture;
- agricultural technologies traditionally used by women, and their displacement by the advent of modern technology;
- women's exposure to chemical pesticides in cotton and in other cash crops, particularly in vegetable cultivation – a traditional area of women's labour that has seen a growing concentration of chemical pesticide use;
- pesticide residue levels in blood and the impact on women's reproductive systems.

Almost no programmes address the problems of rural women. A few donor-driven, men-led women's groups exist, but the token presence of women in these groups without a real voice or decision-making powers is not encouraging. Initiatives which are women-led and which understand the mechanisms of gender relationships can form a sound basis for future action that strives for a society free of discrimination and injustice.

Note

This paper first appeared in *Pesticides News* 37, September 1997. It is based on Nasira Habib, 'Invisible farmers: a study on the role of women in agriculture and the impact of pesticides on them', Penang: PAN Asia and the Pacific and Khoj-Research and Publication Centre, 1996.

10

Day in, day out: lack of protection in India

Daisy Dharmaraj and Sheila Jayaprakash

India is addicted to pesticides. The level of DDT and its metabolic products in the body fat of an average Indian is the highest in the world, and all food has pesticide or chemical residues. The use of pesticides began in the late 1940s and early 1950s, with the high-yielding strains of grains that were susceptible to pest infestation. The media advertise and advocate the use of pesticides. The Planning Commission has recommended use of pesticides as a necessary input for increasing agricultural production. Every budget passed by the Indian parliament gives the pesticide industry tax relief, and no target has been set to reduce pesticide consumption. The only light is that the Directorate of Agriculture has commenced an active campaign to promote integrated pest management (IPM).

More than half of the work in or related to agriculture is done by women, either as cultivators of their family land or as labourers. More men than women are migrating to urban areas and rural non-agricultural livelihoods, and the face of workers in the fields will in future be a woman's.

To understand the extent and type of involvement of women with pesticides, to analyse their vulnerability, and to estimate the effects on their health, PREPARE, a non-governmental organization based in Madras, South India, interviewed 100 women agricultural labourers in ten villages in Tamil Nadu in South India. The researcher visited fields in Padappai where women were at work. She chose respondents at random, struck up a rapport, observed their working environment and tools for controlling pests, and then visited them at home to carry out an interview. Incidents of poisoning and deaths mentioned by interviewees were verified in discussion with neighbours and residents of the villages.

The women interviewed were mostly married and in the reproductive age group. One third were pregnant. One third were breast-feeding, and half worked in the farm throughout the year. The other half spent at least six months in the field. All the women were directly or indirectly exposed to pesticides.

Commonly used pesticides were: monocrotophos, phosphamidon, methyl parathion, endosulfan, BHC, EBDC, dimethoate, carbaryl and decamethrin. These are extremely toxic pesticides, and three (monocrotophos, phosphamidon, methyl parathion) are included in the Prior Informed Consent procedure as unsuitable for use in developing countries. Many of the pesticides are organophosphates, and between them they include pesticides that are potentially carcinogenic, mutagenic, toxic to the liver and kidney, productive of skin problems and respiratory effects. Some may cause birth defects. But only 26 per cent of the women knew that pesticides are harmful: the others were ignorant of the dangers.

Box 10.1 The human impact of pesticide-related crop failures

In the late 1990s increasing reports of suicides among cotton farmers in the Indian states of Gujarat and Andhra Pradesh reached the headlines. The causes were complex. The cotton price was low, farmers were badly in debt, and crop losses reached astronomical levels as a result of the resistance of the major cotton pests, such as the bollworm, to pesticides. The farmers lacked information and training and had little idea of the impact of heavy pesticide use on biodiversity and the ability of insects to build up resistance. Farmers constantly increased the regularity of spraying, some up to fifty times a season, but to no effect. Part of the debt problem was attributable to the cost of pesticides. Most of the farmers who committed suicide did so by consuming pesticides. Largely those committing suicide were men. The phenomenon was widely reported, though the impact on other family members and the household economy has not been investigated. The problems do not end with the death – whether by suicide or accident – or with the man leaving the family to find work elsewhere. Inevitably women remain to pick up the pieces: caring for the family, coping with the debt, and earning the future income for survival.

Source: Reference 1.

The women have no control over the pesticides they use. The owner of the land negotiates with the dealer, who is not trained. In some cases the dealer decides the pesticide to be used, in others the decision is made by the owner, based on experience or discussions with a neighbour.

Only 14 of the respondents could read the labels on the containers, but they barely understood them, and 91 per cent felt the labels were not important. Agricultural workers are largely illiterate. Very few observed that the red triangle marked on the label indicates the high toxicity of the chemical used.

These highly hazardous chemicals are used with little care. Of the women, 21 said that they use their bare hands for mixing the chemicals; 54 either used their hands or sticks; 21 used sticks that invariably soil their hands; 56 applied pesticides on a regular basis. Most women dusted the pesticides on the plants with brushes made from the leaves of neem trees, *Lucas lucifera* (thumbal) and *Vitex nigundu* (notchi), and 32 used a mechanical spraying machine.

Protective gear – used by only 17 per cent of the women – consists of a cloth facemask and polythene covering for the hands. The others disregard even this protection, since it is uncomfortable and takes extra effort. With the water scarcity, it is not surprising to find that only 21 per cent of the women had facilities in the field for immediate cleansing of their hands, face and feet. The others wash only on returning home. Changing clothes in the field is unheard of.

The same hands that apply pesticides nurse babies at the breast, wash vegetables, cook the food, and feed the children. A cycle of poisoning occurs every day in most of these huts. With hardly two or three changes of clothing, women live with chemicals day in and day out. No one has heard of re-entry intervals between spraying and working in the field. Both are done simultaneously.

Attractive leak-proof containers are too tempting to throw away. Although 52 women said that they bury, burn or throw away the containers, the fact remains that most are reused. Shockingly, ice-cream vendors buy these to transport ice cream, milk and other ingredients.

Vomiting, difficulty in breathing and tiredness were seen in more than 75 per cent of the respondents. Skin itching, irritation of the eye and loss of consciousness seem extremely common. These are very serious indications of chronic poisoning. The women have no bargaining capacity, no recourse to action, and are used to tolerating any discomfort in order to appease hunger, each day.

Medical facilities are beyond people's reach, in relation to both distance and money. No landowner provides first aid near the field. In cases of acute poisoning, survival depends on the severity of the poisoning, the pesticide involved, availability of transport, availability of antidotes in the poorly equipped health centres, and most of all on the knowledge and experience of the health personnel. Crab juices, tamarind juice, salt solution, and excreta of pigs serve as first aid, mostly being used to induce vomiting.

In the five years before this interview was carried out, women interviewed cited seven cases of acute poisoning and eight deaths. All deaths except one took place during the act of spraying. When severely poisoned, 60 per cent of the workers have their employment temporarily terminated. Deaths are rarely compensated by any kind of payment. There were two cases of abortion. No birth defects were reported. No blood, enzyme or chromosomal study was conducted.

Note

This is an extract of an article based on the interviews which first appeared in *Pesticide Post*, PREPARE, Madras, India, May 1994.

Reference

1 Parthasarathy, S.G. In *Economic and Philosophical Weekly*, 28 March 1998: 720–26.

Part II

The science of pesticide exposure and health

11

Introduction to Part II

Miriam Jacobs

The effects of pesticides on women's and men's health range from different levels of exposure in the workplace, home or background environment to biological differences in body fat, hormones and metabolism. Both local environment and differences in body fat are likely to have a greater impact on women, who typically spend more time in the home and locality, and naturally store more fat-soluble toxic material, even when exposed to the same amount as men. The fields of public health, epidemiology and the biology of hormones and metabolism can provide the evidence.

Relatively few epidemiological studies have been designed to address gender differences in the harm caused by chronic pesticide exposure. Of the robust studies, the widely banned pesticides and their by-products, dioxins, are the most studied. Very little in the way of data is available on long-term low-dose exposure to organophosphates and other pesticides now in general use. A precautionary approach to the approval and use of these pesticides should be taken until this has changed.

Several of the studies discussed in this section focus on the organochlorine (OC) pesticides (DDT, HCH, HCB) and on dioxin contaminants, because data on this are available. These are now widely banned in most countries, and in 2000 governments concluded the Stockholm Convention on Persistent Organic Pollutants (POPs) to agree on a global phasing out of production and use. These persistent pesticides spread across the globe through a 'grasshopper' effect: they build up in the food chain and are retained in body fats. Production of most of these pesticides has already ceased. The major exception is DDT; the POPs Convention agreed that this should be retained until alternatives for malaria control in developing countries are available.

Nevertheless, human exposure to organochlorines continues through accidental, airborne and dietary exposure. Stores of obsolete pesticides are scattered throughout the world – up to 50,000 tonnes in Africa alone; many of these contain old organochlorines, which are leaking into the soil and environment, affecting humans and wildlife, entering the food chain, and spreading globally. Incineration of these pesticides leads to the formation of dioxins and furans – also POPs. This leads to dietary exposure; evidence is accumulating that DDT and its metabolite DDE are being detected at relatively high levels in feeds destined for animal consumption, where the animals are part of the human food chain [1]. Airborne drift can significantly affect body burdens, and has contaminated breast milk in all reaches of the globe. National dietary calculations will not pick up this sort of exposure, which continues with DDT and other persistent pesticides in spite of their use being banned in most countries. Governments need to ensure that recycling of these contaminants is reduced and eliminated, and that the real dangers of chronic low-dose administration and bioaccumulation are acknowledged and acted upon.

The studies in Part II are chosen to demonstrate the potential and wide-ranging impacts on women and men, girls and boys, highlighting innovative approaches in gender methodology for research. These approaches are relatively rare in scientific literature, and deserve emphasis and development. Many of the concepts should be integrated into future research projects. Failure to ask the appropriate questions, and gather the appropriate tissues and biomarkers at the outset of the study, will lead to ambiguous and inconclusive results and conclusions. With all the studies presented, analytical and methodological detail is referenced, and the original papers are available from the editors.

In the opening study Jenny Pronczuk de Garbino, Nida Besbelli and Mike Ruse of the World Health Organization give a global overview of the difficulties in documenting pesticide exposure of women and men and of the steps being taken by the WHO to address these difficulties. Dr John McLaren Howard of Biolab, London, presents clinical and personal perspectives of individual patient care where gender differences in health outcomes following pesticide exposure required differing treatments.

Ordias Chikuni and Anuschka Polder document a disturbing outcome of local DDT use in Zimbabwe. Pesticides used locally may well impact upon neighbouring areas where pesticides are not used, due to geographical and weather conditions. These impacts are felt most keenly in contaminant residues selectively collecting in breast tissue and breast milk, putting newborns and infants most at risk. Evidence presented in Part I of the volume is seen again, as women in rural areas of Zimbabwe are less well informed about the toxicity of pesticides than men. A regional epidemiological perspective is provided by Lucia Miligi and Laura Settimi, whose studies of chronic occupational pesticide exposure in Italy indicate gender-specific cancer risks for certain crops.

Lennart Hardell and Dieter Flesch-Janys respectively address risks to women from exposure to organochlorine pesticides and industrial by-product contaminants, dioxins and furans, through occupation in agriculture or pesticide-producing factories or simply from background environmental exposure. For women, the implications of exposure to background levels of HCH and dioxins are that these pesticide chemicals have been shown either singly or in chemical mixtures to have links with disease conditions that range from endometriosis (a painful disease where the endometrium grows outside the womb at sites in the pelvic cavity) to breast and uterine cancers. There is evidence that these fat-loving chemicals are both absorbed and retained more effectively in women's bodies than in men's, and that second-generation effects are occurring. Two examples from preliminary studies are given: one a consequence of environmental contamination of a phenoxyherbicide factory in Ufa, Russia; the other a consequence of the use of Agent Orange in Vietnam. Continued exposure to persistent dioxins in Vietnam is linked to alarming evidence of congenital malformation in villages where the mothers had high levels of the dioxin in their breast milk. The Agent Orange-polluted soil continues to affect the Vietnamese food chain.

Although these effects require confirmation, the need for further study should not hamper urgent mitigation. The next generation is likely to be at risk if exposed in the womb, as is the generation after that. Congenital malformations increasingly account for infant deaths, so prevention must be a high priority. Ana García provides suggestions for improving research strategies for pesticides and congenital malformations. While research on male-mediated teratogenesis is important, a greater focus of research on exposed women is needed. Evidence of the teratogenic potential of pesticides, and in general of any chemical released into the environment, is more firmly established regarding maternal exposure than paternal exposure.

In women, sex hormones control development of the reproductive organs, the reproductive cycle, preparation of the uterus for pregnancy, and lactation. In men, sex hormones control the development of the reproductive organs and the formation of sperm (spermatogenesis).

Under normal conditions in humans it is estimated that one in five couples cannot have children, over one-third of early embryos die, and about 15 per cent of pregnancies abort spontaneously. Approximately 3 per cent of newborn babies have developmental defects. Chemicals, including pesticides, can interfere with a number of biological processes in both women and men. Toxic interference can result in sterility, decreased fertility, increased fetus death, increased infant death and increased birth defects. Xiping Xu and Sung-Il Cho describe their research in China that links organophosphate pesticides to these reproductive problems, and show how genotype may increase susceptibility to organophosphates.

During the 1990s, the effects of pesticides and environmental pollution on the animal and human world catapulted to world attention. Endocrine-disrupting chemicals (EDCs) can have a profound and insidious effect on human endocrine systems and thus health and disease. A comprehensive list of endocrine disrupting pesticides can be found in Annex 1.

There are major gender differences in the metabolism of pesticides and steroids. Miriam Jacobs and David Lewis describe how these EDC pesticides work in women and men by disrupting detoxification processes within the cell, tissue organs and entire body. At the molecular level, pesticides exert their effects upon receptors that mediate alterations of hormone availability, action, excretion and biotransformation in concert with certain enzymes, and particularly the cytochrome P450 enzyme system.

The cellular endocrine receptors are involved in a wide range of physiological functions. Each type of receptor in the body has the potential to regulate a distinct endocrine signalling pathway, of which we have only a rudimentary knowledge. The emerging picture is of an interlinked fabric of hormone dynamics where the delicately balanced compensatory systems are easily disturbed.

Hormone dynamics have evolved over a long period of time to deal with hormone and dietary phytochemical exposure; they are not a rapid response system able to deal effectively with the pesticides and other synthetic chemicals of the twentieth and twenty-first centuries. We should look for more than effects on the oestrogen receptor, which has been the main target of studies to date. We should look more closely at the gender differences in tissue distribution of these receptors. A broader perspective for addressing toxicity to the entire endocrine system, from molecule to cell, to tissue, organ systems, reproductive status and gender is essential to improve risk assessments and better protect the most vulnerable sections of the population.

The authors in this section provide an overview of the extensive range of biological functions undermined by pesticides and how they can have differing health impacts on women, men and future generations. The authors make suggestions for future study designs in the light of difficulties they have encountered, to improve documentation and understanding of pesticide exposure risks. Our understanding of toxicity mechanisms may be limited so far, but the evidence available now indicates harmful effects at background levels. Above all, despite the apparent 'lack of conclusive evidence', urgent further precautionary measures are required. In Sandra Steingraber's words, 'We have a moral imperative to act in the face of inconclusive evidence' [2].

References

1 Jacobs, M.N., Covaci, A., Schepens, P. In *Environmental Science and Technology*, 36, 2002: 2797–805.
2 Sherman, J.D. *Life's Delicate Balance, Causes and Prevention of Breast Cancer*, London: Taylor & Francis, 2000.

12

High-risk exposure: gender, age and poverty

**Jenny Pronczuk de Garbino,
Nida Besbelli and Mike Ruse**

Among the large, growing group of chemicals, pesticides have been the most rapidly expanding family over the last forty years. They have proven to be useful for a number of purposes, but also hazardous to human health and the environment. Particular population groups may be susceptible and/or especially vulnerable to their effects. 'Sensitive populations' have a special biological vulnerability if they are exposed to chemicals in a particularly susceptible period of life. Other population groups are 'high risk groups' due to their characteristics and/or behaviour, which renders them more prone to suffer the toxic effects of some chemicals. Women, children and workers exposed to pesticides in the informal sector constitute sensitive and high-risk groups.

Economically disadvantaged populations are at high risk of exposure because they are less able to read or interpret labels, follow instructions, and use chemicals safely. Their living conditions are characterized by indoor air pollution, inappropriate ventilation and the unsafe storage of chemicals. Women tend to be the poorest and most vulnerable group.

Furthermore, malnutrition and chronic health conditions make these groups more sensitive to toxic exposures, as their bodies' natural ways of detoxifying the impact of pesticides are not fully functioning [1]. A well-known example is the relationship between malnutrition and hypoproteinemia, where low enzyme levels result in an enhanced vulnerability to chemicals such as organophosphate pesticides.

Women have a particular susceptibility to pesticides due to their physiological characteristics, lifestyle and behaviour. Most studies on the susceptibility of women to chemicals have focused on reproductive and endocrine problems. Women with high pesticide exposure, as reported in the Colombian flower industry, have shown increased risk of miscarriages [2]. Women working in the informal sectors are more prone to use chemicals in an unsafe way, as they do not receive the training given to formal workforces, and are exposed to polluted environments during periods of special susceptibility.

Epidemiological data

High morbidity and mortality rates, often exacerbated by lack of appropriate diagnosis and treatment, have been reported in many countries. Hundreds of millions of people are exposed to pesticides on a regular basis. These exposures represent a heavy burden on public health, and have an economic and social impact on the communities at risk. An estimated 50 million people work on plantations in developing countries and are in direct contact with pesticides, while over 500 million are exposed through traditional agriculture and as seasonal workers [3]. Even the theoretically 'non-exposed' population – those who do not use or manipulate pesticides – may suffer toxic effects through food or water contamination.

A large number of studies on the prevalence of acute poisoning by pesticides are less than conclusive due to the lack of standardization in the diagnosis, severity grading and follow-up of cases, and to the lack of harmonization in the collection of data [4]. In many studies the gender or age differentiation of cases is not stated. The data tend to be even less conclusive in studies concerning chronic exposures, especially when dealing with neuro-behavioural effects, reproductive health, teratogenesis and carcinogenesis, as both the outcomes and the causality links are difficult to assess and establish.

Few reliable, comparable global data exist on the epidemiology and real magnitude of human exposure to pesticides. In 1972 a World Health Organization (WHO) committee made a first global estimate of the number of acute pesticide poisoning cases. These estimates raised controversy, as the data were obtained through studies undertaken in a limited number of developing countries, and some of the extrapolations were debatable. Data from a large number of country-based studies were available, but unfortunately were not comparable.

Regional estimates have also been carried out in the Americas. A WHO report on small Latin American countries estimated that 1,000 to 2,000 poisoning cases occur every year, with higher numbers for the larger countries. The fatality rates are estimated as varying between 1.5 to 12 per cent [5]. More than half the pesticide poisonings were intentional (suicidal), and only 25 per cent were occupational or accidental. The widespread availability of pesticides and lack of restrictions accounted for their frequent use in suicide attempts, whereas in industrialized countries hazardous pesticides are strictly controlled and less available for intentional, accidental and occupational exposures. Box 12.1 sets out the problems in Sri Lanka, where pesticide poisonings and suicides are particularly high.

In spite of the lack of comparability of data from different sources, and difficulties in assessing the real impact of poisoning by pesticides, existing studies prove undoubtedly that the magnitude of the problem is great, that it mainly affects the developing countries, and in particular the more vulnerable population groups: children, women and workers in the informal sector.

Box 12.1 Pesticide exposure in Sri Lanka

Ravindra Fernando

Among the developing countries with agriculture-based economies, Sri Lanka (population 18.6 million) probably has the highest mortality and morbidity from pesticide poisoning. In 1998, for example, 21,429 patients were admitted to state hospitals with pesticide poisoning and 2,250 died [6]. At least another 500–1,000 die before hospital admission. As many people with minor symptoms do not attend hospitals or are not admitted, the total number of pesticide poisoning cases could be as high as 100,000 annually. The majority of deaths from pesticide poisoning follow suicide attempts. Organophosphates (fenthion), organochlorines (endosulfan) and bipyridyls (paraquat) are responsible for almost all the fatalities.

In Sri Lanka, pesticides are used mainly for agricultural cash crops (rice, tobacco), plantation agriculture (tea, rubber, coconut) and for malaria and filaria vector controls. Women play an important role in agricultural production and are exposed to pesticides. Although spraying is mostly done by men, women assist in other activities, such as mixing pesticides or washing equipment and contaminated clothes, where they are exposed to pesticides. Women also perform other agriculture-related activities in pesticide-sprayed areas. Exposure to pesticides can be occupational, accidental or intentional.

Occupational

Exposure during occupational activities can cause acute or chronic poisoning. Occupational poisoning usually causes mild toxic effects. In acute poisoning cases, symptoms and signs are mild and therefore women usually take home remedies. They very rarely seek medical attention. This makes any statistical analysis of incidence of true occupational poisoning difficult.

Effects of chronic exposure are equally difficult to study, as they are difficult to link to pesticide exposure. More importantly, no in-depth studies have been done to determine outcomes of pregnancy such as abortions, fetal deaths, perinatal mortality and birth defects following pesticide exposure in Sri Lanka. Further research is urgently required because women are not prevented from risk activities, such as tea picking, in the early months of pregnancy. Due to the hot weather, and sometimes for economic reasons, sprayers do not wear protective clothing, gloves or boots, thereby exposing themselves to pesticides.

Accidental exposure to pesticides is common, as concentrated pesticides are stored at home in the absence of proper storage facilities. Easy access causes poisoning in women and children. Many cases of accidental poisoning are common, and fatalities are rarely reported. For example, a 9-year-old child died after drinking water using an 'empty' pesticide bottle, which contained a few millilitres of a toxic bipyridyl.

Accidental poisoning can occur following indiscriminate spraying. On a tea plantation a herbicide was sprayed one morning in an area where there was a very small stream of water. Unknown to the employers and the sprayers, this stream led to the main water tank supplying the houses below the sprayed area. By midday over fifty men, women and children had become ill and had to be hospitalized. Fortunately, all recovered without further complications.

Intentional

Faced with stressful or depressive situations, women and teenagers drink pesticides to end their lives, as pesticides are easily available. Almost all who recover regret their actions. However, the married women who die leave their children orphaned and helpless. Homicidal pesticide poisoning is very rare.

Pesticide import, manufacture, packaging and sales are well regulated by a Pesticide Control Act. However, the easy availability at sales outlets leads to suicidal poisoning and misuse results in occupational poisoning.

Non-availability of adequate health-care facilities leads to high morbidity and mortality rates. Analytical facilities in hospital for toxins in blood or urine are almost non-existent. As a result, doctors have to treat patients blindly, based on the history given by them and the physical signs elicited. Shortages of drugs and lack of intensive care facilities in many hospitals contribute to the high morbidity and mortality rates. Rehabilitation services, such as psychiatric assessment and therapy, are also poor. There are no social workers to support the patients. For example, a young mother who consumes a toxic pesticide because she is depressed as a result of physical and mental abuse by an alcoholic husband will be discharged as soon as she is fit to leave the hospital. She is forced back to an unchanged home environment to cope and suffer as before.

To minimize the impact on health from pesticide exposure, prospective research studies such as the Agricultural Health Study performed in Iowa and North Carolina, USA, are urgently required in countries like Sri Lanka [7]. These should determine, among other things, whether pesticide exposure adversely affects pregnancy outcomes, affects fertility, or leads to malignant diseases and other chronic illnesses.

Appropriate preventive action should be taken based on the results of these studies. Treatment and analytical facilities for pesticide poisoning in all hospitals and health-care facilities should be improved. Supportive therapy for victims and their families should be initiated and continued.

Characteristics of pesticide poisoning: gender issues

Individual pesticide poisoning cases occur via eating or drinking, breathing the fumes, or through contact with the skin (oral, respiratory or cutaneous routes), either at work or through accidental or intentional exposure. The annual reports of different poisons centres[1] and toxicology services, collected at the International Programme on Chemical Safety (IPCS) (report under preparation), record that most workplace exposure affects men, while most intentional incidents occur in women (see Table 12.1).

Epidemic poisonings occur frequently in developing countries as a result of poor regulatory measures and lack of information and education. The undiscriminating, widespread use and harmful potential of pesticides have resulted in epidemic poisonings generated by accidental contamination of food, resulting in high mortality and morbidity rates [8]. These incidents may be due to the contamination of food (flour, sugar) during transportation or storage, eating seeds dressed for sowing (when the warning colouring is washed away), errors in food preparation (similarity with foodstuffs, incorrect packaging, labelling or storage), or contamination of water

Table 12.1 Survey of pesticide poisonings by poisons centres, indicating gender distribution

Country	Year	Women	Men	Unknown	Total	Pesticides as % of total
Australia	1999	38	63	1	102	4.97
Bahamas	1999	4	2	0	6	1.25
Brazil	1998	4521	6203	116	10840	13.69
Chile	1999	735	750	78	1563	10.99
Czech Repub.	1999	113	187	52	352	4.46
France (Lille)	1999	330	471	0	801	3.32
Iran (Mashad)	1998	523	322	0	845	6.90
Ireland	1997				415	3.10
Morocco	1999	253	215	1	469	7.17
New Zealand	1999	373	662	81	1948	9.60
Peru	1997				745	36.00
Poland	1999	2	9	0	11	0.36
Portugal	1998				1559	8.20
Slovenia	1999	11	43	0	54	9.96
Sweden	1998				936	1.90
Switzerland	1998				749	3.30
Taiwan	1998/9	287	618	4	909	18.82
USA	1998				86289	3.90
Uruguay	1999	479	516	10	1005	5.05

Source: IPCS Project on the Epidemiology of Poisoning by Pesticides.

or clothes. In these cases family groups, including children and women, are usually exposed.

In work settings, clusters of workers – mostly men – may be exposed when manufacturing, mixing or applying pesticides, or as a result of crop management activities. In the informal work sector, workplace contamination is frequent and usually accompanied by a lack of personal protective equipment or training of workers on the safe management of chemicals. Plantation workers and farmers are exposed through poor work practices, including a lack of protective equipment and early re-entry into sprayed fields, or use of unregistered compounds. A dramatic example was provided by an episode in Pakistan in 1976, when over 7,500 field workers were heavily exposed to malathion contaminated with isomalathion and about 2,800 were poisoned [9].

While it is commonly believed that plantation workers and farmers are primarily men, many women work in plantations carrying out a range of activities, including spraying. Poverty means that it is not unusual for the whole family, including children, to work on plantations. Family members are not trained in the safe use of pesticides or aware of their risks. They lack protective equipment and knowledge of hygienic practices. It is quite common to observe that women prepare pesticide formulations without any protective clothing, and also that they prepare, and serve, the food in the workplace.

Women's occupational exposure to pesticides may also occur through the help that they provide to field workers in pesticide formulation, transportation and application, as bystanders, and also indirectly, for example, through the washing of contaminated clothing.

In some parts of the world, pesticide poisoning is considered 'endemic', due to the permanently high incidence of both acute and chronic specific pathology related to occupational exposure.

Effects of pesticide exposure on women's health

Poisoning due to pesticides has in general the same characteristics in men and women. However, there may be some special characteristics on the reproductive and endocrine systems. Different types of pesticides have different impacts (see the Technical Annex).

Although it is difficult to assess fully the impact of pesticide exposures both on women and men in a global context, it is known that the number of cases of acute exposure is unacceptably high, and that there are important gender and age implications. Although acute toxic exposures are the primary reason for hospitalization, chronic toxic exposures represent a more permanent, surreptitious menace to human health. Chronic, low-level exposures have been linked to occupational diseases, congenital anomalies, cancer, fertility problems, and behavioural and immune-system disorders. Some of these effects have different health implications according to gender. For example, male workers exposed to the pesticide 1,2-dibromochloropropane

(DBCP) became infertile, suffering from azoospermia and oligo-spermia [10].

Increasing concern is raised by the effect of chemicals that have been shown to modulate endocrine function in animal models, the so-called 'endocrine disrupters', which are suspected of playing a role in the development of male reproductive tract abnormalities and neurobehavioural deficits in children, and have been linked to the rise in hormone-related cancers in women. Many endocrine disrup-tors – including dioxins, polychlorinated biphenyls, organochlorine pesticides, bisphenol A, nonylphenol and phytoestrogens – have been detected in umbilical cord sera [11].

The persistent organic pollutants (known as POPs), many of which are pesticides, are being linked to effects on the reproductive systems of both men and women, as well as to potential effects on the endo-crine and immune systems of children. In women the increasing in-cidence of uterine leiomyoma raises questions on the potential role of environmental factors in tumour aetiology. Although direct evidence for a pathogenic role of the persistent pesticides in leiomyomas is lacking, it has been demonstrated that diverse agents such as organo-chlorine pesticides, dietary flavonoids, botanical compounds and therapeutic antioestrogens have an effect on the myometrial tissues [12].

Many studies suggest a link between chemicals and breast cancer (see elsewhere in this section), although a recent study did not find a link between exposure to DDT and PCBs and an increased risk of occurrence [13].

A recent retrospective study of precocious puberty cases in immi-grant children suggests a possible relationship between transient ex-posure to endocrine disrupters and sexual precocity [14].

An epidemiological study undertaken in Poland on the relation-ship between employment in agriculture and the incidence of congenital malformations, miscarriages, low birth weight, small-for-gestational-age, preterm delivery and stillbirths, demonstrated that employment in agriculture increases the risk of congenital malforma-tions in infants, particularly orofacial cleft, birthmarks in the form of haemangioma, as well as musculoskeletal and nervous system defects. The study found that exposure to pesticides might contribute to still births. The results presented show significant risk of reproduction disorders in women employed during pregnancy in conditions of pesticide exposure. This also justifies the placement of pesticides among factors to which pregnant women should not be exposed [15].

Pesticides have also been linked to chemical intolerance, or reported illness from odours of common environmental chemicals, a controversial entity which is emerging as an important environmental and public health care issue in some countries. The 'chemically intolerant' are primarily women, who may seek medical attention for heart and respiratory problems (bronchitis, asthma and pneumonia) [16].

Main needs identified

The need to prevent and mitigate human pesticide exposure is recognized, and a large number of actions and recommendations have been proposed in recent years by different organizations, with variable success. They include: development of 'pesticide programmes' to set up information and surveillance systems; promotion of educational activities; strengthening epidemiological surveys; developing analytical facilities; updating and strengthening legislation concerning toxic chemicals; facilitating political decisions (application of the International Code of Conduct for Pesticide Distribution and Use, and following the principles of the Rotterdam Convention on Prior Informed Consent); prohibiting or restricting the use of some pesticides; strengthening integrated pest management (IPM); facilitating access to technical information; and supporting the study of biological indicators of exposure.

However, gender-related issues have not been addressed in many of the initiatives. There is a need for more detailed epidemiological studies, dissemination of information and education, and the promotion of gender-related research activities.

Epidemiological studies

The consideration of gender issues in the epidemiological studies is essential. Only the application of standard epidemiological procedures offers the possibility for measuring human morbidity and mortality induced by toxic chemicals, especially by pesticides. Good, comparable epidemiological information is essential for reliable risk assessment and setting up strategies for education and prevention.

There is a need for good quality, comparable human data, stating at least the gender, age and social characteristics of the population groups affected. Although there are numerous epidemiological studies on human pesticide exposure, they tend to be incomplete, and the exercise of assembling data and carrying out a critical evaluation is a difficult task. In settings where epidemiological studies and research are cost-effective, and likely to yield useful information (regionally, countrywide or locally), well-designed studies may yield valuable results. The IPCS project on 'Epidemiology of Poisoning by Pesticides' and the Pan American Health Organization (PAHO) 'Plagsalud' Project in Central America represent initiatives that will help countries to collect information and help characterize pesticide poisoning according to gender. The WHO International Programme on Chemical Safety has developed the INTOX system as a tool for the harmonized collection and analysis of data on chemicals and on cases of toxic exposures (www.intox.org).

Box 12.2   Pesticides and women in the Philippines

Carissa Diaquino

In 1999 the National Poison Control and Information Service of the Philippines received 188 telephone calls identifying pesticides as the toxic agent in poisoning cases. This amounted to 15 per cent of all calls received for the year: 81 per cent of exposures resulted in minor poisoning. Women were involved in 53 per cent of the calls, and 87 per cent of these were intentional exposure. Household pesticides were often used for suicide. The outcome for these cases could not be ascertained because of poor follow-up.

In April 2000, the National Poison Control and Information Service and the Department of Health, in collaboration with the WHO, embarked on a study to estimate the morbidity and mortality associated with pesticides, especially in agricultural regions. Preliminary data indicate that women are involved in up to 41 per cent of reported cases – most cases were intentional. Ages ranged from 1.5 years to 83 years, with most in the 16–20 age group. Agricultural pesticides were the main toxic agent. Of the exposures, 64 per cent resulted in minor poisoning; 32 per cent in moderate poisoning; 78 per cent recovered and no deaths were reported.

Isolated reports indicate increased rates of spontaneous abortions and stillbirths among Filipino peasant women farmers, but well-designed studies documenting health effects of chronic exposure to pesticides are lacking. Acute pesticide poisoning incidents dominate the data.

Information dissemination, training and education

Training and education are strongly needed at different levels and for both genders. Traditionally, information and training activities have set as target groups the users and supervisors, who are instructed on how to use a pesticide safely and recognize the toxic effects [17]. However, these activities address only men, seen as the majority of rural workers. The fact that women may also be involved in the activities is largely ignored. Training and education activities also address regulators (how to register pesticides and legislate their use), and the health-care sector (how to diagnose, treat and follow up and register a poisoning case). In these cases, it is seldom that reference is made to the gender of exposed individuals. Among health personnel, it has been observed that some professionals are not aware of the correct diagnosis and treatment of pesticide exposures, and even less about the specific effects that could be observed in women.

Research

In developing countries the problem of human pesticide exposures is important. From a public health point of view, this represents an alarming situation requiring urgent action. From a research point of view, studies could investigate the impact of short- and long-term exposure to environmental pollutants, exposure-response relationships, biomarkers, role of associated factors (malnutrition, infections) in both women and men. Research studies may offer the opportunity for productive cooperation between the health and environmental sectors and between different organizations in industrialized and developing countries. Studies should be linked to the need for policy changes to reduce exposure to pesticides.

The harmonized and detailed collection of human data by poisons centres, or other health services, using a powerful globally harmonized computerized system is of utmost importance. It will allow the characterization of the disease, an estimation of the burden of disease, the setting up of surveillance mechanisms and the evidence-based planning of primary, secondary and tertiary preventive activities. But it is important to ensure that acute pesticide poisoning incidents reflected in poisons centres' statistics are seen as only one part of the poisoning picture (see Box 12.2). Assessment of the disease burden from acute and chronic toxic exposures affecting high-risk and sensitive groups requires good epidemiological studies, and should help to evaluate the impact of preventive measures.

In summary, the problem of pesticide poisoning and its effects on women and men, and on the health of the most vulnerable population groups, requires appropriate recognition and assessment. Only sound, comparable data will provide the evidence basis for planning prevention, taking into consideration the different needs related to gender and age. Harmonized, comparable studies are required, along with cooperative research and the promotion of access to information, training and education at all levels. The tools and mechanisms for this are already available. International organizations and donors have a very important role to play in coordinating, supporting and promoting activities for the benefit of women's and men's health in countries where the economy is still relying on the heavy use of pesticides.

Note

1. Poisons centres record only acute incidents.

References

1 Hayes, J., Laws, E.R. *Handbook of Pesticide Toxicology*, San Diego CA: Academic Press, 1991.
2 Restrepo, M., Munoz, N., Day, N.E., Parra, J.E., de Romero, L., Nguyen-Dinh, X. In *Scandinavian Journal of Work Environmental Health*, 16(4), 1990: 232–8.
3 WHO/UNEP, *Public Health Impact of Pesticides Used in Agriculture*, Geneva: WHO, 1990.
4 WHO, 'Safe use of pesticides. Fourteenth report of the WHO Expert Committee on Vector Biology and Control', Technical Report Series 813, Geneva: WHO, 1991.
5 PAHO/WHO, 'Pesticides and health in the Americas', Environmental Series 12, Washington DC: PAHO Regional Office for the Americas, 1993.
6 *Annual Health Bulletin*, Colombo: Ministry of Health, 1998.
7 Alavanja, M.C., Sandler, D.P., McMaster, S.B. *et al.* In *Environmental Health Perspectives*, 104(4), 1996: 362–9.
8 Ferrer, A., Cabral, R. In *Food Additive Contamination*, 8(6), 1991: 755–75.
9 Baker, E.L., Zack, M., Miles, J.W., *et al.* In *Lancet*, 7:1(8054), January 1978: 31–4.
10 Slutsky, M., Levin, J.L., Levy, B.S. In *International Journal of Occupational Environmental Health* 5(2), 1999: 116–22.
11 Sakurai, K., Mori, C. In *Nippon Rinsho* (Japan), 58(12), 2000: 2508–13.
12 Hunter, D.S., Hodges, L.C., Eagon, P.K., *et al.* In *Environmental Health*

Perspectives, 108 5, October 2000: 829–34.

13 Laden, F., Hankinson, S.E., Wolff, M.S., *et al.*, In *International Journal of Cancer*, 15:91(4), 2001: 568–74.

14 Krstevska-Konstantinova, M., Charlier, C., Craen, M., *et al.* In *Human Reproduction*, 16(5), 2001: 1020–26.

15 Hanke, W., Hausman, K. In *Med Pr* (Poland), 51(3), 2000: 257–68.

16 Baldwin, C.M., Bell, I.R. In *Archives of Environmental Health*, 53(5), 1998: 347–53.

17 WHO/IPCS, *Multilevel Course on the Safe Use of Pesticides and on the Diagnosis and Treatment of Pesticide Poisoning*, Geneva: WHO, 1994.

13

Measuring gender differences in response to pesticide exposure

John McLaren Howard

In November 1990 I was asked to perform laboratory investigations on a young couple who farmed 90 acres of rural Lincolnshire. They had a six-month history of fatigue and general ill-health and had been investigated through their general practitioner (GP) and local hospital consultant.

By the time I became involved, the man needed at least ten hours of sleep and a further early afternoon rest each day to be able to carry out his farm duties. He was physically weak and complained of mild flu-like symptoms lasting about three days and occurring every two to three weeks. His wife was much more disabled, with more severe symptoms that kept her in bed for at least three full days in each week. Both had been diagnosed as having chronic fatigue syndrome and neither had received any specific advice or treatment.

The man had been responsible for handling and applying a wide range of pesticides and related chemicals on the farm. Blood tests demonstrated exposure to lindane but were otherwise unremarkable. The man's lindane level was 8.8 µg/l and his wife's was 1.9 µg/l. Although organophosphate pesticides had been in regular use up to the start of their illness, none was detected in the blood tests. This is not surprising as these compounds have short half-lives in the circulation system.

Standard liver function tests were normal but the man had an increase in an enzyme called glutathione-S-transferase (GST). Abnormal forms were found in both individuals when affinity chromatography studies were carried out. These findings indicate exposure to a hepatotoxic chemical or chemicals with a high affinity for thiol functional (–SH) groups. It was not typical of exposure to lindane or other organochlorine pesticides, but we were beginning to see this in relation to organophosphorus exposure.

Nutritionally, both individuals had low levels of glutathione per-oxidase (a selenium-dependent antioxidant) and marked intracellular magnesium deficiencies. The husband was zinc deficient as judged by his leucocyte zinc level. Through their GP, advice was given on supplement programmes aimed at correcting these anomalies and providing additional vitamin C and vitamin E.

Three months later, when the tests were repeated, the man was significantly better, with only rare episodes of fatigue. However, his wife's condition had deteriorated slightly. Her symptoms worsened when she restricted carbohydrate intake, as she had done for three weeks prior to retest, but were moderately improved with a fairly high carbohydrate diet. She had stopped this due to weight increase.

The man's GST was at normal levels, but abnormal forms of the enzyme were still detectable by affinity chromatography. Lindane concentration was slightly lower at 6.1 µg/l and all his other test results were within the normal range. His wife's nutrient-related results were also normal but her lindane level had increased to 10.7 µg/l and her GST was now worse than her husband's had been three months earlier. This was despite suspension of the use of pesticides as soon as the original results became available.

Fat cells were analysed for pesticides using gas–liquid chroma-tography. Despite the small samples available the difference between the results was startling. The man's lindane level was approximately 10 times his blood level, while his wife had around 1,000 times as much lindane in her fat cells. She also had detectable levels of two organophosphorus pesticides – mevinphos and tetrachlorvinphos.

Mevinphos and lindane had both been used on the farm although not directly handled by the farmer's wife. Tetrachlorvinphos was eventually traced to anti-flea collars used on the five cats kept on the farm. The woman had fitted these collars and tended the cats. Her husband had hardly any contact with them.

This was my first introduction to a gender-related difference following pesticide exposure. The most likely explanation for the difference seemed to hinge on the increased proportion of fat cells in the woman. She had considerably less exposure than her husband yet attained much higher fat-cell levels of the pesticides. Her symptoms and the blood level of lindane also increased when she was depend-ent on fat stores for energy during self-imposed carbohydrate restriction.

The man has remained well, but his wife has only gradually improved in general health and she has had two miscarriages. Unfortunately, she has now developed breast cancer. There is no possible way to prove any connection between these events and the pesticide exposure but it would, in my opinion, be dishonest and unscientific to ignore the possibilities.

Gender-related issues

This case made me aware of gender-related issues in pesticide exposure. Subsequently, this Medical Referral Unit has performed several thousand pesticide screens and investigated many instances where gender was an important factor.

With acute exposure, the connections between symptoms and the chemical(s) involved are often clear. Such events are usually dealt with by the appropriate Regional Poisons Unit and the Health and Safety Executive.

Chronic illness following a possible pesticide exposure is much more difficult to investigate, and unexplained illness with no specific cause is extremely difficult to investigate in terms of possible pesticide exposure. However, we are seeing increasing numbers of referrals from GPs and hospital consultants who ask us to do just that.

Looking at these requests, over the past two years particularly, one factor stands out. There seems to be increasing concern about hormonally related disease (including some cancers) and infertility. Where it was once difficult to raise even the possibility that pesticides might be involved, we are now quite frequently presented with questions that directly relate to that subject. No doubt, the greater scientific and media publication of the oestrogenic properties of many pesticides and related chemicals has prompted some of these questions, but my experience is that individual doctors and patients are now making some of these connections themselves.

The following selected cases demonstrate important gender-specific features, and laboratory techniques that have helped in the investigation.

Chemical sensitivity reduces sperm motility

Michael, aged 32 and happily married with two healthy children, was referred for infertility studies. The couple had been unable to conceive a third time and Michael was suffering loss of libido.

Investigations locally had revealed a normal sperm count but markedly reduced sperm motility. Three measurements at six-monthly intervals gave results of 52 per cent, 44 per cent and 32 per cent motile sperms with hardly any change in the total count.

Michael's general health records showed that he had put on a lot of weight. He said he had gained 20 kg in a little over two years. He had also noted and was embarrassed by breast development that had not been noted by his medical advisers. No one had inquired into his employment history.

Michael had worked for ten years as an animal-feed salesman, but for the past three years had been involved in the sale of pesticides and in demonstrating dilution and spraying techniques to farmers. Increased exposure to HCB (hexachlorobenzene) and the finding of carbaryl were the only anomalies in blood tests. He had no knowledge of handling HCB but had frequently used carbaryl and other carbamate-type pesticides. He had also handled organophosphorus pesticides, although these were not detected. He had taken great care in handling these substances and they do have a short life in the bloodstream.

Michael's sperm motility measured in our laboratory was 37 per cent (in agreement with earlier tests). We also looked at the unfolding of the DNA (decondensation of the chromatin) and found that 45 per cent of the motile sperms would do this prior to removal of zinc. They stood a high chance of losing their genetic material in vaginal fluid or during passage through the cervical mucus.

Mitochondrial enzymes are the energy source for sperm swimming. Michael had low enzyme activity for three of the four complexes of enzymes measured in his sperms. About 15 per cent of the motile sperms also showed excessive tail-shaking activity without progression, but, according to other tests, this was not the result of anti-sperm antibodies. The implication was that of some other interference with the sperms. We have seen this in toxic metal exposure (especially mercury) but had not previously associated it with pesticides. His toxic metals were well within acceptable levels.

As Michael had been exposed to carbamates and I had found carbaryl in his pesticide screen, I decided to look at the sensitivities of his sperms to a low level of this pesticide. I used phase-contrast microscopy to investigate the *in vitro* effect of 1 µg/l and 10 µg/l carbaryl. There was a mild increase in 'tail shaking without progression' at the 10 µg/l level but this was consistent with the findings in normal controls.

Michael revealed another problem while I was discussing these results with him, which he considered only a mild irritation but gave me a valuable clue. He was getting skin rashes but only when wearing certain highly coloured T-shirts next to his skin. This was unlikely to be a detergent sensitivity as his wife used the same washing powder for the white T-shirts that did not cause any problem.

The main metabolite of carbaryl is alpha-naphthol, to which some people do develop a chemical sensitivity; naphthols are used in the preparation of some chemical dyes. Was this a connection between the skin rashes and the reduction in sperm motility? The phase contrast microscopy of the sperms when suspended in a medium containing just 1 µg/l of alpha-naphthol demonstrated a marked reduction in motility and an increase in 'tail-shaking without progression'. This was only apparent in one out of ten normal controls. I was demonstrating that Michael had developed a sensitivity to alpha-naphthol that was capable of changing sperm motility and inhibiting normal swimming of the sperms at very low exposure levels.

I could not show whether the initiating event was due to carbaryl or other exposure to naphthols, but continued exposure to carbaryl at detectable blood levels was clearly contraindicated. Michael changed his employment within the same company and avoided pesticide exposure as well as clothing that caused a rash. His sperm motility returned to normal within twelve months, and sperms with inappropriate 'tail-shaking without progression' now account for less than 2 per cent of the total motile sperms.

Happily, as I write this, the couple have now conceived. Without changing his diet, Michael has also been losing weight and is no longer concerned by any further breast development. Presumably, a part of the problem related to the oestrogenic nature of some of the pesticides he had been handling.

Nearby spraying contributes to fatigue

Jane, aged 19, was referred for a pesticide screen after reporting severe breathlessness, some nausea and a debilitating fatigue that lasted for around three weeks. This had happened on three occasions and she related it to pesticide spraying of a field next to her home. A local enquiry by the Health and Safety Executive found that the farmer was careful and used only approved pesticides and modern, correctly calibrated, equipment. I have not seen the report and the farmer was reluctant to speak about which pesticides he used. He did, however, assure me of his concern for this young woman and his understanding of and care with the chemicals he used.

Jane's mother and sister had had milder, but similar, symptoms. Her father and two brothers were not affected. No one else in the neighbourhood had reported any problems.

The blood tests demonstrated background levels of a number of organochlorine pesticides but nothing to suggest a specific exposure. A fat cell sample obtained by needle biopsy did contain the organophosporus pesticide diazinon. I have no evidence that the farmer used diazinon, but a simple experiment has helped to show that his spraying was an important factor in her ill health. The farmer was happy to cooperate provided there were no legal implications. I was pleased to be able to tell him that my only concern was an understanding of Jane's medical difficulties.

Jane was provided with a bio-impedance monitor and shown how to apply two sensing electrodes across the thorax. Used in this way, bio-impedance monitors the chest cavity volume and breathing pattern. The equipment recorded the results at one-minute intervals over a period of four hours. The farmer cooperated by using the sprayer for just one hour each day for two weeks. On two of those days, chosen by him and revealed only to Jane's GP, he used his usual spray. For the other twelve days he sprayed water only.

We downloaded the data from the bio-impedance equipment and found three days on which there had been a major change in breathing pattern similar to that seen during a panic attack. When the code was broken, two of these days were the days immediately following pesticide spraying and the third was the first day of pesticide spraying. The results were otherwise unremarkable.

Fortunately, the farmer has been willing to change the use of that field and no longer sprays it with any pesticides. Jane, her mother and sister, have not experienced further problems.

The gender-related factor here might be negated if the women are thought of as being at home during the spraying while the men were away from home. That was not the case. This family runs a business from home that demands similar hours at home for both sexes.

Sensitivity to wood preservative

A hospital allergy consultant referred Karen, aged 18, and her brother David, aged 16, to me. In asking me to investigate their rather odd history he emphasized the different medical outcome in these teenagers following the same initiating exposure. Both had been healthy until the family moved to a renovated eighteenth-century mill house. The teenagers each had an attic room with exposed roof timbers and wood panelling on two of the walls. Both complained of a chemical smell believed to be a wood preservative. The renovation had been done in the 1960s but the attic rooms had been sealed and unused until this family moved in.

The rooms were ventilated during each day to minimize the chemical smell but the youngsters spent long evenings studying in their rooms and, of course, slept there. Both reported dizziness and increasing inability to concentrate on their studies at home and at school. Karen began to have painful, heavy periods for which a gynaecologist could find no explanation. In less than four months, David dropped from second to fifteenth in his class and he began to have more and more time away from school with 'flu-like' illness.

Neither David's GP nor a general medical consultant in a London teaching hospital could explain what was happening. Normal immunoglobulin levels and unchanging white blood cell counts seemed to rule out infection.

The move had been in August 1996; by Christmas of that year both Karen and David were clearly unwell. Their parents hoped that the holiday from school and the festivities would be a turning point. Both began to react to the more unusual foods eaten over the holiday; when they became so ill that both took to their beds, the GP was called.

Understandably, the GP thought it was food poisoning and recommended a simple diet with plenty of fluids. Their parents and the four members of a visiting family had eaten the same foods without problems. Karen and David remained very unwell and two weeks later they were admitted to hospital for tests. Stool cultures and viral antibody studies were normal. They seemed to have developed severe food allergies and were referred to a consultant allergist, who used exclusion diets to identify causative foods. This left them both with different but highly restricted diets. Karen's menstrual problems continued to worsen and David's mental 'fog' increased to the point where he became unable to attend school.

When a visiting friend slept in Karen's room during August of 1997 she also complained of dizziness and was very unhappy about the chemical smell – which Karen and her parents no longer considered a factor. A further attempt was made to find out what wood preservatives had been used in the 1960s renovation. This proved impossible, as the company that did the work had ceased to trade in 1971.

Karen and David were moved to rooms in a modern extension to the house, whereupon their health began to improve although they still had to restrict their diet. Karen continued to have menstrual problems with severe pain and pre-menstrual near-suicidal depression. David still had unexplained 'flu-like' symptoms for about five days in each month.

Over the next few months, their gut problems and most of the shared features of the illness diminished. They did have to remain on highly restricted diets and Karen's menstrual symptoms were unabated. David became hyperactive, unable to sleep and rather aggressive.

I first saw both Karen and David in January 1998. After reviewing the history, tests were performed to exclude toxic metal exposure, to evaluate pesticide exposure and to look at the detoxification pathways. In view of their dietary restrictions, I also looked at their nutritional status with tests that included an essential fatty acid profile.

Some abnormalities were common to Karen and David. The pesticide screens detected pentachlorophenol (PCP) and dinitrocresol (DNOC). Both had abnormal essential fatty acid profiles with normal levels of linoleic acid (LA) but very low levels of gamma-linolenic (GLA) and di-homo gamma linolenic acid (DGLA) in the omega-6 pathway. The enzyme that converts LA to GLA is delta-6-desaturase (D6D), which it is zinc dependent. As David had only a moderate degree of zinc deficiency and Karen had normal white blood cell zinc, the possibility of a chemical inhibition of D6D had to be considered.

Both of their urine samples contained sulphite, indicating poor sulphoxidation. Sulphite is normally converted to sulphate. They also had mild increases in serum levels of primary bile acids (a very sensitive liver function test), and, using affinity chromatography, abnormal forms of liver-derived glutathione-S-transferase (GST) were identified in their blood. Glutathione conjugation in the liver and sulphoxidation are two of the most important detoxification pathways in the body.

Taken together, the results demonstrated a toxic insult almost certainly caused by PCP or DNOC, both of which might have been used for wood preservation in the 1960s.

Oral GLA (as Evening Primrose Oil) was used to improve the essential fatty acids and molybdenum supplements were given to improve sulphoxidation. Karen was given magnesium to correct a marked intracellular deficiency and David was supplemented with zinc to replete his moderate deficiency.

The essential fatty acid and sulphite levels were checked at four-monthly intervals and the pesticide screens and other blood tests were repeated after one year (January 1999). All test results normalized within the year and the youngsters were clinically much improved. David's symptoms had completely cleared and he was back on a normal diet. Karen still had some menstrual problems but these cleared when her GP doubled my recommended dose of GLA and introduced 100 mg pyridoxine (vitamin B6) once each day.

PCP and DNOC have short half-lives in the blood stream. As I first saw Karen and David several months after exposure ceased, I can only assume that they had really high levels while sleeping in the affected rooms. DNOC is not considered to be highly toxic to humans but some people do develop chemical sensitivity after exposure. We occasionally see food sensitivities that develop secondary to this situation. That may well be the case for Karen and David. However, the other symptoms were totally different.

Gender-related factors must be implicated and would include the female hormonal cycle with more evidence of significant hormonal interference in Karen. The results of the biased essential fatty acid metabolism might also have quite different effects through prostaglandin imbalance and disturbances of prostacyclins and leukotrienes. These important biochemicals are produced from the essential fatty acid pathways. Hyperactivity is associated with D6D inhibition and is much more common in males.

Two trends emerging

These cases are, of course, anecdotal. However, they do reflect two trends that are apparent from the requesting and referral patterns in this Unit. I am seeing increased concern over the connection between pesticide exposure and chronic illness. Second, the appreciation of gender-related factors is becoming more common.

The most likely sex differences that are of high relevance in relation to pesticide exposure are the increased fat stores and the increased levels of hormonally sensitive tissues in females. Increased fat exchange, for example in pregnancy and lactation, and cyclic hormonal changes may also result in greater sensitivity to pesticide exposure in women. However, spermatogenesis and sperm activity may also be affected by low-level pesticide exposure, and the effect of increased exposure to oestrogenic chemicals is probably an important factor in male infertility.

Gender-related factors must be taken into account in any consideration of the effects of pesticide exposure on human health and reproduction.

14

Human exposure to airborne pesticide pollutants

Ordias Chikuni and Anuschka Polder

Breast milk samples of women living in Mudzi and Nyanga, in the east and northeast of Zimbabwe, were analysed for traces of the persistent organochlorine pesticides hexachlorobenzene (HCB), hexachlorocyclohexane (HCH), and DDT and its breakdown products.[1] The results indicate airborne transport of these pesticides from Mudzi, which lies in a vector-controlled area with comprehensive spraying programmes during the rainy season (16,839 micrograms per kilogram [μg/kg], or parts per million, of sum-DDT[2] found in milk fat), to Nyanga, which has no history of DDT usage (8,810 μg/kg found). This local dispersion is explained by the prevailing weather patterns and geographical conditions in Zimbabwe. The study observed major differences in knowledge of safe use and toxicity of organochlorine (OC) pesticides between women and men.

Use of DDT in Zimbabwe

Organochlorine compounds take a long time to break down into less toxic substances. After use, they remain in the environment, are distributed there, and enter the food chain. Human exposure to these chemicals is mainly through consumption of contaminated food, but in developing countries unprotected use of the chemicals can be a contributing factor. Because of their high fat solubility the contaminants accumulate in the human body and can be excreted in breast milk, resulting in exposure of the nursing infant. Contamination of breast milk with DDT was first recognized in 1951 [1].

Investigations into possible health and environmental risks have led all industrial countries to restrict or ban the use of DDT. In December 2000, at negotiations to develop an international convention to deal with persistent chemicals, governments agreed that alternatives to DDT for malaria control must be developed to allow its phase-out over time. However, malaria is still one of the leading causes of illness and death in the developing world, and, as an inexpensive pesticide, DDT is still used in anti-malaria operations in many poor countries [2]. Because of their physical properties, DDT and other OCs are spread worldwide. Long-range atmospheric transport of OCs and deposition in colder regions, depending on weather conditions and low and high pressure systems in the atmosphere, is well documented [3]. Several studies in Africa have revealed the contamination and pathways of OC pesticides in the environment [4,5,6].

Usage of DDT in Zimbabwe is related to vector control in areas affected by tsetse flies (*Glossina morsitans*) and malaria [7,8,9]. Over time, this has resulted in accumulation of DDT in the environment [10,11,12]. A previous study [13] revealed the surprisingly high level of 10,060 μg/kg milk fat of sum-DDT in human milk from Nyanga, which is a fruit-growing district in the Eastern Highlands. The pest control on the commercial fruit farms in this area includes usage of HCHs but there is no history of DDT application.

The observations of the high DDT levels in human milk from Nyanga led to the suggestion that the DDT was transported to this area by air. Lying 100–150 km north of Nyanga, the Mudzi area is located in the low veldt (around 400 m above sea level). This is a malaria endemic area, and during the rainy season undergoes an intensive spraying programme, which in the recent past included DDT. During this season humid winds drift from the north to the south, where condensation of the moist air takes place in the colder mountain areas of the Eastern Highlands. The Eastern Highlands, including Nyanga, are situated in the middle of the Inter-tropic Convergence Zone [14] weather system and thus contaminated by airborne OC compounds during the hot and rainy summer.

The study and results

Collection of samples

During the rainy season in 1997–98, 16 human milk samples were collected from mothers living in Mudzi and 28 from mothers living in Nyanga. The average age of the mothers was 22 years in both sampling sites. The average age of the breastfed children at the time of sampling was 8 months in Mudzi and 5.5 months in Nyanga. Mothers breastfeeding either their first or second child participated in this study. The diet of the mothers was quite similar in the studied areas. It was based on *sadza* (thick maize-meal porridge) combined with vegetables and animal products, with a slightly higher use of fish in Nyanga.

Sample extraction, clean-up, and gas-chromatographic (GC) analysis

All the analyses were performed by Dr Chikuni at the Norwegian accredited laboratory of environmental toxicology at the Norwegian School of Veterinary Science in Oslo. The analytical methods used have been described elsewhere [15,16], but some modifications were made. Details of the GC method and tests of quality control are described by the authors elsewhere [17,18].

The mean level of sum-DDT in human milk from Mudzi was twice that found in Nyanga (Table 14.1). The ratio DDT/DDE was only slightly higher in Mudzi. In Nyanga and Mudzi the pp-DDE contributed with 78 per cent and 81 per cent to the sum-DDT, respectively. In Nyanga the mean level of sum-HCH was ten times higher than in Mudzi.

Table 14.1 Residues of OCs in human milk from Nyanga and Mudzi (ppb, µg/kg fat)

	Nyanga (n = 28)		Mudzi (n = 16)	
	Mean	SD*	Mean	SD*
fat %	3.38	1.33	5.10	3.03
HCB	3.91	4.02	1.75	1.73
sum-HCH	399	784	27.7	22.6
pp-DDE	6868	9181	13784	12382
sum-DDT	8810	11018	16839	15407
ratio DDT/DDE	0.17	0.10	0.18	0.06

* Where SD is the standard differentiation (see glossary for definitions).

Implications of the findings

HCB is both a fungicide and a by-product from industrial processes. It is also found as a contaminant in some pesticides. This chemical is globally distributed by the so-called 'grasshopper effect' [19]. The levels of HCB in human milk presented in this study are low compared to industrialized countries like Norway [20]. The slightly higher level of HCB in Nyanga might be explained by the fact that some of the pesticides used in the fruit-growing industry can be contaminated with HCB.

Human milk samples from Nyanga showed a relatively high contamination of HCHs, likely to be a result of the agricultural activity in this fruit-growing district. The mean level of sum-HCH in Nyanga was 14 times higher than in Norway today [21], but 2–10 times lower than in countries like Russia and the states of former Soviet Union where HCHs are still used to a much greater extent in agricultural activities [22,23,24]. The level of sum-HCH in Mudzi was 14 times lower than in Nyanga but was slightly lower than the level in Norway today [25], where use of HCHs was forbidden in 1992. In the present study, β-HCH was the predominant isomer (93 per cent of sum-HCH in Nyanga and 53 per cent in Mudzi). Only small-scale farming is common in the area of Mudzi and the population is rather poor. Use of HCHs in this area is not documented. This indicates a possibility that HCHs are deposited here as an airborne contaminant.

Previous studies in Zimbabwe have shown an extremely high contamination of DDT in human milk in some areas [26,27] – among the highest levels reported in the world. In countries where DDT has been banned since the early 1970s, only the main metabolite DDE is detected today. The DDE levels in the studied areas are 30–70 times higher than levels in Norway [28], and about 10 times higher than levels in human milk samples from the northern part of Russia [29]. The ratio of DDT to DDE was 4 times lower than reported in Kenya [30] but demonstrates nevertheless a continued exposure of DDT.

Because the Mudzi area is malaria endemic, ground spraying is used during the mosquito season in the summer. The hot temperatures volatilize some of the sprayed DDT into pockets of hot air that is carried over by the drifting southeast trade winds [31]. The DDT can then be deposited in the Nyanga area, which has cooler temperatures and high mountains (around 2,000 metres above sea level) providing a catchment area. Cooler temperatures help to condense the drifting DDT particles [32], which are then deposited on the ground. DDT then enters the local environment through the food chain. Mothers are exposed to DDT and transfer the pollutants through their milk to their breastfeeding infants.

Women have less access to information

Through a multi-choice response questionnaire, it was established that 95 per cent of the participating mothers had absolutely no knowledge of the potential toxicity of DDT, whereas men randomly questioned within the same age bracket showed a good knowledge. In Zimbabwe, as in many other African countries, women are active in small-scale agricultural activities near their homes, where they use pesticides available for vector control purposes. Men are often engaged in ground spraying activities on commercial farms and are more familiar with precautions. The gender difference in understanding the potential risks of pesticides could partly be due to the level of education. In the studied areas 19.6 per cent of females and 25.5 per cent of males reach secondary-level education. Only 0.6 per cent of the females and 1.5 per cent of the males reach higher education [33]. The mothers who participated in this study were all living in rural areas and represented a social group with low-income background.

Conclusion

This study shows the possible transport and condensation of particle-bound DDT from a malaria endemic area to the mountains in the Eastern Highlands in Zimbabwe. Human milk investigations have been used as a general biological monitoring tool for the assessment of the levels of environmental pollution by OC pesticides in different parts of Zimbabwe. The study also draws attention to the risk of infants being contaminated by these chemicals through nursing. Women are exposed to the OC pesticides through their daily agricultural activities, through eating foodstuffs polluted by these chemicals, and through general global pollution. Education level can explain gender differences in knowledge of potential toxicity of DDT in countries like Zimbabwe. Because of the well-recognized advantages of breastfeeding, this practice should not be discouraged [34]. Rather, alternatives to, and better practices in the use of, OC pesticides in developing countries should be introduced.

Notes

The authors thank the participating mothers and the health authorities at the Hospital in Nyanga and the Mazarakufa Clinic in Mudzi for permission to collect the milk samples, Wilbert Murambiwa, Maria Mhonda, Sharon Katsande and Elisabeth Lie for their contributions, and the Norwegian Universities' Committee for Development Research and Education (NUFU) for financial assistance.

1. Pesticides analysed were: hexachlorobenzene (HCB), α-, β- and γ-isomers of hexachlorocyclohexane (HCH), *bis*-2,2-(4-chlorophenyl)-1,1,1-trichloro-ethane (*pp*-DDT) and its metabolites *bis*-2,2-(4-chlorophenyl) -1,1,1-trichloro-ethane (*pp*-DDD), and *bis*-2,2-(4-chlorophenyl)-1,1-trichloroethylene (*pp*-DDE).
2. sum of *pp*-DDE + *pp*-DDD + *pp*-DDE.

References

1   Laug, E.P., Kunze, F.M., Pitchett, C.S. In *Archives of Industrial Hygiene*, 3, 1951: 245–6.
2   WWF. *Resolving the DDT dilemma*, WWF Canada and WWF US, 1998.
3   The Arctic Monitoring and Assessment Programme (AMAP). *Arctic Pollution Issues; A State of the Arctic Environmental Report*, Oslo: AMAP, 1997.
4   Chikuni, O., Nhachi, C.B.F., *et al*. In *Science of the Total Environment*, 199, 1997: 183–90.
5   Chikuni, O., Polder, A., Skaare, J.U., Nhachi, C.F.B. In *Bulletin of Environmental Toxicology*, 58, 1997: 776–8.
6   Kanja, L.W., Skaare, J.U., *et al*. In *Journal of Toxicology and Environmental Health*, 19, 1986: 449–64.
7   Mpofu, S.M. In *Scientific News*, 21, 1987: 31–6.
8   Johnstone, D.R., Allsopp, R., Copper, J.F., Dobson, H.M. In *Pesticide Science*, 22, 1988: 107–21.
9   Murray, S.R., Munowenyu, E.M. *Senior Atlas for Zimbabwe*, 1992.
10 Phelps, R.J., Facordi, S., *et al*., In *Transactions of Zimbabwe Scientific Association*, 63, 1986: 8–15.
11 Mpofu, S.M., In *Central African Journal of Medicine*, 32(12), 1986: 285–9.
12 Chikuni, Nhachi *et al*., *op. cit.*, 1997.
13 Chikuni, Nhachi *et al*., *op. cit.*, 1997.
14 Murray, S.R., Munowenyu, E.M. *op. cit.*
15 Brevik, E.M. In *Bulletin of Environmental Contaminants and Toxicology*, 19, 1978: 281–6.
16 Skaare, J.U., Tuveng, J.M., Sande, H.A. In *Archives of Environmental Contaminants and Toxicology*, 17, 1988: 55–63.
17 Chikuni, Nhachi *et al*., *op. cit.*, 1997.

18 Polder, A., Becher, G., Savinova, T.N., Skaare, J.U. In *Chemosphere*, 37(9–12), 1998: 1795–1806.
19 AMAP, *op. cit.*, 1997.
20 Johansen, H.R., Becher, G., Polder, A., Skaare, J.U. In *Journal of Toxicology and Environmental Health*, 25, 1994:1–19.
21 Polder, A., pers. com. 1999.
22 Polder *et al.*, *op. cit.*, 1998.
23 Schecter, A., Fürst, P., Fürst, *et al.*, In *Chemosphere*, 20, 1990: 927–934.
24 Petreas, M., Hooper, K., *et al.*, In *Organohalogen Compounds*, 30, 1996: 20–23.
25 Polder, pers. com. 1999.
26 Chikuni, Nhachi, *et al.*, *op. cit.*, 1997.
27 Chikuni, Polder, *et al.*, *op. cit.*, 1997.
28 Johansen *et al.*, *op. cit.*, 1994.
29 Polder *et al.*, *op. cit.*, 1998.
30 Kanja, L.W., Skaare, J.U., Ojwang, S.B.O., Maitai, C.K. In *Archives of Environmental Contaminants and Toxicology*, 22, 1992: 21–4.
31 Woodwell, G.M., Graug, P.P., Johnson, H.A. In *Science*, 174(14), 1971: 1101–07.
32 Johnstone, D.R., Allsopp, R., Copper, J.F., Dobson, H.M. In *Pesticide Science*, 22, 1988: 107–21.
33 Central Statistical Office. *Zimbabwe Demographic and Health Survey 1994. Harare Zimbabwe*, Calverton, US: Macro International, 1995: 14–15.
34 Jensen, A.A. In *Drugs and Human Lactation*, Elsevier, 1996.

15

Cancer risks in agriculture

Lucia Miligi and Laura Settimi

Agricultural activities may entail exposure to a multitude of biological and chemical hazards such as diseases transmitted by animals, solvents, fertilizers and pesticides. Several investigations have been carried out to evaluate cancer risks posed to farmers by exposure to some of these agents, in particular pesticides.

Most studies conducted on male farmers indicate that this occupational group tends to experience increased risks for selected types of cancer, including leukaemia, non-Hodgkin's lymphoma, multiple myeloma, soft tissue sarcoma, skin melanoma, cancers of brain, stomach and prostate [1]. The available data on women engaged in agricultural activities are scanty. Some studies show that women employed in agriculture, like men workers, experience increased risks for cancer of lymphatic and blood (haematopoietic) tissues [2,3,4,5, 6]. A few observations are also available on cancers of bladder [7,8], ovary [9], thyroid [10] and cervix uteri [11,12].

Studies on cancer risk among women engaged in agricultural activities are of particular interest since women may experience specific exposure situations, and gender differences in response to agricultural hazards may also occur [13,14].

Studies on health effects and farming should include women living on farms, since this group may be exposed to agricultural hazards [15]. Some women, although not classified as farmers in their own right, may be directly engaged in farm activities. Furthermore, household contamination may occur, causing indirect exposure to chemicals and particularly to pesticides.

Cancer linked to pesticides: two recent Italian studies

In Italy, several studies have been carried out in agriculture, and some have focused on women [16,17]. Agriculture has always been an important sector in Italy, particularly before the nineteenth-century Industrial Revolution when manufacturing grew in the North, while Southern Italy retained its agricultural orientation. Changes in the distribution of the Italian workforce in the last thirty years yielded a substantial reduction of 10 per cent in both the agricultural and the industrial workforces and a doubling in the number of people working in office jobs [18], but women remained involved in agricultural activities. In a five-year period to 1999, women made up an estimated 35 per cent of the agricultural workforce [19]. Furthermore, agricultural activities consisted mainly of small and medium-sized farms where a substantial part of the workforce was family members. Farming is still often a family enterprise: family members involved in farm duties are potentially directly – and indirectly – exposed to pesticides.

Two recent Italian epidemiological studies conducted on cancer and pesticides considered men and women separately to understand better the different risks. One was a population-based case-control study that investigates the association between blood and lymph (haematolymphopoietic) malignancies and occupational exposures: it covered agricultural chemicals and involved eleven areas of the country, in nine of which agriculture is prevalent [20,21,22]. Included in the study were all newly diagnosed cases of non-Hodgkin's lymphoma, Hodgkin's disease, leukaemia, and multiple myeloma that occurred in either sex in subjects resident in the areas under study aged 20 to 74. Cases were identified through periodic surveys in hospital and pathology departments and, where available, in the archives of cancer registries.

The control group consisted of a random sample of the general population, aged 20–74 and resident in each of the areas under study. The sample was formed and stratified by sex and five-year groups according to the number of cases in the largest diagnostic group (non-Hodgkin's lymphoma and chronic lymphocitic leukaemia). 2,737 cases were interviewed out of a total of 3,357 eligible cases, (811 non-Hodgkin's lymphoma, 193 Hodgkin's disease, 383 leukaemia, 133 multiple myeloma, among men; 639 non-Hodgkin's lymphoma, 172 Hodgkin's disease, 269 leukaemia, 137 multiple myeloma in women), and 1,779 controls out of a total of 2,391 eligible controls. The overall refusal rate was 10 per cent for cases and 19 per cent for controls. Details of methods used in the study have been given in previous papers [23].

The other study, a hospital-based case-control study, was conducted in five Italian rural areas to examine the association between cancer and farming among agricultural workers [24]. The following cancer sites were selected for the study: lip, oral cavity and oropharynx, oesophagus, stomach, colon, rectum, lung, skin melanoma, skin non-melanocytic, prostate, bladder, kidney, non-Hodgkin's lymphoma, breast, corpus uteri, cervix uteri, and ovary. Altogether, 1,569 newly diagnosed cases in men and 1,044 in women, aged 20–75, were identified from hospital records from March 1990 to September 1992. Of these, detailed information was collected by a standard questionnaire for 1,338 men and 945 women. Data analyses were carried out, comparing each case series to a reference group drawn from other sites. Detailed methods have been described elsewhere [25].

Both investigations used the same approach to infer exposures in agriculture [26]. As a first step, an in-depth interview was conducted using a structured questionnaire. This generated information on known and suspected risk factors for the cancers under investigation. A section of the questionnaire was devoted to agricultural work to collect information on types of crop grown, protective equipment adopted, personal habits during and after treatments, and on where pesticides were stored. A separate questionnaire was used for each crop grown and the subject was interviewed about specific crop diseases, and whether pesticides had been applied. The strategy of eliciting the subjects' recall about specific crop diseases and exposure circumstances was the first step in getting more precise information about exposure. Data were also collected in detail on periods and frequency of treatment, on modes of application and re-entry to the fields after treatment. In total, 23 forms were written up referring to prevalent crops in the study areas. The exposure assessment was performed by experienced agronomists, who reviewed the information collected by the agricultural section of the questionnaire for each subject, and translated it into histories of pesticide exposure.

In addition to the individual exposure assessment by the experts, an *a priori* crop exposure matrix (CEM) was developed for the two studies [27]. This facilitated the reconstruction of exposure to pesticides in an agricultural setting characterized by complex exposure, taking into account the main factors that can influence the use of chemicals for farming (type of crop, crop disease, historical period and geographical area). The exposure linkage system prepared takes into account the diversity in agricultural practices in which exposure may occur and the different uses of chemicals within each crop related to pests and crop diseases. The CEM, which covers the period from 1950 up to 1993, applies to 11 areas and the major crops in the study areas (barley, maize, rice, wheat, flowers, olive trees, orchards, sugar beet, vegetables, and vineyards). The exposure axis is made up of a list of 474 active ingredients and mixtures (1,232 products) in the areas of interest.

In both studies the analysis by exposure assessment concerning the role of pesticide types or active ingredients used is still in progress. The analyses in both studies considered women and men separately. The study on haematolymphopoietic malignancies for women and men who have ever worked as farmers (job titles in the study were coded according to the International Standard Classification of the occupation [28]), based on the ILO code showed no increased risk estimate for non-Hodgkin's lymphoma, leukaemia, multiple myeloma or Hodgkin's disease.

The main findings reported in the study on several types of cancer and agricultural activities, for men employed as farmers or a farm labourer, were as follows:

- Statistically significant increases for women, but not men of skin melanoma and bladder cancer;
- Increased risk for women, but not statistically significant, of lung cancer and pre-menopausal breast cancer;
- Increased risk for men, but not statistically significant, of prostate cancer.

The preliminary analyses performed in both the studies by type of crop shows different risks for women and men. The main results of the two studies can be summarized as:

Flower growing
Women: statistically significant increase of leukaemia.
Men: increased risk, but not statistically significant, of multiple myeloma.

Vine growing
Women: increased risk of leukaemia and not significant increased risks of skin melanoma, skin non-melanoma and bladder cancer.

Men: increased risk, but not statistically significant, of rectal cancer.

Vegetable farming

Women: increased risk of leukaemia, skin non-melanoma and a statistically not-significant increase of bladder cancer.
Men: not significant increased risk for leukaemia and rectal cancer.

Olive farming

Men: increased risk of stomach cancer.

Orchards

Women: increased risk, but not statistically significant, of leukaemia.
Men: increased risk of prostate cancer and not significant increased risk for kidney and liver cancer.

Final remarks

The results of the studies presented here show that women and men experience both similar and different risks from the same environmental agricultural exposure. Several problems that affect studies of cancer and pesticides exposures may refer to either women or men, particularly regarding exposure assessment procedures. In fact, the design and interpretation of epidemiological investigations are sometimes complicated by the complexity of exposure patterns and the difficulty in documenting past exposure. The major difficulty is to evaluate the risks associated with specific pesticides, because most farmers can use a great number of different pesticides. The change in use of specific chemicals over time and the variation in work practices are additional problems. Consequently, misclassification of exposure may seriously affect risk estimates.

Although agriculture in Italy is characterized by small farms, with many different crop types, agricultural practices have changed widely over the past forty years. Since 1960, new chemicals have become available on the market and different modes of application have been introduced. The use of chemicals for farming depends on such factors as type of crop and crop diseases, historical period and geographical area. All these may seriously affect the quality of information. The strategy to collect information on crop grown and on specific crop diseases and exposure circumstances is the first step in getting more precise information about exposure.

In the studies presented here, the crops reported by the subjects were analysed as risk variables, roughly indicative of different patterns of exposures, and the results showed some increased risks for those where the use of insecticides or fungicides happened more frequently (fungicides were usually sprayed ten to twenty times per year in vineyards).

Only a small proportion of women working and living in an environment where pesticides are used are directly engaged in the mixing of or application of pesticides. Preliminary data of this controlled study show that 8.1 per cent of farmers directly engaged in the application of pesticides were women, and 2.5 per cent in the second study. Furthermore, in the Agriculture Health Study [29], only 3 per cent of the applicators with a pesticide applicator licence are women. So women, who are involved in only some aspect of production, may be unaware of the chemical to which they have been exposed. Hence it is very important in the context of epidemiological studies on cancer and pesticides to collect information on all the different activities or all exposure sources where farm women may have been exposed. Sources of exposure should include not only those connected to the work environment during the application of pesticides but also the re-entry tasks and other sources of pesticide residue in the residential environment. It is important to include all possible exposure sources, such as the laundering of clothing contaminated by pesticides, the location of the home in relation to the field where spraying of pesticides occurred, the storage place where the pesticides are kept and any other activity that might have resulted in indirect or secondary exposures.

To clarify the role of pesticide exposure in agriculture, the prospective approach, such as the Agriculture Health study [30,31,32], could eliminate some of the difficulties in assessing historical exposures, and provide useful gendered information, through regular monitoring of the factors that may influence exposure.

Notes

The authors thank the Working group for the Epidemiology of Hematolymphopoietic Malignancies in Italy (WILL) for the original data; and the US National Cancer Institute, Italian Ministry of Agriculture, Italian National Research Council Italian League for the fight against cancer for financial support.

References

1 Blair, A., Zahm, S.H. In *Occupational Medicine*, 6(3), 1991: 335–54; and Blair, A., Zahm, S.H. In *Environmental Health Perspectives*, 103(S8), 1995: 205–8.
2 Zahm, S.H., Weisemburger, D., *et al*. In *Archives of Environmental Health*, 48(5), 1993: 353–8.
3 Kristensen, P., Andersen, A., *et al*. In *Scandinavian Journal of Work Environment and Health*, 22, 1996: 14–26.
4 Zhong, Y., Rafnsson, V. In *International Journal of Epidemiology*, 25(6), 1996: 1117–24.
5 Folsom, A.R., Zhang, S., *et al*. In *Journal of Occupational and Environmental Medicine*, 38(11), 1996: 1171–6.
6 Khuder, S., Mudgi, A. In *American Journal of Industrial Medicine*, 32, 1997: 510–16.
7 Silverman, D.T., McLaughlin, J.K., *et al*. In *American Journal of Industrial Medicine*, 16, 1989: 239–40.
8 Kristensen *et al*., *op. cit.*, 1996.
9 Donna, A., Betta, P.B., *et al*. In *Carcinogenesis*, 5, 1984: 941–2; and Donna, A., Crosignani Probutti, F., *et al*. In *Scandinavian Journal of Work Environment and Health*, 15, 1989: 47–53.
10 Inskip, H., Coggon, D., Winter, P., Pannett, B. In *Occupational and Environmental Medicine*, 53, 1996: 730–35.
11 Stubbs, H.A., Harris, J., Spear, R.C. In *American Journal of Industrial Medicine*, 6, 1984: 305–20.
12 Wesseling, C., Ahlbom, A., *et al*. In *International Journal of Epidemiology*, 25(6), 1996: 1125–31.
13 McDuffie, H.H. In *Journal of Occupational Medicine*, 36, 1994: 1240–46.
14 Blair, Zahm, *op. cit.*, 1995.
15 Alavanja, M.C.R., Akland, G., *et al*. In *Journal of Occupational Medicine*, 11, 1994: 1247–50.
16 Vineis, P., Terracini, B., *et al*. In *Scandinavian Journal of Work Environment and Health*, 13, 1986: 9–17.
17 Donna *et al*., *op. cit.*, 1984, 1989.
18 Sistema Statistico Nazionale Istituto Nazionale di Statistica Imprese Istituzioni e unità locali Fascicolo Nazionale, 6° et 7° censimento generale dell' Industria e dei Servizi, Rome: Istituto Poligrafico dello Stato, 1981.
19 Sistema Statistico Nazionale Istituto Nazionale di Statistica: Forze Lavoro, Rome: Istituto Poligrafico dello Stato, 1999.
20 Vineis, P., Crosignani, P., *et al*., In *Carcinogenesis*, 20(8) 1999: 1459–63; and Vineis, P., Crosignani, P., *et al*. In *Journal of Epidemiology and Community Health* 54, 2000: 431–6.
21 Miligi, L., Settimi, L., *et al*. In *American Journal of Industrial Medicine*, 36, 1999: 40–60.

22 Seniori Costantini, A., Miligi, L., *et al*. In *Epidemiology*. 12(1), 2001: 78–87.

23 Vineis *et al*., *op. cit*., 1999; Miligi *et al*., *op. cit*., 1999; Seniori Costantini *et al*., *op cit*., 2001.

24 Settimi, L., Comba, P., *et al*., 'Cancer risk in farmers: a multi-exposure case-control study'. Proceedings of the International Congress of Occupational Health, Stockholm, 15–20 September 1996; and Settimi, L. Andrion, A. et al. In *American Journal of Industrial Medicine*, 36, 1999: 135–41.

25 Settimi *et al*., 1996; Settimi *et al*., 1999.

26 Miligi, L., Settimi, M., *et al*. Retrospective Pesticide Exposure Assessment in case-control studies. In Proceedings of 9th International Symposium on Epidemiology in Occupational Health. CDC NIOSH, 1994: 332–7.

27 Miligi, L., Settimi, L., *et al*. In *International Journal of Epidemiology*, 22(6) (suppl. 2), 1993: S42–5.

28 International Standard Classification of Occupations, Geneva: ILO, 1968.

29 Alavanja, M.C.R., Sandler, D.P., *et al*. In *Environmental Research, Section A* 80, 1999: 172–9.

30 Alavanja *et al*., *op. cit*., 1999.

31 Gladen, B.C., Sandler, D.P., *et al*. In *American Journal of Industrial Medicine*, 34, 1998: 581–7.

32 Alavanja *et al*., *op. cit*., 1999.

16

Environmental organochlorine exposure and the risk for breast cancer

Lennart Hardell

Breast cancer is the most common female cancer in many western countries. In Sweden in 1997, 27 per cent of all female cancers were located in the breast. During the last two decades the age-standardized incidence of breast cancer has increased 1.4 per cent each year among Swedish women [1]. Oestrogens play a role in the cause of breast cancer [2], and environmental xeno-oestrogens may be potential risk factors [3].

Organochlorine compounds such as the pesticides DDT, hexa-chlorobenzene (HCB), chlordane, and industrial chemicals such as polychlorinated biphenyls (PCBs) may act as endocrine disrupters. Also dioxins, which contaminate certain pesticides (phenoxy herbi-cides and chlorophenols), or which are produced as by-products during combustion of waste or during chlorine bleaching of paper pulp, affect endocrine activity. However, the xeno-oestrogens have much lower oestrogenic potency than oestradiol produced in the ovary. Some dioxins, such as 2,3,7,8-tetrachlorodibenzo-p-dioxin (TCDD), have antagonistic effects (that is, they suppress oestrogenic activity instead of stimulating it).

Results of studies of organochlorines and the risk for breast cancer have been conflicting. With PCBs, some studies have indicated an increased risk, but this has not been confirmed in other investiga-tions [4]. For DDT, analysis of the main and most persistent break-down product, DDE, does not show a strong association with breast cancer. However, a Danish case-control study showed an association with the pesticide dieldrin, which has oestrogenic properties [5]. Hence, certain xeno-oestrogens may increase the risk, but the magnitude is still to be defined. Furthermore, the interaction with oncogenes that are of significance in causing breast cancer has not yet been studied.

We performed a case-control study on the association between breast cancer and breast tissue concentrations of dioxins (PCDDs), dibenzofurans (PCDFs), co-planar (dioxin-like) PCBs, and non co-planar PCBs, HCB and DDE [6,7]. Due to the high cost, analyses were restricted to 22 patients and 19 controls for dioxins and di-benzofurans, and 19 patients and 19 controls for co-planar PCBs (numbered 77, 126 and 169 by the International Union of Pure and Applied Chemistry [IUPAC]). The results are given as pg/g (pico-grams per gram, or parts per trillion) lipid or fat. For non co-planar PCBs, DDE and HCB analyses were performed on 43 cases and 35 controls with concentrations given as ng/g (nanograms per gram, or parts per billion) lipid.

Box 16.1 Fat-loving chemicals stay in women's bodies

Human data suggest that there are significant sex differences in dermal absorption of the organochlorine lindane, which may be three times greater in females than in males [8].

A study by Zarema Amirova and colleagues of workers in a chemical plant in Khimprom, Ufa, Russia, found that many fell ill through occupational contact with phenoxy herbicides. Based at the Environmental Research Centre of the Republic of Bashkortostan, Amirova found that the herbicides made in the factory included: 2,4,5-T (1965/ 67), 2,4,5-TCP (1962/87), 2,4-D (1965 to the present) and 2M-4X (1987–92). Workers were exposed to the contaminant dioxin (2,3,7,8 TCDD) and as a result many suffered from chloracne. Peak exposure values for women workers ranged from 490 to 900 pg/g blood lipid, but from 1,000–90,000 pg/g lipids in men. Although working with a small sample size, preliminary evidence from the studies indicates a tendency for slower elimination of 2,3,7,8–TCDD from highly exposed women.

In a 2,4,5-T exposed cohort, all seven women donors were found to have a 2,3,7,8-TCDD half-life of 9.2 years, whereas the ten male donors were observed to have a 2,3,7,8-TCDD half-life of 6.2 years. In a 2,4,5-TCP exposed cohort, three women showed a 2,3,7,8-TCDD half-life of 11.7 years, whereas the one man had reached this level after 7.5 years.

Fat loving pesticides and chemicals may reside in women's bodies a lot longer than they do in men's bodies.

Source: Reference 9.

Women in the study

Seventy-eight consecutive patients operated on by one surgeon during 1993–95 for a malignant (43) or a benign (35) lesion in the breast were recruited for the study. None of the women had a previous history of malignancy, and all controls were free from a cancer diagnosis. After informed consent, a 10 g tissue sample free from tumour was taken from the breast during the surgical procedure and frozen. The laboratory personnel did not know if the specimen had come from a case or from a control.

Potential confounders, such as a family history of breast cancer, parity, lactation, hormonal therapy, menopausal status and smoking habits, were assessed by a questionnaire. The clinical stage of the breast cancer, hormonal receptor status (oestrogen receptor ER, progesterone receptor PGR), and type of tumour (diploid versus aneuploid tumours) were assessed from medical records.

Methodology and results

Determination of concentrations of organochlorines

Fat was extracted, cleaned and analysed by high-resolution gas chromatography and low-resolution mass spectrometer for PCBs, DDE and HCB determination. The dioxins, dibenzofurans and co-planar PCBs were determined by high-resolution mass spectrometry after enrichment on a PX-21 carbon column [10].

Statistical analyses

Results were calculated for pre-menopausal and post-menopausal women separately, as well as for all subjects together. Analyses were also performed to identify other potential risk or confounding factors. A standard lifetable technique (Kaplan-Meier) was used to decide cut-off values for continuous factors which might be potential risk or confounding factors [11].

Results

Dioxins, dibenzofurans (PCDDs, PCDFs)   After detailed analysis no significant difference in the concentration of TCDD was found between cases and controls. The results were similar if hormone receptor status in the breast cancer was considered. The concentration of octachlorodibenzo-*p*-dioxin (OCDD) was higher in the cases than in the controls, but this difference was found only in the post-menopausal patient group. When the OCDD variable was examined as a continuous risk factor there was a 1.09 (9 per cent), 95 per cent CI = 0.95–1.25, increase in the adjusted elevated risk (Odds Ratio [OR]) for breast cancer per 100 unit (pg/g lipid) increase of OCDD.

PCBs   For non co-planar PCBs no significant difference was found between cases and controls. However, the highest OR was calculated in the post-menopausal patient group with oestrogen receptor positive (ER+) cancer: adjusted OR=1.8, 95 per cent CI=0.4–7.3. The concentrations of the co-planar PCBs were highest in the post-menopausal patient group, which yielded significantly increased risks.

Hexachlorobenzene (HCB)   An increased concentration of HCB was only seen for post-menopausal patients. The risk was significantly increased for post-menopausal patients with ER+ cancer: OR=7.1, 95 per cent CI=1.1–45.

DDE   The concentration of DDE was somewhat higher in the controls than in the cases. No association was found, and the results did not change when menopausal status or hormone receptors were considered.

Discussion

All cases and controls were recruited on a consecutive basis from the same catchment area, ensuring no bias of potential exposure over time or due to regional differences. Factors that could cause breast cancer were assessed by questionnaires and information in the records. The chemical analyses were performed without knowledge of the status of the study subject (case or control).

Organochlorine pesticides and PCBs: a potent mix

It has been suggested that risk factors for breast cancer differ for pre- and post-menopausal women and that organochlorines may be an important causal factor primarily in the post-menopausal group. Furthermore, since some of the organochlorines have oestrogenic properties, increased risk should be found in women with ER+ breast cancer. For co-planar PCBs and HCB this study found the highest risk in post-menopausal women with ER+ cancer. Both oestrogenic and anti-oestrogenic effects have been reported for different PCB congeners [12]. An endocrine effect has been reported for HCB [13].

Our findings seem to support the hypothesis that some environmental oestrogens are risk factors for breast cancer, but the results must be interpreted with caution since they were based on low numbers, and because multiple comparisons were performed. The risk was highest for post-menopausal women with ER+ breast cancer, which gives some biological relevance to the findings. Certainly more investigations are necessary on a potential association between exposure to organochlorines, organobromines and breast cancer. As a minimum, such studies need to contain a large number of post-menopausal women with hormone receptor positive cancer in order to detect possible synergistic effects between different xeno-oestrogens and interaction with oncogenes.

Implications of the findings

This study showed a clear association between the pesticide HCB and breast cancer in women. This risk was highest among post-menopausal women with a hormone receptor positive cancer. Furthermore, a high risk was found for co-planar (dioxin-like) PCBs in the same study group.

Each participant in the study was offered the results of the measurements, but most did not pay much attention to the results. There has been little discussion in the Swedish media on potential environmental risk factors for breast cancer. On the contrary, the anti-oestrogenic effect of TCDD has been, in these circumstances, postulated even to protect against breast cancer. This was not shown in our study. Certainly our results highlight the possibility that the presence of certain pesticides in the environment, such as HCB, may increase the risk for breast cancer through background exposure. Other international studies have not measured HCB or the other compounds of interest in our study, co-planar PCBs and the dioxin congener OCDD.

Although our findings were based on low numbers of cases and controls, they are provocative. Certainly the incidence of breast cancer is still increasing in Sweden. Of all cancers, breast cancer constituted 29 per cent in Sweden in 1998, which parallels the increasing use of pesticides and environmental pollutants. Interaction of certain chemicals may be of great importance, and must be studied.

Studies are hampered by the high cost of chemical analyses, which limits potential for a larger study. Although cancer treatment is making progress, the first goal for all cancer types must be prevention. Much more attention must be placed on pesticides and environmental pollutants in carcinogenesis and it is necessary to reduce such exposure as much as possible.

References

1 *Cancer Incidence in Sweden 1997*, Stockholm: National Board of Health and Welfare, 1999.
2 Kelsey, J.L. In *Epidemiology Reviews,* 15, 1993: 256–63.
3 Wolff, M.S., Toniolo, P.G., Lee, E.W., Rivera, M., Dubin, N. In *Journal of the National Cancer Institute*, 85, 1993: 648–52.
4 Lognecker, M.P., Rogan, W.J., Lucier, G. *Annual Review of Public Health*, 18, 1997: 211–44.
5 Hoyer, A.P., Grandjean, P., Jorgensen, T., Brock, J.W., Hartvig, H.B. In *Lancet*, 352, 1998: 1816–20.
6 Hardell, L., Lindström, G., Liljegren, G., Dahl, P., Magnuson, A. In *European Journal of Cancer Prevention*, 5, 1996: 351–7.
7 Liljegren, G., Hardell, L., Lindström, G., Dahl, P., Magnuson, A. In *European Journal of Cancer Prevention*, 7, 1998: 135–40.
8 Evaluation on the review of lindane (4). UK: Pesticides Safety Directorate, London, November 1999.
9 Amirova, Z., Amerkhanov K., *et al.*, In *Organohalogen Compounds*, 44, 1999: 299–302.
10 Lindström, G., Rappe, C. In *Chemosphere*, 17, 1988: 921–33.
11 Fredrikson, M., 'Epidemiological studies on colorectal cancer. Some design issues and analytical considerations', Medical dissertation, Linköping University, 1997, pp. 22–23.
12 Krishnan, V., Safe, S. In *Toxicology and Applied Pharmacology*, 120, 1993: 55–61.
13 Colborn, T., vom Saal, F.S., Soto, A.M. In *Environmental Health Perspectives*, 101, 1993: 378–84.

17

Explaining breast cancer and chemical links: health hazards for women workers

Dieter Flesch-Janys

An increase in the incidence of breast cancer over the last decades has been observed in many countries. For example, in Hamburg, Germany, the incidence has doubled over the last forty years [1]. This increase cannot totally be explained with changes in known risk factors and improvements in early detection by mass screening programmes [2]. Environmental exposure to certain chemicals may have contributed to this trend [3]. One class of chemicals of concern is the organochlorines.

Several pesticides, widely used in the past, though largely banned or restricted in Western countries over the last two decades (but still in use in many others) belong to this class: DDT, hexachlorocyclohexane (HCH),[1] hexachlorobenzene (HCB), dieldrin and others. The polychlorinated biphenyls (PCBs), used for example in transformers, also belong to this class, as do dioxins (polychlorinated dibenzo-*p*-dioxins), and furans (PCDD/F) which occur mainly as unintended by-products in industrial processes such as pesticide production and waste incineration.

Most of these substances are persistent, accumulate in the food chain and remain ubiquitous in human biological material, especially in fat tissue. Animal and *in vitro* studies confirm that some of these substances exhibit oestrogenic properties (DDT, HCH, some PCBs). On the one hand oestrogens themselves are known to be associated with breast cancer, though the exact mechanism is still unclear. On the other hand, experimental animal and *in vitro* studies have shown that some dioxins and some so-called 'dioxin-like' PCBs exhibit anti-oestrogenic properties. However, the most toxic of the dioxins – namely, 2,3,7,8-TCDD – known from the accident in Seveso, Italy, is considered to be a human carcinogen which produces malignant tumours at different sites in the human body [4]. This conclusion was derived from human studies mainly on occupationally exposed men. So far there is little empirical information regarding the carcinogenic effects in women. In addition, the mechanism by which TCDD exhibits its carcinogenic properties is still poorly understood.

Several studies have investigated the potential link between the body burden of certain organochlorines at environmental levels, but no definite pattern has emerged yet. Only sparse data are available regarding the carcinogenic potency of these substances in women and girls under high-exposure conditions. One example is a group of women workers at a plant in Hamburg, Germany (CH Boehringer), which had produced 2,4,5-T, a herbicide and an ingredient of Agent Orange used in the Vietnam War (See Box 17.1), and the organochlorine insecticide lindane (99 per cent gamma-HCH). The production of these substances started in 1952 and was terminated in 1984, when it was acknowledged that, regardless of efforts to diminish contamination with the dioxin TCDD in the production of 2,4,5-T, there still remained a high contamination with other dioxins known to exhibit similar toxic effects. (All known production of 2,4,5-T has since ceased because of the dioxin contamination, and it has been included for global elimination in the Stockholm Convention on Persistent Organic Pollutants.)

This group of women was monitored until 1989, and an increase in breast cancer mortality was reported at the beginning of the 1990s [5,6]. Compared with the German population, an increase in breast cancer mortality by a factor of 2.5 was observed. However, the number of observed cases (11) was small and precluded a more detailed analysis of whether this increase was associated with exposure to PCDD/F and HCH.

In a consecutive study breast cancer incidence was investigated until 1995 [7]. Additionally, the study tried to reconstruct the exposure to PCDD/F and HCH by including the results of blood and adipose tissue analysis for concentrations of these substances and by utilizing these measurements to assign a individually quantitative exposure estimate for all women in the group as basis for a dose-response analysis.

Box 17.1 Chronic exposure to Agent Orange in the Aluoi Valley, Vietnam

L. Wayne Dwernychuk

During the Vietnam War over 72 million litres of herbicide were applied over southern Vietnam to deprive northern Vietnamese forces of protective forest cover and food. Agent Orange accounted for approximately 60 per cent of all herbicide used during the conflict. Dioxin (specifically 2,3,7,8-TCDD) was a contaminant in Agent Orange.

A new study has been assessing dioxin residues in the environment of Aluoi Valley. A collaborative effort of Hatfield Consultants Ltd (HCL), the Vietnamese government 10–80 Committee, the Thua Thien Hue Province Department of Health, with support from the Canadian International Development Agency, the Canadian Space Agency, Revenue Canada, Environment Canada, and the Canadian National Research Council, has examined soils, food and human blood and breast milk [8]. The Aluoi Valley was an integral proportion of the Ho Chi Minh Trail, through which supplies were transported from northern to southern Vietnam during the conflict. In 1999, HCL and the 10–80 Committee undertook additional studies in the Aluoi Valley. Soils from three former US Special Forces bases and other aerially sprayed regions of the valley were collected for dioxin analyses. Foods, human blood and human breast milk were also collected for analysis in Canada. In addition, a nutrition and preliminary health survey was undertaken in the valley, in collaboration with the Department of Health and Epidemiology (University of British Columbia, Canada).

Results of the 1999 investigation confirmed earlier studies that elevated levels of dioxin existed in valley soils and human food, with the highest level of contamination found in the vicinity of the former US Special Forces base at A So (formerly named A Shau). Fish and duck tissues, human blood and human breast milk collected from the village nearest the former base had the highest levels of dioxin contamination, relative to other regions of the valley. As a result of the contaminated food chain in the vicinity of the base, adults and children born after the war are continuing to ingest contaminated foods.

Health studies suggest that inhabitants of the village situated nearest the most highly contaminated former base experience a higher level of birth defects relative to other villages studied in the valley.

Many other former South Vietnamese and US military installations throughout Vietnam could serve as 'dioxin reservoirs' that are continuing to contaminate local food chains, and humans living in the vicinity [8].

The terrible urgency for mitigating and addressing the health and environmental impacts affecting two generations of Vietnamese are demonstrated in a preliminary study from HCL and the Vietnamese 10–80 committee. Reservoirs of dioxin contamination from Agent Orange around former US army bases are slowly releasing their poison into the environment, contaminating the major local food sources. Women, men, girls and boys will continue to be chronically exposed, suffering compromised health effects in this way for many more generations without urgent humanitarian aid.

Soils, pond-raised fish and ducks in the area have been found to have dioxin (I-TEQ) levels which exceed Western standards for residential and agricultural soils and the guidelines for unrestricted human consumption (foods). Dioxin levels in human blood and breast milk are higher than those found in industrialized countries.

Many people in the valley are already living at a very basic subsistence level – mainly centred around vegetable, fish and poultry foods raised near their own households.

One area of concern for the Vietnamese government has been the possibility of exposed populations having a higher than expected prevalence of birth defects. A number of abnormal fetuses have been recorded over the years. Making a connection between past/present dioxin exposure and the prevalence of birth defects presents problems that need to be carefully addressed.

Vietnam is unique; a careful research design is required to address interrelated factors, ongoing exposure, and pre-existing genetic issues in the shape of relatively high frequency of genetic errors, neural tube defects and palato-glossal defects that can be observed among ethnic minorities. The most heavily exposed have the highest macro- and micro-nutrient deficiencies.

The debate on how to separate the chemical causes of birth defect rates should not prevent immediate realistic impact mitigation programmes.

Source: Reference 9.

Description of study methods

The study covered 398 women workers of the Hamburg plant which had produced herbicides and insecticides (2,4,5-T and HCH including lindane) from 1952 to 1984. Detailed working histories in twenty-two plant departments were extracted from company records. Incidence follow-up covered the time period 1952–95. Women employees known to be alive in 1995 were interviewed by a mailed

Figure 17.1 Illustration of the course of TCDD blood levels for two persons (Person A: usual background levels. Person B: exposure to 20 ng/kg/yr from age 20 to 29)

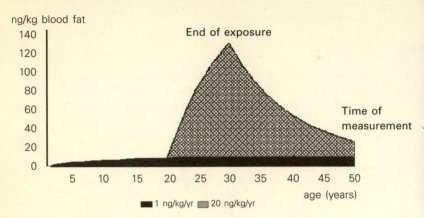

Note: Shaded areas illustrate the quantification of exposure.

questionnaire. When a woman reported that cancer had been diagnosed within that period, medical records were obtained to verify the diagnosis. For deceased women death records were used and date of diagnosis of a cancer of the breast was set to date of death. Exposure to PCDD/F, especially 2,3,7,8-TCDD, and beta-HCH, was assessed by measuring blood levels in a subgroup. Using these blood levels and the occupational histories, together with information regarding the contamination with PCDD/F and HCH for every production department, an estimate of a dose rate was derived. The accumulation and elimination of these substances in the human body were taken into account. The half-life was estimated from a special elimination study [10, 11]. Using these dose rates an exposure indicator reflecting the cumulative exposure until the end of follow-up ('area under the curve'; in nanogrammes per kilogram [ng/kg, or parts per billion] [blood fat x years] for PCDD/F; in microgrammes per litre [µg/l, or parts per million] [blood x years] for beta-HCH) was estimated for every woman [12]. The procedure is illustrated in Figure 17.1.

Standardized incidence ratios (SIR) were calculated for all cancer sites with two or more observed cases using reference incidence data from the cancer registry of the German state Saarland for the years 1970–92 (data were extrapolated for 1960–69 and 1993–95). In the analysis all women who did not respond to the questionnaire were treated as non-cancer cases. Overall cancer incidence was also calculated excluding non-responders. In order to assess dose-response relationships the cohort was divided in tertiles of PCDD/F and beta-HCH exposure. In addition, time-dependent proportional hazard models (internal comparison) stratified by birth year were calculated using the lowest one-third cases as the reference. Relative risks for different combinations of exposure were calculated.

Results

Out of 398 women, 4 could not be contacted. For 334 (83.4 per cent) women, cancer incidence could be assessed. A total of 61 cancer cases (57 confirmed by medical records) were identified (34 deceased,

Table 17.1 Standardized cancer incidence ratios for selected cancer sites

Localization	ICD-9	Pyr	Obs	Exp	SIR	95% CI
All*	140–208	11704	57	52.0	1.10	0.83–1.42
Digestive	150–159	12016	6	13.8	0.43	0.16–0.95
Breast	174	11910	23	14.9	1.55	0.98–2.32
Uterus	182	11983	5	3.8	1.31	0.42–3.05
Ovary	183	12016	4	2.6	1.55	0.42–3.96
Other genital, ill defined	184	11963	3	0.6	5.45	1.12–15.9
Bladder	188	11996	2	1.1	1.81	0.22–6.55
Kidney	189	12016	2	1.2	1.71	0.21–6.17
Lympho-hematopoietic	200–208	12016	4	2.8	1.44	0.39–3.68

Notes
ICD: International Classification of Diseases, Version 9.
Pyr: Amount of person years = sum of observation time over all individuals.
Obs: Number of observed cases.
Exp: Number of cases expected had the incidence been the same as the incidence in Saarland.
SIR: Standardized incidence ratio.
CI: Confidence interval.
* All skin cancers were excluded.
Reference data 1970–1974 were used for 1960–1969; 1991–1992 for 1993–1995.

Table 17.2 Summary of key studies of breast cancer and exposure to PCDD/F and beta-HCH

Authors	Type	Size	Subst.	Exp. measure	Effect	Comment
Bertazzi 1997; Baccarelli et al. 1999	Seveso (accident) cohort/mortality incidence	6,000 Zone A+B[a] 39,000 Zone R[a] 233,000 controls	TCDD	Zone A median 71.5 ppt Zone B median 16.8 ppt	10/13.2[b] 67/88.6 11/16.3	Zone A+B Zone R Zone A+B
Kogevinas 1993	Cohort (occupational), incidence	169 exp. 532 exp. unlikely	TCDD	No biological measurements	1 (0.86)[b] 8 (0.91)	
Mussalo-Rauhamaa 1990	Case/control	44/33[c]	beta-HCH[b]	>0.1 ppm (fat)	OR 10.5[d]	
Hoyer 1998	Prosp. nested case/control	240/477[c] (cohort n=7712 follow up 1976–96)	beta-HCH	118.9 ng/g	OR 1.36 (4th quartile) n.s.[e]	A significant effect for dieldrin was observed median 24.4 ng/g lip. OR 1.96 (III q) 2.05 (IV q)
Zheng 1999[a,b]	Case/control	304/186[c] (benign breast disease), adipose tissue	beta-HCH	Median 27.1 (cases) /25.2 ppb lipid adjusted	OR 0.6 (highest vs lowest) n.s[e]	

[a] Zone A: most contaminated, B: second contaminated, R: uncontaminated.
[b] Observed/expected cases.
[c] Number of cases/controls.
[d] Odds ratio.
[e] Statistically not significant.
Source: References 13–18.

Box 17.2 Women's exposure to the TCDD dioxin

The study of effects of TCDD exposure following the Seveso accident [13] is of special interest. The available blood levels show mean concentrations in women from the area with the highest exposure (Zone A) of 71.5 ng/kg blood lipid, well in the range of exposure of the women in the study described here. However, no increase in breast cancer has been observed to the latest follow-up date, although other cancers, such as uterine cancers, have increased [15]. On the contrary, data showed a numerical decrease in breast cancer risk. There may be several reasons for this discrepancy to the present study. The observation period in Seveso adds up to 20 years while in the present study up to 43 years are covered. It may be that the effect in Seveso will show up later.[2] Another difference is the timing of exposure, which was accidental in the Seveso study but chronic in this occupational study. However, animal data do not indicate differences in effects due to differences in these exposure conditions. Finally, TCDD alone is known to have anti-oestrogenic activity, which can be important for oestrogen receptor positive (ER+) breast cancers.

An international effort to investigate the impact of occupational exposure to TCDD in pesticide production workers and sprayers found no increase in breast cancer risk, but there were few exposed women in the study [15]. Furthermore, the exposure classification was based solely on work histories. No biological measurements were available.

Women's exposure to HCH

Numerous case-control studies with contradictory results are published in the context of ubiquitous environmental exposure to HCH. Some [16] reported a strong elevated risk (odds ratio 10.5) for women with more than 0.1 parts per million (ppm) beta-HCH in adipose tissue compared to women with less than 0.1 ppm, but study size was very small. A Danish study of 240 cases and 477 controls [17] observed a statistically non-significant elevated odds ratio of 1.36 for women with the highest beta-HCH levels, although a strong significant effect was observed for dieldrin, another organochlorine. On the contrary, a study with 304 cases and 186 controls did not find an elevated risk [18], but the results may have been influenced by the use of women with benign breast disease as controls because of a potential association of beta-HCH with this disease. The extent of exposure in all these case-control studies was an order of magnitude lower than in the study of the occupationally exposed women described here.

27 alive), including 23 breast cancer cases (11 deceased, 12 alive: all confirmed by medical records). Table 17.1 shows the standardized incidence ratios for selected cancer sites in the body. Total cancer was slightly elevated, but the 95 per cent confidence interval (CI) included one. Breast cancer showed an incident ratio (SIR) of 1.55 with the assumption that all non-responders had been non-breast cancer cases. Excluding non-responders from the analysis yielded a SIR of 1.84. Cancers of uteri and ovary (International Classification of Disease [ICD] numbers 182, 183) were also elevated. The significant increase in 'ill defined cancer' of the genital tract (ICD 184) was based on three cases; however, all were self-reported and no medical documents were available.

In Germany current background levels range between 2–4 ng/kg blood lipid for the dioxin TCDD; 10–15 ng/kg for I-TEQ (International Toxic Equivalencies – a summary measure for all PCDD/F). Thus with respect to PCDD/F the observed levels are 10–15 times higher. Regarding the estimated levels at the end of exposure this factor increases to about 20–50 times higher. With respect to beta-HCH it is assumed that background levels are usually below 1 µg/l, thus the elevation factors are about 10–30. These data indicate substantial exposure of the cohort for dioxins and beta-HCH compared to the German population. It should be noted that the background concentrations in other countries do not differ substantially from the German data.

A comparison of an occupationally exposed group always carries the problem that there may be factors where these groups differ, which may contribute to the effect. This study took steps to ensure that this did not occur, and that the results were therefore attributable to dioxins and beta-HCH.

Discussion

The group of women workers described here is one of those with the highest occupational exposure to dioxins PCDD/F and beta-HCH worldwide, confirmed by measurements of blood levels in a subgroup. The data allowed for the construction of an exposure indicator to obtain an estimate for the dose-related effect on breast cancer incidence.

It is unlikely that the results have been biased by the choice of the reference population since the statistical tools used yielded comparable dose-response results as those from SIR analysis. Nevertheless, some factors complicate the interpretation of the findings: the cohort is small, and adjustment for known risk factors for breast cancer (age at menarche, menopause, number of pregnancies) was not possible due to the lack of complete data. However, there is no indication that any of these factors would be strongly related to the exposure indicators. Finally, due to the high correlation of exposure to PCDD/Fs and beta-HCH the respective contributions of beta-HCH and PCDD/F to elevated breast cancer risk could not be separated. Few studies address the relationship of exposure to PCDD/F and beta-HCH to breast cancer. The relevant recent studies are listed in Table 17.2, with comments in Box 17.2.

In conclusion, women working in the Hamburg factory experienced an increased incidence of breast cancer, confirming the finding of the mortality study. While a separation of the effects of the dioxins and furans and HCH was not possible, there was a statistically significant increase in breast cancer risk in the groups with the highest estimates of PCDD/F and beta-HCH exposure.

Note

1. Isomers of HCH have been used for pesticides: mixed isomers of HCH, alpha-HCH and beta-HCH are now largely banned for use in agriculture. The 99 per cent gamma-isomer of HCH, lindane, has remained in use, but the European Community banned most uses in 2000.
2. Since this was written, evidence of increased breast cancer risk with TCDD exposure has been reported from the Seveso Women's Health Study [19].

References

1 Flesch-Janys, D., Baumgardt-Elms, C. *et al*. In Langfristige Trends der Brustkrebsinzidenz und -mortalität in Hamburg, *Hamburger Ärzteblatt* 2000 (in press).
2 Feuer, E.J., Wun, L-M. In *American Journal of Epidemiology,* 136, 1992: 1423–36.
3 Davis, D.L., Bradlow, H.L. *et al*. In *Environmental Health Perspectives,* 101, 1993: 372–7.
4 IARC monographs on the evaluation of carcinogenic risks to humans, vol. 69: 'Polychlorinated dibenzo-*para*-dioxins and polychlorinated dibenzofurans', Geneva: IARC Press, WHO, 1997.
5 Manz, A., Berger, J. *et al*. In *Lancet,* 338, 1991: 959–64.
6 Flesch-Janys, D. Berger, J. *et al*. In *Organohalogen Compounds,* 13, 1993: 381–4.

7 Flesch-Janys, D. Becher, H., *et al.* In *Organohalogen Compounds,* 44, 1999: 379–82.

8 Schecter, A., Dai, L.C., Päpke, O., Prange, J., Constable, J.D., Matsuda, M., Thao, V.D., Pisac, A.L. In *Journal of Occupational and Environmental Medicine,* 43, 2001: 435–43.

9 Dwernychuk, L.W., Dinh Cau, H., *et al.* In *Chemosphere,* 47, 2002: 117–37.

10 Flesch-Janys, D. Becher, H. *et al.* In *Journal of Toxicology and Environmental Health,* 47, 1996: 363–78.

11 Jung, D., Becher, H., Flesch-Janys, D., *et al.* In *Organohalogen Compounds,* 25, 1995: 185–9.

12 Flesch-Janys, D., Steindorf, K., Gurn, P., Becher, H. In *Environmental Health Perspectives,* 106, 1998: 655–62.

13 Bertazzi, P.A., Zocchetti, C. *et al.* In *Epidemiology,* 8, 1997: 646–52.

14 Baccarelli, A., Pesatori, A. *et al.* In *Organohalogen Compounds,* 42, 1999: 43–7.

15 Kogevinas, M., Saracci, R. *et al.* In *Cancer Causes and Control,* 4, 1993: 547–53.

16 Mussalo-Rauhamaa, H., Häsänen, E. *et al.* In *Cancer,* 66, 1990: 2124–8.

17 Hoyer, A.P., Grandjean, P., *et al.* In *Lancet,* 352, 1998: 1816–20.

18 Zheng, T.Z., Holford, T.R. *et al.* In *Cancer,* 85, 1999: 2212–18.

19 Warner, M., Eskenazi, B. *et al.* In *Environmental Health Perspectives,* 110, 2002: 625–8

Birth defects in an agricultural environment

Ana M. García

Congenital malformations are anatomical structural defects present at birth. Almost 3 per cent of all newborns have congenital defects requiring medical care. The lives of one-third of these babies are threatened as a result of the defect [1]. As global infant mortality declines, congenital malformations account for an increasing proportion of infant deaths.

Two main features of congenital malformations justify the priority on prevention: very early onset and a limited chance for complete recovery [2]. Therefore, the search for risk factors that could cause these anomalies acquires particular significance. A limited number of agents have been identified definitely to act as human teratogens (environmental agents causing congenital defects). Others are considered likely to cause congenital defects, although more data are needed. Pesticides have been a focus of research on congenital malformations: the evidence is suggestive, but not fully consistent [3].

Exposure and mechanisms for teratogenesis

The major risk of congenital malformations in children is related to maternal exposure to teratogens during the first phase of pregnancy. Many chemicals can cross the placenta and act on the embryo during the most vulnerable period – the first three months of pregnancy, particularly between 15 and 60 days after conception [4]. Results from animal studies present ample evidence of the teratogenicity of many pesticides. Several types and chemical classes of pesticides have been shown to have teratogenic effects on the developing embryo of different animal species. Table 18.1 gives examples of widely used agricultural pesticides that have known teratogenic activity in some animal species.

Table 18.1 Examples of pesticides frequently used in agriculture and shown to cause congenital malformations in animal studies

Chemical class or type of pesticide	Active ingredient	Congenital malformation
Organophosphates	Dimethoate	Polidactyly, urogenital anomalies
Carbamates	Carbaryl	Skeletal defects
Fungicides	Benomyl	Nervous system defects, eye defects
Herbicides	Paraquat	Skeletal defects

Source: Reference 7.

Male or female mutation of germ cells (precursor cells for spermatozoa in the male and for ova in the female) can produce genetic defects in subsequent generations expressed as congenital malformations. A large number of pesticides demonstrate mutagenic effects. A review of the genetic activity of 65 pesticides [5] found nine pesticides genetically active in most of the bioassays, and 26 genetically active in a smaller number of tests. Only 30 pesticides gave negative results in all tests. A mother's question – whether the reproductive function of her 12-year-old daughter might be genetically injured from the domestic use of organophosphates – stimulated a study on genotoxicity from domestic use of organophosphates [6]. The researchers found overt genotoxic effects from domestic application of commonly used organophosphate pesticides.

Limitations of epidemiological research on humans

The results from experimental studies with animals can suggest the existence of risks for human beings, but definite evidence should come from epidemiological research of exposed people. This evidence is not yet available. A review of 45 epidemiological studies carried out between 1966 and 1999 on occupational pesticide exposure and congenital defects found major limitations [8]. These included:

• Only 24 studies focus on exposed women: as environmental teratogenesis is more firmly established for maternal exposure during pregnancy than for paternal exposure, a greater focus of research on female exposure to pesticides is needed.

- A large number of studies simply assessed pesticide exposure indirectly through occupational titles ('agricultural workers', 'farmers', 'applicators').
- Over 800 pesticide active ingredients are in use, with varying degrees of toxicity and a wide diversity of biological actions, but only a very small number of the studies (5 related to paternal exposure and 2 to maternal exposure) assessed exposure to specific active ingredients.
- Definitions of exposure and identification of specific patterns of exposure were inadequate: comparisons of the results of different studies are limited, as the population in each study is likely to be exposed to different pesticides or combinations of pesticides.
- Some studies assessed the risk of any kind of congenital malformations, while others categorized congenital defects by affected anatomical region; but congenital malformations include a wide range of different defects, some with plausible relationships to environmental exposures, some with known genetic determinants, some unlikely to be related to chemical action.

Table 18.2 Research needs regarding pesticides exposure and cancer

- Evaluation of the effects of individual pesticides and combination of pesticides.
- Improvement of exposure assessment methods: more 'crude estimates' of exposure will not make major contributions to knowledge; assessment of validity and reliability of exposure assessment strategies is needed.
- Improvement of the knowledge on inert compounds (chemicals without pesticide action present in pesticide formulations).
- More basic knowledge on mechanisms of action is needed and should be applied for the studies' design and interpretation.
- More attention is needed to populations understudied (migrants, women, seasonal workers).
- Evaluation of gene–environment interactions.

Note: This proposal is equally valid for research on pesticides and congenital defects.
Source: Reference 9.

• Many of the studies included a small number of cases to properly assess the relationship between exposure and specific congenital malformation or specific teratogenic patterns.

Table 18.2 presents a proposal of research needs regarding pesticides exposure and cancer and these needs are equally relevant for research on congenital malformations.

Agriculture in the Mediterranean area: pesticides and birth defects

A study in Valencia, Spain, of the relationship between occupational exposure to pesticides in agricultural work and congenital malformations sought to avoid some of the flaws limiting previous research, while attempting to address some of the research needs identified in Table 18.2. Maternal and paternal risks were evaluated, and relevant risk periods for exposure were considered for both parents. The hypothesis investigated was that exposures defined as male and/or female involvement in agricultural work and/or direct handling of specific pesticides during relevant time periods related to conception and pregnancy increase the probability of having a child with some selected birth defects [10,11].

In this study, 261 case children born with some selected congenital malformations and 261 control children without congenital malformations were selected from eight public hospitals serving the main intensive agricultural zones of Valencia during 1993 and 1994. The mothers and the fathers of the selected children were located and interviewed in order to collect information on socio-economic data, habits (smoking, alcohol), and medical, reproductive and occupational history. Additional detailed information on pesticide exposure was collected for those parents involved in agricultural work.

The number of women reporting themselves as 'pesticide applicators' was very low, although a slightly higher number of women reported having directly handled pesticides, and a still higher number had been involved in agricultural tasks. It is possible for these women to be exposed to pesticides when they are working on crops, even if they do not directly handle the chemicals; also, while women are rarely directly involved in pesticide treatments tasks, they are frequently involved in re-entry activities (harvesting), where the potential for pesticide exposure is high because pesticide residues are present in foliage and soil [12].

Table 18.3 presents the adjusted estimates for the risk of congenital malformations in relation to maternal and paternal agricultural work and pesticide handling obtained in the Valencia study. When the risk estimates are greater than 1 it means that the risk of having a child with congenital malformations is increased in mothers and fathers exposed during agricultural work or handling pesticides as compared to the risk for unexposed people. The analysis was repeated for the 'acute risk period' (exposure around conception and first trimester of pregnancy) and 'non-acute risk period' (exposure out of the acute risk period). There was a statistically significant risk of having a child with congenital defects for mothers involved in agricultural work during the acute risk period: mothers reporting having been involved in agricultural activities around the conception and/or during the first trimester of pregnancy carried a risk more than three times higher of having a child born with congenital defects

Table 18.3 Adjusted risk estimates for congenital malformations in relation to maternal and paternal agricultural work and pesticide handling in Valencia

Exposure variable		Adjusted risk estimates (ratio)	95% confidence interval
Mothers			
Agricultural workers	during ARP	3.16	1.11–9.01
	during NARP	1.06	0.65–1.70
Handling pesticides	during ARP	1.87	0.16–22.26
	during NARP	2.88	0.50–16.41
Fathers			
Agricultural workers	during ARP	1.50	0.72–3.13
	during NARP	0.87	0.51–1.50
Handling pesticides	during ARP	1.48	0.82–2.68
	during NARP	1.62	0.86–3.05

Notes
ARP – Acute risk period: exposure between one month before conception and first trimester of pregnancy for the mothers and between three months before conception and first trimester of pregnancy for the fathers.
NARP – Non-acute risk period: exposure out of the acute risk period.
Source: References 10, 11.

than mothers not reporting such activities, and this result was unlikely to be explained because of chance (as seen in 95 per cent confidence intervals). For the fathers, a smaller increase of the risk was related to direct handling of pesticides, but statistical significance was not reached. Because of the small number of women reporting direct handling of pesticides, results from this analysis are uncertain. As noted, pesticide exposure is very likely in agricultural work without the direct handling of pesticides.

Other routes of exposure: contamination at home

Domestic contamination can be an important source of exposure for the families of occupationally exposed workers. Evidence exists of 'para-occupational' exposures in workers' family members when toxic substances are carried to the household, mainly on contaminated work clothing and equipments, with subsequent 'pollution' of the home environment [13,14]. High concentrations of occupational chemicals have been measured at the houses of workers exposed in their workplace, and different diseases and health effects have been reported in their families. Some examples of these para-occupational exposures have been described in relation to agricultural workers and pesticides [15].

In the Valencia study questions were introduced to evaluate the significance of home contamination from the occupational activity. The aim was to assess the risk derived from mothers' exposure to pesticides as a consequence of paternal occupational exposure. These questions covered two main issues: washing of work clothes, and home storage of both pesticides and their application devices. However, the results were not conclusive. None of the factors investigated demonstrated a significant increase in risk.

Conclusion

According to available knowledge from experimental studies with laboratory animals, several active ingredients of pesticides have the potential to act as teratogens in human beings – to cause congenital malformations (gross structural defects present at birth) in the children of exposed people. The association between environmental exposure to teratogenic agents and congenital defects is more biologically plausible for maternal than for paternal exposure, although the potential for an increase of the risk exists for exposure of any parent.

Epidemiological studies of the association between congenital malformations and pesticide exposure reported in the literature are not conclusive. Although several limitations have been identified in relation to these studies, a precautionary approach is required with regard to the availability and use of pesticides. The risk from maternal exposure is expected to be both more likely and higher than the risk derived from paternal exposure; more studies which focus on mothers are needed. Research needs to define exposure better, in particular to describe exposure to specific active ingredients and patterns of pesticide use.

A study in a Mediterranean agricultural area shows a statistically significant increase of the risk for congenital malformations in the children of mothers exposed to agricultural activities during the first phase of pregnancy. Para-occupational routes of exposure for women and other family members of workers occupationally exposed to pesticides should be properly evaluated. Future study designs should try to avoid previous limitations in order to provide more robust findings on the health risks of pesticide exposure for women and men.

Incomplete though they are, the data available suggest that harm is plausible and this requires immediate action in public health terms. It needs to be acted upon directly with a precautionary approach, to reduce exposure now.

References

1 Shepard, T.H. *Catalog of Teratogenic Agents*, Baltimore: Johns Hopkins University Press, 1992.
2 Czeizel, A.E. In *Epidemiology*, 6, 1995: 205–7.
3 García, A.M. In *American Journal of Industrial Medicine*, 33, 1998: 232–40; García, A.M. In *Proceedings from the 27th Conference of the European Teratology Society*, Oxford, 4–9 September 1999.
4 Brent, R.L., Beckman, D.A. In *Bulletin of the New York Academy of Medicine*, 66, 1990: 123–63.
5 Garret, N.E., Stack, H.F., Waters, M.D. In *Mutagenesis Research*, 168, 1986: 301–25.
6 Lieberman, A.D., Craven, M.R., Lewis, H.A., Nemenzo, J.H. In *Journal of Occupational and Environmental Medicine,* 40, 1998: 954–7.
7 Hayes, W.J., Laws, E.R. (eds) *Handbook of Pesticide Toxicology*, San Diego: Academic Press, 1991.

8 García, *op. cit.*, 1998.

9 Zahm, S.A., Ward, M.H., Blair, A. In *Occupational Medicine: State of the Art Reviews*, 12, 1997: 269–89.

10 García, A.M., Benavides, F.G., Fletcher, T., Orts, E. In *Scandinavian Journal of Work, Environment and Health*, 24, 1998: 473–80.

11 García, A.M., Fletcher, T., Benavides, F.G., Orts, E. In *American Journal of Epidemiology*, 149, 1999: 64–74.

12 Popendorf, W. In *Review of Environmental Contaminants and Toxicology*, 128, 1992: 71–117.

13 Knishkowy, B., Baker, E.L. In *American Journal of Industrial Medicine*, 9, 1986: 543–50.

14 McDiarmid, M.A., Weaver, V. In *American Journal of Industrial Medicine*, 24, 1993: 1–9.

15 Loewenherz, C., Fenske, R.A., Simcox, N.J., Bellamy, G., Kalman, D. In *Environmental Health Perspectives*, 105, 1997: 1344–53.

19

Reproductive health and pesticide exposure

Xiping Xu and Sung-Il Cho

Reproductive health is a significant public health concern. Only one-quarter to one-third of fertilized human eggs are likely to survive to term [1]. Occupational and environmental exposures to toxins may result in a wide range of adverse reproductive outcomes, such as reduced semen quality, ovarian dysfunction, infertility, fetal loss, growth retardation, stillbirth and birth defects [2]. The biological process of reproduction involves several key stages: production of healthy germ cells in the male and the female, formation of a viable conceptus, growth and development of the fetus in a favorable maternal environment, successful delivery of the baby in an adequate time window, and subsequent growth and development of the baby into a healthy adult [3]. Any factor that disrupts one or more links in the chain results in a reproductive failure with specific manifestations. This multifaceted vulnerability of the reproductive process to external influence poses a challenge to researchers. An assessment of the reproductive risk of a certain exposure must use an appropriate study design and data analysis method to address a broad range of possible endpoints while focusing on the most relevant outcomes [4].

Issues in the evaluation of adverse reproductive outcomes

Spontaneous abortion

The most serious adverse outcome from conception to birth is death of the fetus. Fetal loss can occur at early stages of the reproductive process or later in gestation, but most losses occur early, between fertilization and the clinical detection of pregnancy. Most studies of spontaneous abortion address the events between detected pregnancy and the twentieth week of gestation. Urine pregnancy tests in routine clinical use may not confirm a pregnancy until five to six weeks after the last menstrual period. Therefore, spontaneous abortions occurring during this period may not be documented clinically [5].

Time to pregnancy

Time to pregnancy is another useful measure in the study of environmental exposures [6]. A prolonged waiting time to pregnancy in a couple actively trying to conceive may indicate reproductive failure at any of several stages from the formation of germ cells onward: this is known as reduced fecundability. The two approaches, detection of fetal loss and reduced fecundability, complement each other up to the twentieth week of gestation, and may be used to assess the effects of environmental exposures experienced by men or women. Low values of semen parameters such as sperm concentration and motility have been associated with prolonged time to pregnancy [7]. Therefore, an ideal research design for assessing the effect of environmental toxin on reproductive health is a simultaneous prospective study of women and their partners that partitions the contribution of women and men and provides insight into the mechanism of toxicity associated with an environmental exposure.

The necessity of considering multiple outcomes

Reproduction as a group of interconnected processes is a useful paradigm for interpreting observations on specific outcome. Different outcomes may be dependent on one another. For example, if a certain toxic exposure increases the frequency of spontaneous abortion, a higher dose may increase loss at a very early stage, paradoxically reducing the frequency of clinically observable spontaneous abortion [8]. However, such an effect may be detected as a delay in time to pregnancy. On the other hand, if a certain exposure is associated with delayed time to pregnancy measured in months, this effect may be arising from prolonged menstrual cycle length, reduced fecundity, frequent early pregnancy loss, or a combination of these factors [9,10].

The use of biomarkers for hormone measurements

The development of urinary biomarkers for reproductive hormones made it possible to measure outcomes more precisely. Sensitive and specific assay methods for human chorionic gonadotropin (hCG) have been developed and applied to both laboratory and epidemiological studies [11,12]. A urine analysis documenting a rising hCG pattern with a subsequent fall indicates an early pregnancy loss, and this could not be detected by conventional clinical pregnancy tests. Precise identification of conception time significantly improves the assessment of time to conception and gestational age. Urinary biomarkers are able to pinpoint ovulation and project hormone profiles of the menstrual cycle [13]. These advances enable researchers to detect subtle effects of environmental pollutants on reproductive health that were difficult to verify by conventional methods.

Reproductive toxicity of the organochlorine DDT

DDT was extensively used in the past as a pesticide in agriculture and as a vector control agent. In 1963, 81,000 tonnes were manufactured and 27,000 tonnes were used in the USA [14], but health and environmental concerns have led to widespread bans. Governments negotiating the international Convention on Persistent Organic Pollutants agreed that alternatives to DDT for malaria control must be developed to allow the phase-out over time of this persistent pesticide. DDT was heavily used in China in the 1960s and 1970s but was banned in the early 1980s. In reproductive health studies, we found a significant association between serum concentration of p,p'-DDE and a history of spontaneous abortion in Anqing, China [15]. Further investigation with innovative methods and improved study design is warranted; however, there is sufficient information to direct policies effectively that protect women and their ability to have healthy pregnancies.

Toxicity of organophosphate pesticides

The use of organophosphate pesticides has increased worldwide over the past few decades, as they have largely replaced the organochlorine insecticides that are environmentally persistent and even more detrimental. Yet, organophosphate pesticides, too, are known for their potentially fatal effects in humans [16]. Various organophosphates share chemical and biological properties including metabolism and mode of action. After entering the human body, most organophosphates are bioactivated and become even more potent acetylcholinesterase (AChE) inhibitors than their parent compounds [17].

Most of the organophosphates are rapidly absorbed orally, through the skin, and via the lungs, and are quickly distributed to various body tissues. They are primarily metabolized and detoxified in the liver and are eliminated from the body by urinary excretion. Urinary metabolites such as alkylphosphates and para-nitrophenol can be used as a biomarker for exposure [18].

In developing countries, farmers and agricultural workers continue to have significant daily exposure to organophosphates [19]. More than 100 organophosphate insecticides are in use, including methyl parathion, malathion, diazinon and monocrotophos. In 1990, WHO reported that these four organophosphates, along with carbaryl (a carbamate insecticide), were the pesticides most commonly used in developing countries (see Annex 1 for list of pesticides of concern).

Epidemiological studies of organophosphates and reproductive health

Methyl parathion is known to cross the placenta [20]. Reproductive toxicity of methyl parathion has been identified in a limited number of experimental studies on various species including rats, mice, pigs and pheasants. Most epidemiological studies of the reproductive toxicity of pesticides do not specifically concentrate on one compound, mainly because subjects are exposed to multiple pesticides. However, in many cases it is possible to infer that organophosphates make up the majority of a mixed exposure.

Several studies have addressed the association between pesticide exposure and various reproductive outcomes. An investigation of the time to pregnancy of wives of fruit growers relative to pesticide exposure of male workers [21] studied 91 pregnancies in 43 couples between 1978 and 1990. The authors found a longer time to pregnancy among the exposed than the unexposed group. Studies of women farm workers in Washington state [22] and in Finland [23] found increased risks for spontaneous abortion and stillbirth. One investigation found a substantially increased risk of fetal loss in the second trimester [24]. A study in India among couples who worked as sprayers in the vineyards and lived in the area found a significantly higher prevalence of spontaneous abortion and stillbirth than in the control group [25]. A cross-sectional study of female workers and the wives of male floriculture workers to examine various pregnancy outcomes found an increased odds ratio of spontaneous abortion in both female workers (2.2; 95 per cent CI, 1.82–2.66) and the wives of male workers (1.79; 95 per cent CI, 1.16–2.77) [26] (a ratio greater than 1 indicates increased risk). A study of 1,016 couples whose men were directly exposed to pesticides from spraying and mixing compared them to 1,020 unexposed couples [27]. The frequency of spontaneous abortion was significantly higher in the exposed group (risk ratio = 1.7; 95 per cent CI, 1.6–1.9), with similar results observed for smokers and nonsmokers. Other investigators have found significant associations between pesticide exposure and haemangioma in the newborn (a benign tumour of the blood vessels, often appearing as a birth mark that spontaneously disappears within the first year of life) [28], perinatal mortality [29], and birth defects [30]. Another study found that women's exposure to organophosphates was associated (although not statistically significantly) with delayed time to pregnancy [31].

Box 19.1 Reproductive health studies in men: three studies at the Anqing Pesticide Production Factory, China

Occupational pesticide exposure and semen quality [32]

A total of 32 male workers with exposure to methyl parathion and 43 who had no exposure were recruited from two nearby factories. The men provided a single semen sample immediately at the end of a working shift and five urine samples over the next twenty-four hours for pesticide metabolite analysis. Semen samples were analysed for sperm concentration, motility, and normal morphology percentages according to the 1987 WHO criteria. Quantitative exposure to parathion was assessed. Median pesticide residue from personal monitoring among the pesticide workers (eight-hour time-weighted average) was 0.02 mg/m^3. Within the exposed group, the mean end-of-shift urinary *p*-nitrophenol levels were 0.22 and 0.15 mg/l for the high- and low- exposure subgroups, respectively. Statistical analysis of individual semen parameters revealed a significant exposure effect in the reduction in sperm concentration (35.9 x 10^6 vs 62.8 x 10^6, p < 0.01) and motility percentage (47 per cent vs 57 per cent, p = 0.03) but not in the percentage of sperm with normal morphology (57 per cent vs 61 per cent, p = 0.13). The mean semen parameter was significantly lower in the exposed group than that in the unexposed group. The effect persisted after adjustment for confounders including age, length of sexual abstinence and smoking status.

Adverse reproductive effects of organophosphate pesticides [33]

The adverse reproductive effects of organophosphate pesticides was measured by taking blood and urine measurements of serum follicle-stimulating hormone (FSH), luteinizing hormone (LH), testosterone and a metabolite of testosterone. Single blood and semen samples were collected at the end of a work shift. Three first-void urine samples were collected from each worker on three consecutive days. Urinary p-nitrophenol levels one hour after the work shift correlated with serum ($r = 0.71$, $p < 0.01$) and urinary ($r = 0.51$, $p = 0.04$) FSH. Pesticide exposure alone was significantly associated with serum LH ($\beta = 0.79$; 95 per cent CI, 0.42–1.16). With adjustment for age, rotating shift work, current cigarette smoking, and current alcohol consumption, pesticide exposure significantly increased serum LH by 1.1 units (95 per cent CI, 0.34–1.82). Serum FSH was slightly elevated ($\beta = 1.38$; 95 per cent CI, 0.09–2.85) and serum testosterone was decreased ($\beta = -55.1$; 95 per cent CI, −147.2–37.0) with increased pesticide exposure. Stratifying by exposure status, we found a significant negative correlation among the exposed group between urinary FSH and both sperm count ($r = -0.61$, $p < 0.01$) and sperm concentration ($r = -0.53$, $p = 0.03$).

Prevalence of sperm aneuploidy [34]

Twenty-nine semen slides (13 from exposed and 16 from unexposed men) were randomly chosen for aneuploidy (where the chromosome number of a cell is not an exact multiple of the normal basic number), using methods described elsewhere. The specific chromosome abnormalities of interest were disomy for chromosome 18 and the three different types of sex chromosome disomy: XX, XY, and YY. The crude proportions of all aneuploidy combined were 0.30 per cent and 0.19 per cent for sperm from exposed and unexposed men, respectively. Statistical analysis yielded significantly different crude risks of aneuploidy: 3.03 and 1.94 per 1,000 sperm from exposed and unexposed men, respectively, for a statistically significant rate ratio of 1.56 (95 per cent CI, 1.06–2.31). Occupational exposure to organophosphate pesticides moderately increases the prevalence of sperm aneuploidy, and increased sperm aneuploidy leads to reduced male fertility and increased risk of spontaneous abortion in women.

Genetic susceptibility to parathion reproductive toxicity

Gene–environment interactions may help to explain why exposure to toxins usually affects only a portion of an exposed population. Several metabolic traits are associated with environmentally induced disorders, including paraoxonase polymorphism and parathion toxicity [35]. The enzyme paraoxonase has two major functions: metabolism of fats (particularly high-density lipoproteins) and of paraoxon [36]. Once parathion enters the body, it is bioactivated by liver cytochrome P450 enzymes into paraoxon, an acetylcholinesterase inhibitor that is more potent than its parent compound. Other liver enzymes subsequently detoxify paraoxon. In mammals, any oxon such as paraoxon or methyl-paraoxon that escapes liver detoxification can be excreted in urine. It has been suggested that phenotypic polymorphisms of serum paraoxonase [37] may benefit individuals subjected to repeated low-level exposure by catalysing the detoxification process [38], but the process of its metabolism of organophosphates remains largely unknown [39]. As part of our study we conducted a genetic epidemiological investigation of the

---

Box 19.2 Genetic polymorphism and susceptibility to organophosphate toxicity [41]

Among 60 pesticide factory workers and 89 textile factory workers, we studied the Gln_{192} variant of PON1, which has a more reduced detoxifying capability than the wild-type Arg_{192} homozygotes. Semen samples were evaluated, and serum FSH, LH, testosterone, and their urinary metabolites were measured. Exposure was assessed by urinary p-nitrophenol levels over a 24-hour period. The men were classified into four groups according to exposed vs unexposed, and homozygote variant genotype vs wild-type hetero/homozygotes. The three exposed groups had significantly lower sperm counts (χ^2 = 11.0, p = 0.01) but higher serum levels of LH (χ^2 = 9.8, p = 0.02) than the unexposed wild-type hetero/homozygote group. These results suggest a modifying effect of the PON1 genotype on the reproductive toxicity of organophosphates. Limited evidence is available for other genotypes. Epoxide hydrolase was shown to be associated with the metabolism of some organophosphates. Animal studies support this finding: exposure of male rats to malathion showed a significant increase in the activity of epoxide hydrolase [42]. Thus, polymorphism of this enzyme may also have a modifying effect.

interaction between the human paraoxonase PON1 genotype and pesticide exposure in relation to biological markers of exposure and male reproductive outcomes. We found that this interaction modifies male reproductive toxicity [40]. The effect of genotype upon pesticide toxicity should always be considered in risk assessments, and the most vulnerable and genotypically at-risk sectors of the population should be the basis for intervention and protection, rather than the 'average population'.

Conclusion

The past few decades have seen a significant methodological advance in research on reproductive outcomes, and application of these methods will greatly improve the ability to investigate research questions that have been difficult to answer with conventional methods.

There have been strong suggestions of adverse effects of DDT and its metabolite DDE on reproductive outcomes in both women and men. While overall epidemiological data are not yet conclusive, improved research methods incorporating sensitive biomarkers for the assessment of subtle changes will help clarify the unresolved issues in the future studies.

The adverse effects on reproduction of organophosphate exposure in both women and men have been demonstrated. A genetic polymorphism associated with susceptibility to organophosphate toxicity has been identified. Further research will concentrate on clarifying the mechanism of the observed effect. Quantitative and comparative risk assessment studies are needed for individual chemicals, with improved measurement of exposure to account for adverse effects on multiple endpoints. Protective measures to reduce exposure, particularly among workers of reproductive age, should be emphasized.

References

1 Witschi, E. In Fraser, F. Mckusick, V. (eds) *Congenital Malformations*, Amsterdam: Excerpta Medica, 1970, pp. 157–69.
2 Sharara F.I., Seifer, D.B., Flaws, J.A. In *Fertility and Sterility*, 70, 1998: 613–22.
3 Savitz, D.A., Harlow, S.D. In *Environmental Health Perspectives*, 90, 1999: 159–64.
4 Savitz, Harlow, *op. cit.*, 1999.
5 Wilcox, A.J. In *American Journal of Industrial Medicine*, 4, 1983: 285–91.

6 Baird D.D., Wilcox A.J., Weinberg C.R. In *American Journal of Epidemiology*, 124, 1986: 470–80.
7 Ayala, C., Steinberger, E., Smith, D.P. In *Journal of Andrology*, 17, 1996: 718–25.
8 Weinberg, C.R., Wilcox, A.J. In Rothman, K.J., Greenland, S. (eds) *Modern Epidemiology*, Philadelphia: Lippincott-Raven, 1998.
9 Baird, Wilcox, Weinberg, *op. cit.*, 1986.
10 Catalano, P.J., Scharfstein, D.O., *et al.* In *Teratology*, 47, 1993: 281–90.
11 O'Connor, J.F., Birken, S., *et al.* In *Endocrinology Reviews*, 15, 1994: 650–82.
12 Lasley, B.L., Lohstroh, P. *et al.* In *American Journal of Industrial Medicine*, 28, 1995: 771–81.
13 Lasley, B.L., Shideler, S.E. In *Occupational Medicine: State of the Art Reviews*, 9, 1994: 423–33.
14 WHO. *DDT and its Derivatives: Environmental Aspects*, Geneva: WHO, 1989.
15 Korrick, S.A., Chen, C., Damokosh, A.I. *et al.* In *Annals of Epidemiology*, 11, 2001: 491–6.
16 WHO. *Public Health Impact of Pesticides Used in Agriculture*, Geneva: WHO, 1990.
17 Davies, H.G., Richter, R.J., Keifer, M., *et al.* In *Nature Genetics*, 14, 1996: 334–6.
18 Murray, W.J., Franklin, C.A. In Ballantyne, B., Marrs, T.C., Aldridge, W.N. (eds) *Clinical and Experimental Toxicology of Organophosphates and Carbamates*, Oxford: Butterworth–Heinemann 1992.
19 Jeyaratnam, J. In Jeyaratnam, J. (ed.) *Occupational Health in Developing Countries*, Oxford: Oxford University Press, 1992, pp. 255–64.
20 Ackermann, H. 'Transfer of organophosphorous insecticides to the embryo-formation of PO derivatives and development of toxic symptoms' (German). In *Tagungsber Akad Landwirtsch*, 126, 1974: 23–9.
21 De Cock, J., Westveer, K., *et al.* In *Occupational and Environmental Medicine*, 51, 1994: 693–9.
22 Vaughan, T.L., Daling, J.R. *et al.* In *Journal of Occupational Medicine*, 26, 1984: 676–8.
23 Hemminki, K., Niemi, M.L., *et al.* In *International Journal of Epidemiology*, 9, 1980: 149–53.
24 McDonald, A.D., McDonald, J.C. *et al.* In *British Journal of Industrial Medicine*, 45, 1988: 148–57.
25 Rita, P., Reddy, P.P., Reddy, S.V. In *Environmental Research*, 44, 1987: 1–5.
26 Restrepo, M., Munoz, N., *et al.* In *Scandinavian Journal of Work Environment and Health*, 16, 1990: 232–8.
27 Rupa, D.S., Reddy, R.R., Reddy, O.S. In *Environmental Research*, 55, 1991: 123–8.
28 Restrepo, M., Day, N.M. *et al.* In *Scandinavian Journal of Work Environment and Health*, 16, 1990: 239–46.

29 Taha, T.E. Gray, R.H. In *Bulletin of the World Health Organization*, 71, 1993: 317–21.
30 Nurminen, T., Rantala, K., *et al.* In *Epidemiology*, 6, 1995: 23–30.
31 Curtis, K.M., Savitz, D.A., *et al.* In *Epidemiology*, 10, 1999: 112–17.
32 Padungtod, C., Savitz, D.A., *et al.* In *Journal of Occupational and Environmental Medicine* 42, 2000: 982–92.
33 Padungtod, C, Lasley, B.L., *et al.* In *Journal of Occupational and Environmental Medicine*, 40, 1998: 1038–47.
34 Padungtodm, C., Hassold, T.J., Millie, E. *et al.* In *American Journal of Industrial Medicine*, 36, 1999: 230–38.
35 Weber, W.W. In *Environmental and Molecular Mutagenesis*, 25, 1995: 102–14.
36 Mackness, M.I., Mackness, B. *et al.* In *Current Opinion in Lipidology*, 7, 1996: 69–76.
37 Geldmacher, M. *et al.* In *Humangenetik*, 19, 1973: 353–6.
38 Weber, *op. cit.*, 1995.
39 Mackness *et al. op. cit.*, 1996.
40 Padungtod, C., Niu, T., Wang, Z. *et al.* In *American Journal of Industrial Medicine*, 36, 1999: 379–87.
41 Padungtod, Niu, Wang, *et al.*, *op. cit.*, 1999.
42 Reidy, G.F., Rose, H.A., Stacey, N.H. In *Toxicology Letters*, 38, 1987: 193–9.

20

Unsafe sex: how endocrine disruptors work

Miriam Jacobs

> Almost all aspects of life are engineered at the molecular level, and without understanding molecules we can only have a very sketchy understanding of life itself.
>
> Francis Crick

Endocrine disrupting chemicals are substances that can cause adverse effects by interfering in some way with the body's hormones or chemical messengers, consequently causing adverse health effects. Under the control of the central nervous system hormones are secreted by the endocrine glands into the bloodstream travelling through the body to specific organs, where they exert control on other cells by binding to specific cellular sites called receptors. The receptors control or regulate key bodily functions and processes including development, growth and reproduction. The endocrine glands include the thyroid, ovaries, testes and adrenals. They produce different hormones in a complex chemical control system. This multi-faceted feedback regulatory system is found in nearly all animals, but is deficient in the developing fetus and infant.

Endocrine disrupting chemicals (EDCs) differ from toxic substances such as carcinogens, neurotoxicants and heavy metals, because they can interfere with normal blood hormone levels or the subsequent action of those hormones, but do not have a classical toxic effect. The effects can disrupt the hormonal regulation of normal cell differentiation, growth, development, metabolism and reproduction throughout life. Endocrine disruption can occur at levels far lower than those of traditional concern to toxicologists. Sometimes high doses shut off effects that occur at low levels, and sometimes low and intermediate doses produce greater effects than those observed at high doses. The variation from the accepted

---

Box 20.1 Health effects linked to EDCs

- Increased incidence of breast, testicular and prostate cancers.
- Decreases in sperm counts and quality.
- Increased incidence of defects in the male reproductive tract.
- Changes in sex ratio (declining proportion of males).
- Neurological and behavioural disorders in children.
- Impaired immune and thyroid function.

---

wisdom, that the dose makes the poison, calls into question many regulatory assumptions about traditional toxicological safety testing for EDCs.

Pesticides and other chemicals can interfere with a number of biological processes in both women and men. The outcome of such toxic interference can include sterility, decreased fertility, increased fetus death, increased infant death and increased birth defects. For example, in reproductive toxicology, the organochlorine (OC) pesticides aldrin, dieldrin and hexachlorocyclohexane (HCH, from which lindane is derived) are associated with hormonal imbalances, spontaneous abortion and premature labour.

Endocrine disrupting potential of pesticides

Many reports suggest an increasing incidence of breast cancer in women [1,2,3,4] and in men decreased sperm counts and increased incidence of testicular cancer [5,6,7]. Adverse wildlife effects include birth defects, reproductive failures, and sexual abnormalities [8,9, 10,11]. These have stimulated research into both the chemical and molecular actions, and the clinical and epidemiological effects, of a large variety of natural and synthetic oestrogens present in the environment. The growing body of evidence on the hormone-like effects of many synthetic chemicals, including pesticides, in fish, wildlife and humans, has led to the setting up of endocrine disruption screening programmes relating to persistent organic pollutants (POPs).

Pesticides are one group of synthetic EDCs. It should come as no surprise that many pesticides interfere with hormone pathways, as they are designed to interfere with these systems. The trichlorophenoxyacetic acid herbicides (2,4-D, 2,4,5-T, MCPA), for example, work by disrupting the normal growth hormone systems of plants. Various insecticides (diflubenzuron) also disrupt the hormonal systems controlling the moulting and development of insects. The herbicides atrazine and simazine have been shown to be powerful disrupters of oestrogen mechanisms in rodent models [12].

The OC pesticides are among the first compounds to be tested in the US Environmental Protection Agency's endocrine disrupter screening programme for 87,000 chemicals [13].

Biological differences in hormones and hormone metabolism

In utero, natural sex hormones are largely responsible for development into females, or totally responsible for male development, as the default pathway for fetal development is phenotypically female. In the male fetus, androgens stabilize the Wolfian duct development, and actively remove the Müllerian duct (which is the precursor to the female uterine system).

The most important factors guaranteeing the homeostasis of female and male sexual functions include differentiation and reproduction. Main target tissues include bone and skin, the cardiovascular system, the brain and central nervous and immune system.

Endocrine hormones are lipophilic (fat loving), moving easily through cell membranes to activate or suppress the nuclear receptors (receptors in the nucleus of the cell) that directly act upon DNA. In synthesis with each other they contribute to the control of broad aspects of growth, development and adult organ physiology. The Steroid Hormone Receptor (SHR) family is extensive, but currently the research emphasis is on a sub-classification, the oestrogen receptors (ER). The other members of this family and other nuclear receptors of unknown functions also play key roles in endocrine disruption [14], both gender and non-gender specific. For example, a clear link between DDT and pancreatic cancer was recently reported in the *Lancet* [15], and the persistent DDT metabolite *p,p'*-DDE has been shown to have anti-androgenic potential [16].

Molecular mechanism of endocrine action

Receptor based

The nuclear receptor family have structural features in common. These include a central highly conserved DNA binding domain (DBD) that targets the receptor to specific DNA sequences, termed

---

Box 20.2 Steroid hormone and nuclear receptors [19]

AR   = androgen receptor
AhR   = aryl hydrocarbon receptor
ERα   = oestrogen receptor α
ERβ   = oestrogen receptor β
CAR   = constitutive androstane receptor
LXR   = liver X receptor
FXR   = farnesoid X receptor
RAR   = retinoic acid receptor
RXR   = retinoid X receptor
PXR   = pregnane X receptor
PR   = progesterone receptor
GR   = glucocorticoid receptor
PPAR = peroxisome proliferator-activated receptor
VDR   = vitamin D receptor

---

hormone response elements (HREs). A terminal portion of this receptor includes the ligand-binding domain (LBD), which interacts directly with the hormone. The ligand is the activating compound. Embedded within the LBD is a hormone dependent transcriptional activation domain. The LBD acts as a molecular switch that recruits coactivator proteins and activates the transcription of target genes when flipped into the active conformation by hormone binding. The currently accepted theory of steroid hormone binding suggests that in the absence of the hormone, each receptor is associated with certain 'chaperone' proteins (these are other proteins which protect and aid the receptor). Binding of the steroid hormone with the receptor protein causes a large shape change. This molecular switch results in the removal of the heat shock complex and allows the receptors to pair up (dimerize). Then DNA binding to a HRE occurs, to produce a complex that can trigger or suppress the transcription of a selected set of genes [17,18].

Most research is based on the oestrogen receptors (ER)

Due to the early identification of ER alpha and links between DDT and breast cancer, the oestrogen receptors have received most EDC research attention. So far they are known to exist as two subtypes, each one encoded by a separate gene. These are ER alpha [20] and the recently discovered ER beta [21] and its isoforms. The ERs differ in tissue distribution and relative ligand-binding affinities, which may help explain the selective action of oestrogens in different tissues [22]. This has important gender implications due to the differences in tissue physiology between women and men.

Tissue differences in ER distribution in women and men

While women have ER alpha and ER beta in breast, uterine and ovarian tissue, men have ER beta in the prostate and ER alpha in the testes. Both women and men have ER alpha in the adrenals and kidneys, and ER beta in the brain, thymus, lung, vascular system, bladder and bone [23,24]. ER alpha dominates specifically in the reproductive tissues, while ER beta plays an important role in the physiology of several tissues. Female and male sex hormones can be understood to act as functional antagonists: such that an excess of oestrogenic hormones may depress male development or male functions. There are also situations in which male and female hormones may act synergistically (and, for example, show effects upon bone density or the promotion of liver tumours). This complexity is the consequence of the multiple targets of these hormones within mammals, including target tissue other than the sex organs, as the tissue distributions of the ERs indicate.

Receptors and 'cross-talk'

The receptors often have ligands in common (although with different binding affinities), and there is also a great deal of 'cross-talk' and 'ligand promiscuity'. That is, the same chemical may be able to bind with different receptors, and, if they do, the binding strength may differ greatly between different receptors. This can occur for both hormones produced within the body and environmental chemicals. Pesticide examples include methoxychlor metabolites and DDT, which have different binding affinities in the ERs, and trans-nonachlor and chlordane, known to activate both known ERs, and the pregnane X receptor (PXR), but with different affinities [25,26, 27,28]. As these receptors are present in different ratios in different cell types and tissues, the response on cellular, tissue and systemic levels may be quantitatively very different, and may vary over time. The choices of appropriate test systems for risk assessment must be strategically designed to cover such multiple actions and interactions.

Disease scenarios: how much inhibition, how much activation?

The proliferative role of ER alpha in breast cancer is well established, but there is increasing evidence that ER beta is part of the disease picture, through antiproliferative activity, thereby having therapeutic implications. The distinct differences in activational mechanisms between the different ERs and their isoforms will have a direct effect upon possible disease scenarios – such as ER-positive and ER-negative breast cancers, testicular and prostate cancers, and perhaps also brain injury.

ER beta and men

Perinatal exposure of the male fetus to potent oestrogens is known to increase the incidence of cryptochordism and hypospadias at birth, and small testes, reduced sperm counts, epididymal cysts, prostatic abnormalities and testicular cancer in adult animals. ER beta appears to be preferentially expressed at significant levels in spermatocytes at various developmental stages in the testes, specifically the gonocytes, spermatogonia and spermatocytes. This suggests that EDCs with an affinity for ER beta may find their way into precursors of sperm and cause disturbances in their function, disrupting male reproductive functions [29,30].

Timing is all important. During fetal testicular development, if one phase of development is out of phase with the following step (such as Müllerian duct regression), developmental problems ensue in the adult that may not become apparent until later developmental stages, such as puberty, have been completed. This is reflected particularly in the reports of falling sperm counts [31], incidence of testicular cancer [32], and decreased fertilization rates in couples with paternal pesticide exposure [33]. Interestingly, high sperm density in organic farmers has been reported in a Danish study of reproductive effects of pesticides in male greenhouse workers [34].

ER beta and ovaries

Steroid hormone expression in ovarian surface epithelial cells (the tissue of origin for over 90 per cent of ovarian cancers) has been recently found to be disrupted in ovarian cancer cells taken from postmenopausal women [35]. Oestrogens, androgens and progestins regulate normal ovarian cells. Down-regulation or mutational inactivation of receptors (including the receptors ER, AR CAR and PXR) may be a key feature of ovarian epithelial transformation, which may lead to diseases such as endometriosis,[1] some cases of sterility and ultimately uterine/ovarian cancers.

Examples of other signalling pathways

As p,p'-DDT, has been found to be capable of activating cellular signalling events in ER-negative breast cancer cells [36], it is highly likely that some organochlorine pesticides may function through other signalling pathways.

Other key nuclear receptors: a multifaceted communication system

Members of the same nuclear receptor family share a common partner, retinoid X receptor (RXR). There may be competition for RXR for the dimerization stage of receptor activation of DNA. There may even be a cascade effect, where metabolites produced through the activities of one receptor are specific signalling molecules (and ligands) to modulate the next receptor, a link in a nuclear receptor intercommunication web.

The pathways of EDC pesticide activity are largely unknown and there are a huge number of confounding factors, some of which have only been recently identified. The hierarchy of ligand activation differs between the receptors as well as for receptors isolated from different species, and in many instances molecules that were previously regarded as metabolic intermediates are in fact 'intracrine' signalling molecules within tightly coupled metabolic pathways for altering gene expression.

Aromatase disruption in women

Aromatase is a key enzyme (cytochrome P450) in the production of oestrogen. It catalyses the conversion of androgens, androstenedione and testosterone via three hydroxylation steps to estrone and oestradiol [37,38]. Aromatase is expressed in many tissues, including the ovaries, the testes, the placenta, the brain, adipose tissue of the breasts, abdomen, thighs, buttocks and bone osteoblasts.

Adipose tissue is the major site of oestrogen biosynthesis in postmenopausal women, with the local production of oestrogen in breast adipose tissue implicated in the development of breast cancer. Inhibition of this pathway is one method that is exploited pharmacologically in ER-positive breast cancer treatments to inhibit oestrogen production. Another approach is to inhibit oestrogen action by antioestrogens, which interact with the oestrogen receptor in the tumours. Developmental inhibition of the aromatase pathway can give rise to excess androstane metabolites, excessively stimulating ER beta, and may possibly give rise to polycystic ovarian syndromes in women. It is possible that the perturbation of the steroid biosynthesis pathways in this way may be further confounded by defects in ER beta expression and management of excess androgen hormone products, with insufficient oestrogen products.

EDC pesticides that may affect this pathway include those that have been observed to bind with the ER, but also have anti-androgenic potential, particularly the organochlorines and their isomers, such as DDT, methoxychlor and the fungicide vinclozolin.

EDCs and the young

Endocrine effects are mediated through multiple sites of action, and EDCs are able to alter endogenous hormone pathways, as well as acting directly upon receptors. Foetal exposure to EDCs at critical times will have harmful health effects that do not become evident until puberty and adulthood, and again there will be gender differences and not just age-related susceptibilities. Vulnerability to the adverse effects of EDC exposure escalates during dynamic periods of growth and development. Children may metabolize compounds faster, but they detoxify more slowly and have greater body burdens due to higher dietary intakes in relation to body size, compared to adults.

What should be done?

There are still many aspects of EDC pesticide effects that we do not understand. Under the circumstances, researchers and government regulators should consider adoption of the following measures as a matter of urgency:

- Phase out by 2020 the production and use of chemicals that affect the endocrine system and set a clear timetable prioritizing action on the most harmful chemicals, taking into account the need to protect the most vulnerable groups.

- Address the problems associated with endocrine disruptors as a whole, not just oestrogen mimics.
- Integrate low-dose considerations into regulatory science.
- Use pre-screening computer techniques as a means of reducing animal usage for the extensive US EPA screening of 87,000 chemicals.

The full range of effects of EDC pesticides, from exposure routes to health outcomes, on women men, and subsequent generations can only be unravelled with an integrated multidisciplinary approach. This needs to include the use and development of gender-specific biological methodology at the molecular, cellular, tissue, physiological and epidemiological levels, within a wider framework of participatory socio-economic and cultural analyses. It means the design and coordinated use of data-collection methods specifically for women, and girls, men and boys. The health situations of postmenopausal women, elderly women, and the roles of race, ethnicity, culture and changing societal conditions also need to be integrated into study designs.

To understand fully and protect ourselves from EDC pesticides we need to ask the right questions and develop and utilize accurate tools. A prioritized agenda needs to be clearly set out at international and local levels to have the maximum impact on reducing our exposure to EDCs, protecting our health and that of future generations.[2]

Notes

1. Abnormally located uterine tissue may block or stick to the womb, ovaries or fallopian tubes, causing infertility. The endometrium is very responsive to hormone mimics. Epidemiological and clinical studies have indicated a link between POPs exposure, endometriosis, infertility and uterine cancers, but the significance and precise mechanism is unknown.

2. For further details and full references see M.N Jacobs, 'Unsafe sex: how endocrine disruptors work', PAN UK briefing paper No. 4, January 2001.

References

1 Davidson, N.E., Yager, J.D. In *Journal of the National Cancer Institute*, 89, 1997: 1743–4.
2 Davis, D.L., Telang, N.T., Osborne, M.P., Bradlow, H.L. In *Environmental Health Perspectives*, 105 (Suppl. 3), 1997: 571–6.
3 Bradlow, H.L., Davis, D.L., *et al*. In *Environmental Health Perspectives*, 103, 1995: 147–50.

4 Bradlow, H.L. Davis, D., Sepkovic, D.W. *et al.* In *Science of the Total Environment*, 208, 1997: 9–14.

5 Sharpe, R.M., Skakkebaek, N.E. *Lancet*, 341, 1993: 1392–5.

6 Auger, J., Kunstmann, J. M., *et al.* In *New England Journal of Medicine*, 332, 1995: 281–5.

7 Adami, H.-O., Bergström, R., *et al.* In *International Journal of Cancer*, 59, 1995: 33–8.

8 Colburn, T., Vom Saal, F.S., Soto, A.M. In *Environmental Health Perspectives*, 101, 1993: 378–84.

9 Guillette, L.J., Arnold, S.F., McLachlan, J.A. In *Animal Reproduction Science*, 42, 1996: 13–24.

10 Colburn, T., Dumanoski, D., Myers, J.P. *Our Stolen Future: Are We Threatening Our Fertility, Intelligence, and Survival? A Scientific Detective Story*, New York: Dutton, 1999.

11 Crain, D.A., Rooney, A.A., *et al.* In Guillette Jr, L., Crain, D.A. (eds) *Environmental Endocrine Disruptors, an Evolutionary Perspective.* New York: Taylor & Francis, 2000, pp. 1–21.

12 Stevens, J.T., Breckenridge, C.B., *et al.* In *Journal of Toxicology and Environmental Health*, 43, 1994: 139–53.

13 US EPA Endocrine disrupter screening program www.epa.gov/scipoly/oscpendo/index.htm

14 Parker, M.G. In *Current Opinion in Cell Biology*, 5, 1993: 499–504.

15 Porta, M., Malats, N., *et al.* In *Lancet*, 354, 1999: 2125–9.

16 Kelce, R.W., Stone, R.C. *et al.* In *Nature*, 373, 1995: 581–5.

17 Weigel, N. In *Biochemistry Journal*, 319, 1996: 657–67.

18 Alberts, B., Bray, D. *et al. Essential Cell Biology*, New York and London: Garland Publishing, 1997.

19 Jacobs, M.N, Lewis, D., 'Steroid hormone receptors and dietary ligands – a selected review'. In *Proceedings of the Nutrition Society*, 61, 2002: 1–18.

20 Brzozowski, A.M., Pike, A.C., *et al.* In *Nature*, 389, 1997: 753–8.

21 Kuiper, G.C.J.M., Lemmen, J.G., *et al.* In *Endocrinology*, 139, 1998: 4252–63.

22 Paech, K., Webb, P., *et al.* In *Science*, 227, 1997: 1508–10.

23 Paech *et al.*, *op. cit.*, 1997.

24 Kuiper, G.C.J.M., Carlsson, B., *et al.* In *Endocrinology*, 138, 1997: 863–70.

25 Jones, S.A., Moore, L.B., *et al.* In *Molecular Endocrinology*, 14, 2000: 27–39.

26 Kuiper *et al.*, *op. cit.*, 1998.

27 Barkhem, T., Carlsson, B., *et al.* In *Molecular Pharmacology*, 54, 1998: 105–12.

28 Waxman, D.J. In *Archives of Biochemistry and Biophysics* 369, 1999: 11–23.

29 Gustafsson, J-Å. In *Journal of Endocrinology*, 163, 1999: 379–83.

30 Hess, R.A., Bunick, D., *et al.* In *Nature*, 390, 1997: 509–12.

31 Auger *et al.*, *op. cit.*, 1995.
32 Adami *et al.*, *op. cit.*, 1994.
33 Tielemans, E., van Kooij, R., *et al.* In *Lancet*, 354, 1999: 484–5.
34 Abell, A., Ernst, E., Jens, P. In *Lancet*, 343, 1994: 1498.
35 Lau, K.-M., Mok, S.C., Ho, S.-M. In *Proceedings of the National Academy of Science USA*, 96, 1999: 5722–7.
36 Shen, K., Novak, R.F., In *Advances in Experimental Medicine and Biology*, 407, 1997: 295–302.
37 Martucci, C.P., Fishman, J. In *Pharmacology and Therapeutics*, 57, 1993: 237–57.
38 Brodie, A., Lu, Q., Long, B. In *Journal of Steroid Biochemistry and Molecular Biology*, 69, 1999: 205–210.

21

Pesticides and P450 induction: gender implications

David F.V. Lewis

Many chemicals are able to influence the pathways in the body (endogenous pathways) governing the regulation of steroid hormones, leading to them being called 'hormone-disrupting chemicals' or 'endocrine disrupters'. A large family of enzymes, the cytochrome P450 (CYP), are essential in the process of synthesizing steroids in the body, and are present in all forms of life apart from the most primitive bacteria [1]. In addition to their roles in fatty acid metabolism and steroid biosynthesis, P450s act as catalysts for oxygen in the metabolism of a large number of foreign chemicals, including pesticides, pharmaceuticals, agrochemical solvents, food additives, packaging migrants and many other industrial chemicals.

These enzymes are mainly found in the livers of mammals where they activate molecular oxygen to detoxify tissue dioxygen ultimately to form water. Certain P450 enzymes present in the liver also are associated with the oxidative metabolism of steroids, such as oestradiol and testosterone, as part of the normal body mechanisms necessary for the maintenance of these hormone levels [2]. More recently, the roles of various P450s outside the liver have been investigated and, in particular, variation in the combination of enzymes in women's bodies, principally in breast tissue [3], placenta [4] and in the feto-placental unit [5].

Induction of P450 enzymes

The range of P450 enzymes in mammals is around fifty individual enzymes, most of which possess known physiological roles [6]. Their expression is regulated by a number of different hormonal factors within the body [7]. However, the liver P450s include several enzymes that can break down foreign organic compounds (xenobiotic-metabolizing) which have their levels modulated by certain inducing agents (see Table 21.1). Some regulation of this process is mediated by nuclear receptor proteins [8,9] such as the Ah receptor [10,11,12, 13] the oestrogen receptor [14], the glucocorticoid receptor [15], the pregnane X receptor [16,17,18,19], the constitutive androstane receptor [20,21,22], the liver X receptor [23,24,25,26,27] the farnesoid X receptor [28], and the peroxisome proliferator-activated receptor [29,30,31].

Various pesticides and industrial chemicals can act as inducers of several drug-metabolizing P450s. The pesticides include DDT, aldrin, endrin, dieldrin, heptachlor, lindane, arochlor, TCDD, PCBs and other organochlorine compounds (OCs) [32,33]. For example, TCDD and planar PCBs are able to induce CYP1, whereas DDT, aldrin, heptachlor, dieldrin and non-planar PCBs primarily induce CYP2B [34]. Many organophosphate (OP) pesticides, however, tend to be metabolized by various P450s (CYP2A, CYP2B and CYP3A), and their interaction with the enzyme can activate the OP to form toxic metabolites [35]. Although both classes of pesticides have been inves-

Table 21.1 P450 families and known chemical inducers

CYP	Substrates	Inducers	Receptors[3]
1A	Caffeine	TCDD	AhR, ER
2A	Coumarin	PB, organophosphate pesticides	FXR/LXR?
2B	Phenobarbital (PB)	organophosphate pesticides, DDT, aldrin, heptachlor, dieldrin (and non-planar PCBs)	CAR
2C	Tolbutamide	PB	RAR/RXR
2D	Debrisoquine	PB	None[1,2]
2E	p-nitrophenol	None[1]	None[2]
3A	Erythromycin	Ethanol, organophosphate pesticides, Dexamethsone	GR, PXR
4A	Lauric acid	Clofibrate	PPAR

Notes

[1] Constitutively expressed – non-inducible form.
[2] Induction is not receptor mediated.
[3] See p. 180 above for abbreviations.

Source: Reference 36.

tigated in experimental animals, and metabolism in humans has been studied using expressed enzymes in some instances, the majority of data in this area have focused primarily on OCs rather than OPs. This chapter describes the gender implications or possible differential gender effects arising from exposure to OCs, as this is where sex differences are likely to manifest themselves more clearly.

P450 induction, metabolism and fetal development

Table 21.1 summarizes the more important P450s involved in xenobiotic metabolism, including those whose mechanisms of induction involve ligand binding to nuclear receptors. TCDD is the most potent high-affinity ligand known for CYP1 induction, as minute (nanomolar) quantities can give rise to hundredfold increases in CYP1 levels [37]. DDT is able to induce CYP2B by up to forty times its normal constitutive levels (see Table 21.2). Such changes in P450

Table 21.2 P450s associated with testosterone metabolism in the rat

CYP	Fold induction by phenobarbital	Testosterone metabolism	Gender selectivity	Receptor mediation[1]
1A2	0	6β-hydroxylation	Female dominant	AhR
2A1	2	7α-hydroxylation	Female dominant	FXR/LXR[2]
2B1	40	17α,16α-hydroxylation	Male dominant	CAR
2C6	2	2α, 16α and 17α-hydroxylation	None	RAR/RXR
2D1	0	6β-hydroxylation	Male dominant	None
2E1	0	none	Female dominant	None
3A1	12	6β-hydroxylation[3]	Male specific	PXR/GR
4A1	0	none	none	PPAR

Notes

[1] Full names of receptors on p. 180 above.
[2] FXR (bile acid receptor) suppresses CYP7 levels whereas LXR (oxysterol receptor) activates CYP7 which is involved in the 7α-hydroxylation of cholesterol 155 [38].
[3] Major pathway via this isoform.
Source: references 39–51.

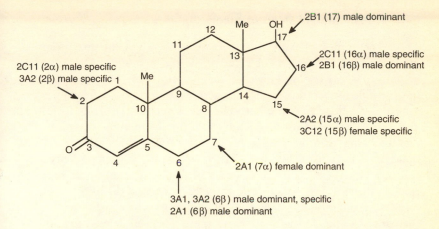

Figure 21.1 Testosterone metabolism via rat liver P450s (showing numbering system of the steroid nucleus)

expression will inevitably affect the homeostatic mechanisms governing steroid hormone (such as testosterone) concentrations in both sexes [52,53]. The clear gender difference in the levels of rat liver P450s and their expression due to exposure to OCs such as DDT may adversely affect the normal course of androgenic imprinting in the fetus and disrupt fetal development.

The development and maintenance of sexual characteristics is regulated by hormonal control. The biosynthesis and metabolism of steroid hormones are both carried out by P450 enzymes but in different tissues [54]. Consequently, the P450 system of Phase 1 enzymes has a role in the homeostasis of sex hormone levels which will exhibit gender differences with respect to, for example, the major sex steroids such as oestradiol and testosterone (see Figure 21.1). For example, with testosterone metabolism in men, five enzymes are male specific and three are dominant. Women only have one specific P450 enzyme and one dominant enzyme. Changes in this homeostatic system via external agents such as OC pesticides [55] can lead to considerable disruption in the natural balance operating in the endocrine system, with concomitant health effects and hormone disruption (particularly where receptor mediation is indicated). Indeed, a development role for the Ah receptor/CYP1 loop has been postulated [56] but also CYP1 regulation may be mediated by the oestrogen receptor [57].

Risk assessment of P450 inducers

The cytochromes P450 are the major drug metabolizing enzymes in most biological systems. Their activity is the first step in pathways leading to detoxication. However, detoxication may be impeded, or not possible for certain chemical structures, especially where chlorine (and other halogens) is present. Thus OCs such as DDT, PCBs [58] and TCDD are refractory to metabolism due to the presence of several blocking chlorine ring substituents. These chemicals tend to build up in fatty tissue because of their relatively high lipophilicity as measured by their log P values (where P is the octanol/water partition coefficient). It is possible, nevertheless, to assess the likely degree of bioaccumulation for many foreign compounds by consideration of their log P value, and in some cases there is a well-defined relationship between log P and toxicity [59].

Another approach, which is complementary to this, uses some form of molecular modelling to construct three-dimensional structures of the receptors or enzymes involved in production of the biological activity. This technique has been successfully applied to both PPAR and hER ligands [60,61] using homology models of the nuclear receptors involved.

Box 21.1 Method for estimating the endocrine effect of a pesticide

One method of estimating the likely biological effect from exposure to a given chemical is to perform a Quantitative Structure–Activity Relationship (QSAR) study. This involves consideration of (usually) a series of compounds for which the biological activity (such as induction, metabolism or receptor binding) is known, and then performing a statistical analysis between various structural/physico-chemical descriptors for the given compounds and the activity data. If successful, this leads to a specific mathematical equation by which the potential activity of a new chemical can be estimated from its structural characteristics [62,63,64,65,66].

Conclusions

It would appear that receptor-mediated processes control the expression of many P450s associated with the development [67] and maintenance of sexual characteristics in the fetus, infant and adult [68]. Pesticides and other agents which interfere with those homeostatic processes are likely to give rise to endocrine hormone disruption, together with other undesirable effects such as uncontrolled tissue growth, cell proliferation and, possibly, carcinogenesis.

Note

The financial support of GlaxoWellcome Research and Development Ltd, Merck, Sharp and Dohme Ltd, the European Union (EUROCYP project) and the University of Surrey is gratefully acknowledged.

References

1   Lewis, D.F.V. *Cytochromes P450: Structure, Function and Mechanism*, London: Taylor & Francis, 1996.
2   Zimniak, P., Waxman, D.J. In Schenkman, J.B., Griem, H. (eds) *Cytochrome P450*, Berlin: Springer Verlag, 1993, pp. 127–44.
3   Hellmold, H., Rylander, T. *et al.* In *Journal of Clinical Endocrinology and Metabolism*, 83, 1998: 886–95.
4   Hakkola, J., Pasanen, M. *et al.* In *Biochemical Pharmacology*, 51, 1996: 403–11.
5   Hakkola, J., Pelkonen, O. *et al.* In *Critical Reviews in Toxicology*, 28, 1998: 35–72.
6   Estabrook, R.W. 'Impact of the human genome project on drug metabolism and chemical toxicity,' British Toxicology Society Meeting, Guildford, 19–22 April 1998.
7   Gibson, G.G., Skett, P. *Introduction to Drug Metabolism*, London: Chapman & Hall, 1994.
8   Lewis, *op. cit.*, 1996.
9   Honkakoski, P., Negishi, M. In *Biochemical Journal*, 347, 2000: 321–37.
10 Burbach, K.M., Poland, A., Bradfield, C.A. In *Proceedings of the National Academy of Sciences USA*, 89, 1992: 8185–9.
11 Hahn, M.E. In *Comparative Biochemistry and Physiology*, 121C, 1998: 23–53.
12 Okey, A.B., Vella, L.M. In *European Journal of Biochemistry*, 127, 1982: 39–47.
13 Hankinson, O. *Annual Review of Pharmacology and Toxicology*, 35, 1995: 307–340.
14 Kuiper, G.G.J.M., Lemmen, J.G., *et al.* In *Nature,* 389, 1997: 753–8.
15 Krust, A., Green, S. *et al.* In *EMBO Journal*, 5, 1986: 891–7.

16 Jones, S.A., Moore, L.B. *et al.* In *Molecular Endocrinology*, 14, 2000: 27–39.

17 Kliewer, S.A., Willson, T.M. In *Current Opinion in Genetics and Development*, 8, 1998: 576–81.

18 Bertilsson, G., Heidrich, J., *et al.* In *Proceedings of the National Academy of Science USA*, 95, 1998: 12208–13.

19 Blumberg, B., Sabbagh, W., *et al.* In *Genes and Development*, 12, 1998: 3195–205.

20 Choi, H.-S., Chung, M., *et al.* In *Journal of Biological Chemistry*, 272, 1997: 23565–71.

21 Forman, B.M., Tzameli, I., *et al.* In *Nature*, 395, 1998: 612–15.

22 Honkakoski, P., Zelko, I., *et al.* In *Cellular Biology*, 18, 1998: 5652–8.

23 Schmidt, A., Vogel, R., *et al.* In *Molecular and Cellular Endocrinology*, 155, 1999: 57–60.

24 Forman, B.M., Ruan, B., *et al.* In *Proceedings of the National Academy of Science USA*, 94, 1997: 10588–93.

25 Lehmann, J.M. Kliewer, S.A. *et al.* In *Journal of Biological Chemistry*, 272, 1997: 3137–40.

26 Janowski, B.A., Will, P.J., *et al.* In *Nature*, 383, 1996: 728–31.

27 Peet, D.J., Turley, S.D., *et al.* In *Cell*, 93, 1998: 693–704.

28 Wang, H., Chen, J., *et al.* In *Molecular Cell*, 3, 1999: 543–53.

29 Kliewer, Willson, *op. cit.*, 1998.

30 Willson, T.M., Brown, P.J. *et al.* In *Journal of Medicinal Chemistry*, 43, 2000: 527–50.

31 Lewis, D.F.V., Lake, B.G. In *Toxicology in Vitro*, 12, 1998: 619–32.

32 Waxman, D.J., Azaroff, L. In *Biochemical Journal*, 281, 1992: 577–92.

33 Okey, A.B. In *Pharmacology and Therapeutics*, 45, 1990: 241–98.

34 Waxman, Azaroff, *op. cit.*, 1992.

35 Gonzalez, F.J., Gelboin, H.V. In *Drug Metabolism Reviews*, 26, 1994: 165–83.

36 Rendic, S., DiCarlo, F.J. In *Drug Metabolism Reviews*, 29, 1997: 413–580.

37 Lewis, *op. cit.*, 1996.

38 Russell, D.W. In *Cell*, 97, 1999: 539–42.

39 Lewis, *op. cit.*, 1996.

40 Russell, *op. cit.*

41 Weigel, N. In *Biochemical Journal*, 319, 1996: 657–67.

42 Kliewer, S.A., Moore, J.T., *et al.*, In *Cell*, 92, 1998: 73–82.

43 Laudet, V., Auwex, J., Gustafsson, J.-A., Wahli, W. In *Cell*, 97, 1999: 161–3.

44 McKenna, N.J. Xu, J. et al., In *Journal of Steroid Biochemistry and Molecular Biology*, 69, 1999: 3–12.

45 Kliewer, S.A., Lehmann, J.M., Willson, T.M. In *Science*, 284, 1999: 757–60.

46 Makishima, M., Okamoto, A.Y., *et al.*, In *Science*, 284, 1999: 1362–85.

47 Parks, D.J., Blanchard, S.G., *et al.* In *Science*, 284, 1999: 1365–9.

48 Baes, M., Gulick, T., *et al.* In *Molecular and Cellular Biology*, 14, 1994: 1544–52.
49 Neubert, D. In *Regulatory Toxicology and Pharmacology*, 26, 1997: 9–29.
50 Edwards, P.A., Ericsson, J. In *Annual Review of Biochemistry*, 68, 1999: 157–85.
51 Honkakoski, Negishi, *op. cit.*, 2000.
52 Okey, *op. cit.*, 1990.
53 Zimniak, Waxman, *op. cit.*, 1993.
54 Lewis, *op. cit.*, 1996.
55 Wiseman, A., Goldfarb, P., *et al.* In *Journal of Chemical Technology and Biotechnology*, 71, 1998: 3–5.
56 Stegeman, J.J., Seppa, P.L., *et al.* In *Marine Environmental Research*, 42, 1996: 306–3.
57 Honkakoski, Negishi, *op. cit.*, 2000.
58 Waller, S.C., He, Y.A., *et al.* In *Chemical Research in Toxicology*, 12, 1999: 690–99.
59 Hermens, J.L.M., Opperhuizen, A. *QSAR in Environmental Toxicology – IV*, Amsterdam: Elsevier, 1991.
60 Lewis, Lake, *op. cit.*, 1998.
61 Jacobs, M.N. 'Molecular modelling of oestrogenic compounds in the human oestrogen receptor and investigation of the activity of oestrogenic compounds in breast cancer cell lines', M.Sc. Dissertation, University of Surrey, 1998.
62 Lewis, *op. cit.*, 1996
63 Lewis, D.F.V. In *Drug Metabolism Reviews*, 29: 589–650, 1997.
64 Lewis, D.F.V. In *Drug Metabolism Reviews*, 31: 755–814, 1999.
65 Jacobs, M.N., Lewis, D.F.V. In *Organohalogen Compounds*, 41: 517–20, 1999.
66 Jacobs, Lewis, *op. cit.*, 1999.
67 Stegeman, et al., *op. cit.*, 1996.
68 Zimniak, Waxman, *op. cit.*, 1993.

Part III

A precautionary approach to policy and regulation

22

Introduction to Part III

Barbara Dinham

The precautionary principle in relation to pesticides says that action should be taken to avoid potential harm to humans, animals and the environment, particularly if the impact is uncertain, and the paths of exposure are unknown. Policies that regulate pesticides draw heavily on evidence from risk assessments, which in turn rely predominantly on laboratory tests and standardized exposure limits. Risk assessments have been criticized for being gender-blind – or 'one-eyed science' – and for failing to take account of social and economic concerns. The papers in this section examine problems, policies, and policy responses to pesticides and pesticide risks.

Pesticides are, in fact, highly regulated, and rightly so. Globally, around a thousand pesticide active ingredients are used, in combinations of tens of thousands of products. However, pesticide registration systems are based on policy decisions that frequently favour the use of pesticides and encourage a pesticide culture. Leslie London and Andrea Rother point out that confidence in a well-developed regulatory system can be misplaced, as it is not always capable of delivering the monitoring required to protect pesticide users and others exposed through proximity or the environment.

Risk assessment strategies will treat data as scientific, objective and value-free even when the risks are unclear and uncertain. Scientific discovery is constantly pushing new frontiers, but little is known about long-term low-level exposures. Toxicology failed for twenty years to detect the impacts of persistent organochlorine pesticides when they were released in the late 1940s and 1950s – and the worst of these pesticides were not finally globally banned from production and use until 2000. Not until the 1990s was the potential of certain pesticides to disrupt hormone systems recognized. Risk assessment is represented as an objective science. However, Meriel Watts shows that decisions incorporate a high degree of subjectivity. Different perceptions of risk by scientists and regulators are demonstrated by the wide variety of acceptable residue and exposure levels used under different regulatory systems.

The science of risk assessment has paid limited attention to gender and to social and political issues, and has largely ignored the different physiology of women, men and children. The threshold limit values for chemical exposure, for example, are often based on young, fit men. Standard risk assessment strategies exclude potential differences arising from women's physiology, pregnancy, the smaller body weight of children, effects of poor diet on exposure and other complex factors related to standard of living, high workload, physical capacity, poor general health (in particular the prevalence of AIDS in developing countries), gender division of labour, and local work practices.

Studies show that women are more likely to be risk-refusers, and prefer to avoid risk, whereas men tend to be more accepting. Whatever the reasons, whether it is a higher value placed on good health or greater concern than men about their children's exposure, the concern with avoiding risks is not recognized as legitimate by policymakers. Whereas policymakers, regulators and scientific experts indicate that they 'assess' risks, they believe that critics and the public 'perceive' risks, implying an irrational and emotional response. A risk assessor's perception of risk aversion may lead them to ignore warning signs of chemical impacts. The extract from Mary O'Brien's book demonstrates the false assumptions underlying risk assessment strategies.

The symptoms of pesticide exposure can be downplayed and ignored, even by sections of the medical profession. Those exposed to pesticides sometimes become highly sensitized to chemicals: multiple chemical sensitivity (MCS) is a syndrome which affects some of those exposed to continuous low levels of chemicals. It appears that more women than men suffer from MCS, but doctors and regulators have failed to treat the physical response seriously, and often dismiss it as an emotional reaction. The limited research in this field has found some physiological explanation, as oestrogen may enhance the effect of chemicals on the nervous system, and increase sensitivity to stress and drugs. The causes and symptoms of chemical sensitivity and chronic long-term effects of low doses of exposure to chemicals need to be better understood, and the diagnostic procedures need improvement. In the meantime this condition, like other 'perceived risks', needs to be treated seriously by the medical profession and regulators.

Exposure to mixtures of different pesticides has only recently surfaced as an important concern. Yet women and men are exposed to multiple chemicals through multiple pathways: use, proximity, residues in food and water and airborne exposure, for example. The position may be further complicated, as David Watt's chapter shows, by pesticide exposures through use and residues in homes, housing and even leisure activities.

Stereotyped views of who uses pesticides, and how individuals and groups are exposed, can prevent policymakers from fulfilling their obligation to protect the public from potential hazards. Similarly, many doctors regard non-specific illnesses as malingering, general malaise, or psychological symptoms, and will rarely report these cases to the authorities. Leslie London and Hanna-Andrea Rother point out how health care providers with inadequate awareness of pesticide problems fall back on gender stereotypes and sexist values. A group of women reporting pesticide poisoning were diagnosed as suffering from 'mass hysteria', when they had been exposed to the ozone-depleting chemical and highly toxic pesticide methyl bromide.

Even when evidence of serious problems with a specific pesticide is identified, the policy response may be limited, and can demonstrate a misplaced use of 'gender' to allow general continued exposure. Andrew and Jenny Watterson look at the response of UK regulators to dinoseb after it was demonstrated to have adverse effects on reproduction. Trade-union calls for a ban were ignored, in favour of representation from the employer farmers' union to allow continued use by male farm workers. The decision was used to exclude women from employment, yet the adverse reproductive effects associated with dinoseb included damage not only to the fetus but also to sperm and the thyroid. In another instance, research indicated a possible link between lindane and breast cancer in 1938, but it took another sixty years before the pesticide was banned in the UK – although, ironically, regulators issued warnings for male forestry workers using lindane.

In South Africa women provide 70 per cent of labour in farming activities, and 90 per cent of hired labour, and pesticide usage is among the highest in Africa. Like women in all farming systems, South African farm workers are involved in a wide range of farm jobs and exposed through both use and related activities. Yet, like policies in almost all countries, no recognition is given to specific pesticide users, their conditions of use, and the potential differential impacts of pesticides on women, men and children.

Because poisoning statistics are inaccurate and overreflect the problem of pesticide-related suicides, public policy on pesticides may seriously underestimate the wide range of other physical and social effects and fail to develop precautionary policies. Research on the impacts of pesticides is fundamental to policy, but is often gender blind. Infertility concerns have focused on research on sperm counts, while there is a lack of corresponding research on the effects on the unborn fetus and on women's reproductive cycle. While endocrine disrupting pesticides may increase the potential for breast cancer in women, they can also increase the risk of testicular cancer in men. Research may be forced by limited funds to focus on either males or females, but needs to demonstrate that it is cognizant of linked implications.

Pesticide research is predominantly undertaken by the industry that promotes the products. Independent scientists and researchers are constrained by the boundaries of existing knowledge, as well as by funds, and too often conclude that 'more research is necessary'. The result is that scientific data remain limited, fragmented, contradictory or inconclusive. Regulators have trouble in taking action on this basis, and prefer to wait for scientific certainty, when in reality concerns and limited evidence should encourage a precautionary approach. In relation to pesticides, one precautionary tool – now fully implemented in Sweden – has been the principle of 'comparative risk assessment', which will register the pesticide with the least risk. Regulators need to find ways to extend the concept beyond substituting one chemical with a less toxic one, and in taking account of all concerns, to promote more sustainable, ecological, health-conscious pest management strategies.

The authors in this section provide important insights into the gap between pesticide policy tools and decision-making procedures, and law and regulation – and into the even wider gap between regulation in industrialized countries and in developing countries. In principle, a pesticide is registered as a public service. In practice registration is a limited response, which has not adequately assessed all risks or all routes of exposure, and fails to discriminate between risks to women, risks to men, and risks to children. Policy decisions should be based on medical, scientific, economic and agricultural evidence, but should also reflect the attitudes of both women and men to the negative aspects of pesticide use. The precautionary principle needs to be developed into a decision-making tool, fully underpinned by gender-sensitive considerations. Assistance must be extended to developing countries, where the conditions of pesticide use are dramatically more hazardous, to implement precautionary regulatory strategies.

23

Failing laws: assumptions and realities for women in South African agriculture

Leslie London and Hanna-Andrea Rother

> We must spray pesticides on our fields. It's the law.
>> Elderly woman from KwaZulu Natal, South Africa, 1997[1]

To redress inequities created by apartheid, national policy in South Africa encourages agriculture as a lead developmental activity and contributor to economic and social reconstruction in rural areas [1]. However, South Africa's agricultural workforce remains an extremely oppressed sector. Women in South Africa provide a large portion of the agricultural labour force and constitute more than half of the seasonally employed [2]. Women in Africa, in general, conduct at least three-quarters of agricultural work [3, 4]. It is estimated that in rural South Africa, women provide 70 per cent of total labour used in farming activities and 90 per cent of hired labour [5].

Work and living conditions in South African agriculture are poor, with wage levels and labour rights lagging far behind other industrial sectors [6,7,8]. Women are particularly disadvantaged in the kind of agricultural work they do, their lack of security, high rates of casualization and in the provision of the poorest protection under existing labour standards. As a result, they form the most marginal element of an already marginalized labour sector. Women in the food industry responsible for secondary processing of agricultural products are also subject to harsh working conditions and a wide variety of occupational health hazards [9,10].

At the same time, usage of pesticides in agriculture is widespread and particularly intense in export-driven production sectors. For example, in 1996 over 1.4 million kg of active ingredient of pesticides were used in agriculture in South Africa [11], which represents the largest agrochemical market in sub-Saharan Africa [12]. In comparison with many other developing countries, South Africa has far more chemicals registered for use, as a result of which the potential for hazardous interactions between chemicals is substantial. For example, in the deciduous fruit industry alone, over one hundred different chemical agents were recorded for use in 1989 [13].

Although South Africa has a formal regulatory authority for the registration and monitoring of pesticides, the control of pesticide storage, usage and disposal is poor, as is typical of many developing countries generally. Safety measures on commercial farms are limited, with little investment in technologies for monitoring or exposure reduction. There is also increasing pressure for usage of pesticides as a result of market incentives related to globalization, aggressive sales by pesticide companies, and economic policies to promote small-scale agriculture that seek to improve competitiveness of new entrants to the agricultural markets [14]. Because of the latter forces, new entrants to the agricultural sector are under increasing pressure to make use of pesticide inputs to achieve competitiveness, and prove the soundness of current economic policies. South Africa also remains locked in a 'pesticide culture' by regarding pesticide's efficacy in the control of pests as the norm. This pesticide culture underplays pesticides' potential hazards by explicitly or implicitly rationalizing the ongoing support for pesticide use in terms of the need for food security and economic development [15].

As a result of all these factors, pesticide usage poses a significant threat to women in both small-scale and commercial agriculture, as well as in secondary manufacturing. Yet, the infrastructure for the control of pesticide hazards in South African (e.g. laws, surveillance, monitoring, law enforcement, and training) is poorly geared towards protecting the health of politically and economically marginalized communities, particularly women. Registration procedures of pesticides, for example, do not take into account the practical difficulties experienced by women small-scale farmers and farm workers in South Africa. This can, and does, give rise to a situation where a pesticide that may be seen as relatively safe for use (and registered as such) is in practice a serious threat to women's health under field use in rural areas [16]. Analysis of the key issues underlying this situation is illustrated below through a number of case studies.

Women's exposure to pesticides is significantly underestimated

The traditional view held among researchers, epidemiologists, safety personnel and policymakers is that high-exposure jobs are typically men's work, and that because women in some countries do not generally spray pesticides, they are thus not exposed. However, this is not necessarily the experience in the developing world, where women are often expected to undertake hazardous activities, although these are not recognized as skilled tasks, or acknowledged as having significant exposure. For example, empirical evidence from a pilot study in the rural northern KwaZulu Natal (KZN) province found that women were widely responsible for the mixing of the chemical solutions for backpack and tractor sprayers used by men [17]. Although women did not physically apply the pesticides in this area, women were usually present during application activities either weeding or harvesting in an adjoining section of the sprayed field or working in a field just sprayed. Men were often absent from the production setting, or held their wives responsible for functions that they saw as routine or less critical. In many ways, the gendered nature of risk perceptions on the part of both men and women helps to reinforce myths surrounding women's work in agriculture being low risk. In reality, women are at greater risk of accumulated exposure because of long working hours from an earlier age and multiple exposures (at

---

Box 23.1 Women's perceptions of health risks

In rural KwaZulu Natal, South Africa, some women believe that pesticide containers containing residues can be 'cleaned' for reuse. They suggested two methods: soaking the container for a week in a cattle dung solution, or rinsing it with hot water. The women were aware that containers hold a 'poison'; however, the risk is quantified by the perception that it could be removed [19]. There is a lack of scientific evidence that pesticide residues are removable to make containers safe for storing goods intended for human consumption. Legislation in South Africa stipulates that pesticide containers must be disposed of and that it is an offence to reuse them. The perception that the risks from pesticide residues in containers can be removed may increase accumulated exposure.

work and in domestic settings), with potential exposure to pesticides through:

- working conditions (e.g. spray drift, coming into contact with sprayed plants, early re-entry into a field);
- eating contaminated plants and produce;
- pesticide residues in water, air and soil;
- washing of contaminated clothing;
- drinking contaminated water;
- pesticides used in malaria control programmes;
- intense use of a multitude of pesticides, both in agriculture and domestically [18].

Women's perception of the health risks from exposure to pesticides varies. These perceptions often increase their exposure to pesticides (see Box 23.1). Evidence from commercial agriculture in South Africa also points to many practices in which women are given low-skills jobs that carry high risks of exposure, precisely because of their status as casual or seasonal workers on farms (see Box 23.2).

Box 23.2 **High risk exposure at work**

In the fruit farming industry, thinning of fruit on the trees is an important activity to ensure quality. Women workers, frequently relatives of the permanent farm workers, are almost exclusively employed – ostensibly because of the need for meticulous work, but presumably underpinned by the need for a ready pool of temporary labour. The timing of thinning frequently coincides with the period of peak application of fungicides to the fruit trees, providing a significant risk of exposure. Hand protection tends to interfere with dexterity; thus dermal absorption is poorly controlled.

Another common practice in the fruit industry is application of herbicides from a hose with a series of punctures carried horizontally behind a moving tractor. The hose is hand held by a number of women, and the herbicide drips constantly from the puncture holes. Because this job requires little skill, and is regarded as suited for temporary labour, women frequently undertake this work, often with little or no protective clothing. Herbicides commonly used in the fruit industry include paraquat, or the phenoxyacetic-acid herbicides thought to be endocrine disruptors.

Women's morbidity

Despite notorious problems in accuracy, reporting of acute poisoning by pesticides is generally used as the hallmark for assessing pesticide-related morbidity and disease burden [20]. While there is much evidence that poisoning due to pesticides is widely under-reported, these data are often the only information available on which to plan public health interventions. If under-reporting is uniform, the use of these data to identify trends or priorities could be justified. However, if the patterns of under-reporting are confounded, public policy on pesticides may be significantly misinformed.

For example, much of the surveillance data available in South Africa point to pesticide poisoning being a problem amongst men, where routine notifications of pesticide poisoning suggest that two-thirds of poisonings involve men and that less than 11 per cent are occupationally related [21]. Where pesticide poisoning is a problem for women, the circumstances are generally thought to be deliberate ingestion, with occupational exposure being a rare cause.

However, data from an intervention study in a farming district 120 km from Cape Town, which aimed to improve notification for pesticide poisoning through various modalities [22] illustrated a tenfold increase in acute morbidity when reporting systems were improved. More importantly, the study found that 61 per cent of cases were found to involve women, and the majority were occupationally

---

Box 23.3   Poisoning in the field

In November 1994, 20 farm workers, including 19 women, were poisoned while weeding an onion field in a rural district in the Western Cape Province. The field lay alongside an orchard that was being sprayed with a mixture of an organophosphate and two fungicides, which drifted over the workers. Despite evacuating as soon as they could smell the pesticide, all 20 subjects developed nausea, vomiting, headache and disturbed vision, and were admitted to the local hospital. Only because of a local campaign to notify all poisonings to the Department of Health was this case brought to public attention. South African legislation does not mandate re-entry intervals that would have protected these women.

Source: Reference 23.

related. This was the reverse of the typical national profile based on routine notification and illustrates the consequences of relying on flawed gender-biased surveillance data, in terms of which women would not have been seen as an important occupational risk group.

Medical diagnostic skills are poor – and gendered!

One of the difficulties in establishing the true burden of disease due to pesticides is the poor awareness amongst health care providers of the adverse impacts of pesticides. This is particularly accentuated by gender stereotypes and sexist values.

A case study from a rural factory in the Western Cape Province in South Africa in 1985 illustrates the inadequacy of rural health care providers to detect pesticide-related morbidity. The plant was part of a highly profitable company responsible for drying deciduous fruit for retail sale in South Africa and overseas. Located in a small rural town, amidst extensive local fruit farming production, it employed around 200 workers, the majority being women employed for three months during peak season to assist with sorting, packing and other activities related to the dried fruit production.

Part of the production process involved application of an insecticide to the fruit early in the drying production process. The agent usually applied was a pyrethroid, but due to increasing insect resistance over successive years the company arranged a subcontractor to fumigate the fruit under plastic sheeting. However, the fumigant leaked out from the plastic and caused widespread morbidity in the form of headaches, nausea, dizziness, salivation and weakness throughout the workforce, resulting in closure of the factory the next day. Twenty-five women were diagnosed by the local general practitioner as suffering from 'mass hysteria'. Only after investigation by a union-linked health programme did it emerge that methyl bromide had been used to treat the fruit, and that poor industrial hygiene had resulted in accidental exposures [24]. The propensity of general practitioners to label non-specific ailments as 'malingering' or psychological reinforces the fiction that women are not at high risk for pesticide-related illness and illustrates the gendered nature of biomedical knowledge in this area. Moreover, none of these cases was reported to the health or labour authorities, thereby reinforcing the myth that women have little exposure to hazardous pesticides.

Women's overall morbidity burden is higher

Women in rural agricultural communities in developing countries have to cope with multiple environmental and social hazards, such as child and adult under-nutrition, alcohol abuse, ergonomic hazards, coercive social relations, lack of adequate health care and a greatly increased burden for domestic duties, in addition to agricultural production [25]. The potential for interactions between these social and environmental hazards, and the hazards posed by pesticide exposure are poorly explored and may add a significant additional dimension to women's morbidity and mortality in farming areas. For example, heavy alcohol consumption, common in parts of South Africa where historically farm workers were paid with alcohol (the DOP system) [26], may influence the metabolism of many pesticides, either increasing or decreasing toxicity, or their influence on other hazards. Chronic under-nutrition in adult male farm workers appears to have adverse impacts on sub-clinical neurological function [27] and may well have similar interactions for women farm workers exposed to pesticides known to be neurotoxic. Pesticide regulations and toxicological risk assessment data in South Africa used for pesticide registration do not take into account the above factors for the pesticides used in South Africa. Toxicological risk assessment estimations used in assessing a pesticide's health and safety profile are based on hazards and exposures for healthy European males and not for African women [28].

Furthermore, social hazards may interact with pesticides in complex ways. Suicide amongst young women farm workers and family members is a relatively common occurrence and is facilitated by easy access to pesticides on farms. Where reviews of such poisonings have been conducted, the main source of pesticides for deliberate ingestion is usually a farm store. Domestic violence is another area where, as a result of the replication of patriarchal relations on the farm generally, women carry a magnified burden of gender-related illness.

Social and cultural burdens of poor health

In both developed and developing countries, the knowledge of the nature of the adverse effects of pesticides is poorly known, particularly for chronic effects with multiple competing causes. This is amplified in developing countries, where there is a real paucity in local understanding of health effects from pesticide exposure, and where training and awareness programmes are severely under-resourced. However, it is precisely in these countries where the consequences of such lack of information may be most significant. The social and cultural norms of African societies continue to ensure that women are marginalized and disadvantaged. For example, in societies where accusations of witchcraft are culturally embraced, health effects from pesticides may not be seen as a consequence of exposure to toxins, but as the result of a curse, bewitching or similar traditional belief. Another example is that Ndebele women in Southern Africa are not considered 'married' until they have borne their first child. If unable to bear a child they may be subject to divorce and ill-treatment. Infertility amongst men is on the rise globally; scientific data point to increased exposure to pesticides as one possible cause [29,30]. However, if an African man is infertile from exposure to pesticides, the woman will have to bear the brunt of this social and cultural shame, as barrenness in most traditional African cultures is identified as the fault of women. As a result, failure of a woman to conceive a child is grounds for her to be divorced, ridiculed and subjected to possible community ostracism [31].

Solutions and challenges

A number of routes to address these gendered obstacles are suggested:

- There are generic difficulties in organizing farm workers, but this is particularly the case with women. Worker organizations need to develop specific means to integrate gender into their recruitment strategies, and to ensure that health and safety concerns are central concerns.
- Training and information-provision need to address the gender issues raised above. Traditionally, training has been dominated by men or by gender-insensitive perspectives. Models of training need to empower workers in ways that build gender sensitivity. A first step would be to conduct gender awareness workshops for trainers. Health and safety materials produced need to incorporate a gendered context.
- South Africa has pioneered a number of human rights innovations, including a Bill of Rights in the new Constitution, and institutions to support the building of a human rights culture in civil society, including a Human Rights Commission and a Commission for

Gender Equality. Application of human rights approaches on farms may go some way to addressing gender imbalances.
- Research agendas need to be changed to fill the gaps caused by incorrect assumptions about women's exposures and morbidity. Moreover, the social sciences need to inform health research, and encourage good public health practice and policy, by identifying the social and cultural context in which pesticide risk perceptions are interpreted and acted upon, as well as providing structures for pragmatic incorporation of risk perceptions into traditional health research methodologies, health and safety programmes, and public policy. Pesticide research data, in general, should reflect and incorporate the context within which African women are exposed to pesticides.

Ultimately, it is policy and legislative reform that are needed to ensure an appropriate framework for protecting women from the burden of pesticide-related illness. Such legislative and policy changes need to be practically implemented and publicly embraced by all stakeholders, rather than remaining 'politically correct' rhetoric. Pesticide-related health and safety messages, structured with a gender-sensitive slant, need to be spread through popular media in order to challenge cultural and social barriers.

Note

1. In response to a question asked by Hanna-Andrea Rother about pesticide usage, safety and health issues.

References

1 Lipton, M., Ellis, F., Lipton, M. *Land, Labour and Livelihoods in Rural South Africa – Volume Two: KzaZulu–Natal and Northern Province*, Durban: Indicator Press, South Africa, 1996.
2 Donaldson, A., Roux, A. In *Development Southern Africa* 11(1), 1994: 131–43.
3 Arumugam, V. *Victims Without Voice: A Study of Women Pesticide Workers in Malaysia*. Malaysia: Tenaganita/PAN Asia and the Pacific, 1992.
4 Rosas L., Reeves, M. 'Women farmworkers and pesticides – stories from the fields', *Global Pesticide Campaigner*, 8(4), 1998.
5 Lipton, Ellis, Lipton, *op. cit.*, 1996.
6 Donaldson, Roux, *op. cit.*, 1994.
7 Emanuel, K., *Poisoned Pay: Farmworkers and the South African Pesticide*

Industry, Report for London: the Pesticide Trust/Johannesburg: Group for Environmental Monitoring, 1992.

8   Robins, T., Salie F., Gwagwa T. In *South African Medical Journal* 88, 1998: 1117–27.

9   London, L., Joubert, G., Manjra, S, Krause L. In *South African Medical Journal*, 81, 1992: 606–12.

10 London, L., In *Social Science and Medicine* 37, 1993: 1521–7.

11 Kleynhans, J. Cited in Rother, A., London, L., *et al.*, 'National Consultative Workshop on Pesticide Policy in South Africa', Pesticide Policy Project, Occupational and Environmental Health Research Unit, University of Cape Town, 6–7 April 1998.

12 Dinham, B., *The Pesticide Hazard: A Global Health and Environmental Audit*, London: Zed Books, 1993.

13 London, L., Myers, J.E. In *South African Journal of Science*, 91, 1995: 515–22.

14 National Department of Agriculture. 'Cotton farming for small-scale or emergent farmers', *Agricultural News*, 13, 1997: 11.

15 Rother, A., London, L. 'Pesticide health and safety policy mechanisms in South Africa: the state of the debate', Occupational and Environmental Health Research Unit, Working Paper No. 1, Department of Community Health, University of Cape Town, 1998.

16 London, L., Rother, A. In *Environmental Solutions*, 10(4), 2000: 339–50.

17 Plant Protection Research Institute, 'Jozini field trip report', Agricultural Research Council, 22–26 April 1997.

18 Rother, A. In *African Newsletter on Occupational Health and Safety*, 10(2), 2000: 42–6.

19 Rother, A. *op. cit.*, 2000.

20 WHO, *Public Health Impact of Pesticides Used in Agriculture*, Geneva: WHO.

21 Department of Health, 'Pesticidal poisoning in South Africa, 1980–1994', *Epidemiological Comments* 22(5), 1995: 112–38.

22 Baillie, R., London, L. In *South African Medical Journal*, 88, 1998: 1105–9.

23 Department of Health, *op. cit.*, 1995.

24 Thompson, L. Food and Allied Workers Union, pers. comm., 1987.

25 Sims, J. *Women, Health and Environment: An Anthology*, Geneva: WHO, 1994.

26 London, L. 'Alcohol consumption amongst South African farm workers: a post-apartheid challenge', *Drug and Alcohol Dependence*, 2000.

27 London, L., Nell, V., Thompson, M.L., Myers, J.E., In *Scandinavian Journal of Work, Environment and Health*, 24, 1998: 18–29.

28 Thrupp, A., 'Exporting risk analyses to developing countries', *Global Pesticide Campaigner*, 4(1), 1994: 3–5.

29 Carlsen, E., Giwercman, A., Keiding, N., Skakkebaek, N.E., In *British Medical Journal*, 305 (6854), 1992: 609–13.

30 Swan, S.H., Elkin, E.P., In *Bioessays* 21(7), 1999: 614–21.

31 Rother, H.A., unpublished research, Kanyemba, Zimbabwe, 1990.

24

Safety at work and gender bias: attitudes to risk in setting policy

Meriel A. Watts

Public policy decisions and decision-making procedures regarding pesticides seldom take into account gender differences. Other chapters have revealed that there is clear evidence of physiological gender differences that affect the outcome of pesticide exposure, and in many situations a marked degree of difference in exposure. However, there is also evidence, at least within several Western countries, of a gender difference in attitude towards pesticides, those attitudes arising from underlying value systems and finding expression in the degree of risk attached to the use of pesticides. Remembering that it is a function of public policy to express public values and intentions [1], if those values and the expressions of them differ between females and males, then the pesticide policy process must be cognizant of those differences, as well as of the differences in vulnerability to pesticides. For it must be remembered that pesticides are registered, theoretically at least, as a public service. They have never been demonstrated to be a necessity of life, although that is frequently an assumption of many pesticide policies. Therefore policy decisions regarding their continued use should be subject not only to medical, scientific and agricultural evidence but also to a determination of societal attitudes towards the acceptability of their adverse effects as an expression of public values.

These attitudinal differences may be easily brushed aside if the view is held that the risk assessment of pesticides is a purely technical matter, that since the estimated risks are scientific they are an objective and value-free depiction of actual risk. There is, however, a wealth of evidence that risk assessment of pesticides is in fact riddled with uncertainty, estimates, judgements, and indeed incorporates a high degree of subjectivity [2,3,4,5,6,7,8]. Where there is subjectivity, there is scope for personal and institutional value systems to influence the outcomes of decisions [9]. One study effectively illustrated this point with an analysis of the Canadian inquiry into the effects of the herbicide alachlor [10]. Estimates of exposure to the herbicide varied from 2.7 mg/kg to 0.0000009 mg/kg, depending on the assumptions made, those assumptions being either protective of health, on the one hand, or protective of monetary gain, on the other. Hence attitudes and the underlying value systems they express are already a part of pesticide policy, including in the area of risk evaluation.

That differences in value systems explain to a large degree the differences in perception of risk from pesticides between the public and the experts is not the subject here. Suffice it to say at this point that the attitudes of the public should be regarded as legitimate expressions of their values (see Box 24.1). The subject is briefly touched on, for a note of explanation is required about the terminology used here. It is normal to refer to the *assessment* of risks by scientific experts, and the *perception* of risks by the public, the former term implying a degree of objectivity, rationality, and freedom from values, and the latter implying emotion, fear, irrationality and ignorance. It is argued elsewhere [11] that such distinctions are not warranted and indeed are purposely used to undermine the validity of public views. Language is a powerful instrument and should be used with integrity in public policy. Therefore the traditional assignment of terminology is rejected here, in favour of a more inclusive approach in which the terms 'assessment' and 'perception' are applied equally to the public and to technical experts.

This chapter will review the evidence of gender differences in attitude towards pesticides, those differences being evident amongst members of the public and amongst toxicologists. They are underscored by the disparity between genders with respect to grassroots activism in the area of hazardous chemicals in general, including pesticides, and in the apparent susceptibility to low dose exposure as manifested by multiple chemical sensitivity (MCS).

Box 24.1 Risk assessment: better decision-making tools

Mary O'Brien

Imagine a woman standing by an icy mountain river, intending to cross to the other side. A team of four risk assessors stands behind her, reviewing her situation. The toxicologist says that she ought to wade across the river because it is not toxic, only cold. The cardiologist says she ought to wade across the river because she looks to be young and not already chilled. Her risks of cardiac arrest, therefore, are low. The hydrologist says she ought to wade across the river because he has seen other rivers like this and estimates that this one is not more than four feet deep and probably has no whirlpools at this location. Finally, the EPA policy specialist says that the woman ought to wade across the river because, compared to global warming, ozone depletion and loss of species diversity, the risks of her crossing are trivial.

The woman refuses to wade across. 'Why?' the risk assessors ask. They show her their calculations, condescendingly explaining to her that her risk of dying while wading across the river is one in 40 million.

Still the woman refuses to wade across. 'Why?' the risk assessors ask again, frustrated by this woman who clearly doesn't understand the nature of risks.

The woman points upstream, and says, 'Because there is a bridge.'

The risk assessors in this story are evaluating the risks of only one option: wading across an icy river. The woman is evaluating her alternatives, one of which involves crossing the river on a bridge. The woman doesn't really care whether getting wet in the icy stream will kill her or not, because it doesn't make sense to her to even become chilled in the light of her options. This is the fundamental difference between risk assessment and alternatives assessment.

The addition of toxic chemicals to our food

When scientists and risk assessors become convinced that risk assessments are not considering important information (infants' special physiology, cultures with particular diets, habits of particular species), they will strive to make the risk assessment more complicated and more data-rich (i.e. full of more information). Meanwhile, these scientists and risk assessors generally fail to ask whether the hazardous activity that is being assessed is even necessary or ethical.

In 1988, Congress asked the National Academy of Sciences to establish a committee within the National Research Council to study scientific and policy issues surrounding pesticide residues that the federal government permits to be present on foods eaten by the infants and children. Five years later, the committee published its findings in a book called *Pesticides and the Diets of Infants and Children*. The book noted that the levels of pesticides currently 'permissible' for adults are not necessarily 'safe' for children for a number of reasons.

Children or infants may absorb a greater proportion of pesticide inside the body, and they may not break down (detoxify) or get rid of (excrete) pesticides as readily as adults. Even more critical, the committee wrote, infants and young children may eat much more of certain foods (e.g. apples via apple juice and apple sauce) per body weight than adults, and so may receive more of certain pesticides than was 'expected' for an average adult.

The committee's recommendations are numerous, and they focus on producing more comprehensive risk assessments so we won't allow 'too much' pesticide residues on foods that infants and children eat.

For instance, the committee recommended that studies of the effects of pesticides on laboratory animals should focus on health damage effects to which infants and children are particularly vulnerable during certain periods, such as damage to the immune system, to the developing reproductive system, and to the nervous system. When such information is missing (as it is most of the time), extra 'safety factors' should be plugged into the numerical risk-assessment formulas. These safety factors would result in a reduction of the amount of pesticides that would be considered 'safe'. The committee recommended that we learn more about what foods infants and young children eat, and in what amounts. They recommended more frequent testing of the amounts of pesticides that are present on foods in the store. They recommended that we learn more about which chemicals transform into other, possibly more toxic chemicals as food is processed (for instance, when tomatoes are heated for canning). They recommended adding the amounts of different pesticide residues on a food together if they cause the same adverse effects (for instance, a particular interference with the nervous system). Adding similar pesticides together would result in lower allowable amounts for any one of these pesticides. They also recommended that we learn more about how cancer rates are affected by exposure to a cancer-causing pesticide at a certain time of life.

Overall, the committee's recommendations 'support the need to improve methods for estimating exposure and for setting tolerances [acceptable amounts of a pesticides on any given item of food] to safeguard the health of infants and children'.

More important, the committee did not recommend producing food organically, or altering agricultural methods to reduce dependency on pesticide use. It did not recommend allowing zero amounts of a particular pesticide on children's food if that pesticide is not one that 'needs' to be used to produce the crop. It did not question whether pesticides 'have' to be on children's food; nor did it call for a study of the availability of alternatives to using pesticides. It simply made recommendations for figuring out how much pesticide we should permit on children's food ...

In the end, will we best protect our children by very carefully calculating how much pesticide to feed our children, or will we best protect our children by feeding them foods grown without pesticides? This is not the kind of question the National Research Council's committee of experts asked. Most risk assessors don't ask about the necessity of undertaking the hazardous activities they assess.

Source: Reference 12.

Public assessment of risk

Attitudinal surveys reveal that the public has considerable concern about the risks of pesticides to health and the environment. Few of them differentiate between females and males, but where they do they consistently reveal that women assess the risk from pesticides to be greater than men do, at least in the USA, Canada and New Zealand. This gender difference appears to occur with respect to other hazardous technologies and to environmental attitudes generally.

During the 1990s a series of studies were carried out into the effects of gender on the assessment of risk by the public. The studies consistently revealed that, for a variety of health and environmental risks, including those posed by nuclear and chemical technologies, the level of risk was assessed to be higher by women than by men [13,14,15,16]. The only exception to this was in a finding that for non-white Americans, there was no significant difference between men and women in the assessment of risks relating to nuclear and chemical technologies [17].

These findings are well supported by New Zealand and US attitudinal surveys relating to pesticides, genetic engineering and general environmental attitudes. In New Zealand, the Lifestyle and Environment Survey [18] found that most concern about pesticides was shown by women aged between 30 and 39 (51 per cent compared to 44 per cent for all respondents). Women were more likely to eat organic food (27 per cent of women aged between 30 and 39 compared with 19 per cent of all respondents) and to use natural pesticides (32 per cent of women aged 40+ compared with 21 per cent of all respondents). They also dominated the 'deep green' segment of environmental attitudes (70 per cent). A survey of the general public found a similar, consistent difference in attitude by men and women to genetic engineering. In answer to every relevant question in the survey, women assessed the risks as higher than did men: 49:37 per cent and 54:43 per cent. Equally, in the relevant questions women assessed the acceptability and benefits to be lower than did men: 53:61 per cent; 48:64 per cent; 61:71 per cent [19].

A recent US study [20] found that women were 14 per cent more likely to be risk-averse to pesticide usage than men, that men chose chemical pesticides over non-chemical pesticides more often than women, and that having children resulted in an increased concern about pesticides (the authors cited a number of supporting studies).

A survey of members of the public in Australia found, once again, that concern for the environment was higher amongst females than males. A total of 54 per cent of women were concerned about pollution compared with 46 per cent of men; 53 per cent of women and 47 per cent of men were concerned about nature conservation; and 42 per cent of women and 29 per cent of men were concerned about 'social and environmental issues'. Men were more concerned about economic issues (61:48 per cent) [21].

The same gender differences have been reported with respect to lay assessment of genetic engineering. Psychological research from the Institute of Food Research, reporting on a UK survey of attitudes, noted that 'compared to men, women indicated less need for the technology, gave lower ratings about improvements to the quality of life, reported lower benefits and greater risks, expressed less favourable attitudes to all three applications [animal, plant and microorganisms], expressed greater concern, and agreed more strongly that ethical issues were involved' [22].

Grassroots activism

This assessment of greater risk, by women, is consistent with what others [23] referred to as women's leadership in political efforts to reduce health and environmental risks [24]. In early twentieth-century USA, middle-class women were a powerful force in the 'progressive conservation crusade', saving many old forests from the 'men whose souls are gang-saws', as they were described by Mrs Robert Burdett, president of the California Federation of Women's Clubs in 1900. Women have been prominent in tree-saving movements around the world, movements such as the Chipko movement of India and the Greenbelt movement of Kenya founded by Wangari Maathai. But it is women's involvement in the movement to curtail the risks from chemical technology that is most striking. During the 1980s in the USA, 80–85 per cent of grassroots activists in the 'antitoxic movement' were women [25]. Similarly it is the author's experience within New Zealand that women have traditionally been, and still are, the leaders and the mainstay of the anti-pesticides movement. 'Why do women do it?' asked Kate Short of the Total Environment Centre in Sydney. The answer is: because they bear children and they and their children bear the consequences. Their wombs and their breast milk are contaminated with DDT, benzene and dieldrin [26].

There may well be other reasons too, including that women generally have less to lose socio-economically than men by challenging the status quo; that women are more inclined to be egalitarian and men to be technological enthusiasts [27,28]; women to be risk-refusers and men to be risk-acceptors; and that women tend to be more vulnerable to chemicals than men, especially in the area of MCS.

Multiple chemical sensitivity

MCS is a syndrome of effects experienced usually as a result of ongoing low-level exposure to chemicals, including pesticides. Organophosphate insecticides have been implicated by several US authors as likely key causes of onset [29,30,31,32,33]. The effects experienced and the levels of chemicals at which effects occur are not supported by toxicological data. This, together with the lack of an agreed physiological mechanism for the syndrome, has hampered its medical and scientific acceptance, and controversy still surrounds the subject. Although there is still doubt in some quarters as to the actual existence of the syndrome, there is a wealth of supportive medical, scientific and patient literature [34].

One of the very few aspects of MCS on which there appears to be general agreement is that there is a greater incidence of the problem amongst women than amongst men, with studies reporting that 70–80 per cent of cases were women [35]. Women, white-collar workers and others who experience minimal chemical exposure in their routine lives (relative to occupationally exposed people), appear to be more susceptible [36]. A survey of 112 patients with MCS, found that 80 per cent were women [37]. Dr Finn Levy noted that about 80 per cent of MCS patients at his occupational medicine clinic were women, well educated, with good intellectual resources, and who functioned well until chemical exposure [38]. The Interagency Workgroup [39], in acknowledging the preponderance of women amongst MCS sufferers, added that 'the reasons for this preponderance are unknown' [40]. Dr Iris Bell provided one possible clue: when reporting on studies on animals indicating that females are more sensitive to stress and drugs than are males, she commented that this is perhaps an effect of oestrogen [41]. Evidence that oestrogen may enhance the effect of chemicals on the nervous system was subsequently provided [42].

It may well be that this gender difference in the expression of MCS is one of the reasons for the lack of acceptance in some quarters of the existence of the syndrome as an effect of chemical exposure. A study carried out in 1990 stated that MCS patients are typically middle-aged, well-educated women, with an interest in emotional disorders, and who have developed a lifestyle and friendships around their illnesses – implying that this indicates a preexisting psychological gender-based disturbance or neurosis, rather than an outcome of an effect of chemicals or unrecognized and misdiagnosed reactions to chemicals [43]. These conclusions have been repeated by many of the sceptics of MCS [44,45,46], even though the authors had acknowledged that the methodology of their study was lacking in rigour, resulting in a general denial of the genesis of the syndrome in ongoing low-level exposure to mixtures of chemicals. Their conclusions, together with irrefutable evidence that more women than men are reported as suffering from the syndrome, has left it with a stigma that may be preventing many involved in toxicology from exploring the field, even with the increasing recognition of the likely adverse effects of ongoing exposure to low levels of mixtures of chemicals [47,48,49].

The stigma attaching to women and MCS also collides with the assessment by women of higher risk from pesticides, and their greater refusal to accept that risk. The result is the intentional, or otherwise, depiction of those averse to risk from pesticides as emotive, fearful, ignorant and irrational.

'Experts' assessing risks

Unfortunately for the critics of women's attitudes towards the risks from pesticides, this same disparity between genders appears to be mirrored in the opinions about risks by female and male toxicologists, presumably with the same or similar levels of training and knowledge. A survey of members of the British Toxicological Society found that female toxicologists judge risk from chemicals to be higher than do their male counterparts [50]. A similar pattern occurred with female and male physical scientists judging risks from nuclear technology [51]. These two studies confirm the findings of an earlier one [52] which reported that not only were female toxicologists more concerned by chemical risks than were male toxicologists, but also that the former 'were less favourably impressed with the benefits of chemicals' than the later.

Conclusion

The findings of a difference in assessment of risk by female and male toxicologists effectively remove the charge that the gender difference in perception of risk may be an issue of ignorance. It also therefore questions the assumption that lay assessment is based on ignorance simply because it differs from that of technical assessors. Conversely it lends weight to the theory that the difference in assessment of risks between males and females may well result from differences in value systems or world-views. Since the objective of public policy is supposedly to reflect the values and needs to all of society, both male and female, pesticide policy should reflect these gender differences. At the least, there should be a balance of women and men involved in all pesticide policy decisions. This includes the toxicological assessment of pesticides in the risk assessment process. For this process involves substantial numbers of judgements to be made that are outside the scope of science, and hence must logically derive from the value system of the person making them. Further attitudinal research on pesticides should also be structured to enable gender segregation of answers, so that the gender differences are recognized and policy is forced to address them.

References

1 Considine, M. *Public Policy: A Critical Approach*, Victoria, Melbourne: Macmillan, 1994.
2 Shrader-Frechette, K.S. *Risk Analysis and Scientific Method*, Dordrecht: Reidel, 1985.
3 Shrader-Frechette, K.S. *Risk and Rationality: Philosophical Foundations for Populist Reforms*, Berkeley: University of California Press, 1991.
4 Graham, J.D., Green, L.C., Roberts, M.J. *In Search of Safety*, Cambridge, MA: Harvard University Press, 1988.
5 Fan, A., Howd, R., Davis, B. In *Annual Review of Pharmacology and Toxicology*, 35, 1995: 341–68.

6 'A review of the California EPA's risk assessment practices, policies and guidelines', Sacramento: California EPA, 1996.

7 Slovic, P. *Trust, Emotion, Sex, Politics, and Science: Surveying the Risk Assessment Battlefield*, Chicago: University of Chicago Legal Forum, 1997, pp. 59–99.

8 Brunk, C.G., Haworth, L., Lee, B. *Value Assumptions in Risk Assessment: A Case Study of the Alachlor Controversy*, Waterloo, ON: Wilfrid Laurier University Press, 1998.

9 Schierow, L.-J. 'Environmental risk analysis: a review of public policy issues', Washington DC: Congressional Research Service, Committee for the National Institute for the Environment, 15 July 1998.

10 Brunk, Haworth, Lee, *op. cit.*, 1998.

11 Watts, M.A. 'Ethical Pesticide Policy: Beyond Risk Assessment', PhD thesis, University of Auckland, 2001.

12 Mary O'Brien, *Making Better Environmental Decisions: An Alternative to Risk Assessment*, Cambridge, MA: MIT Press, in association with the Environmental Research Foundation, pp. 3–4, 50–53.

13 Flynn, J., Slovic, P., Mertz, C.K. In *Risk Analysis*, 14(6), 1994: 1101–08.

14 Kraus, N. Malmfors, T., Slovic, P. In *Risk Analysis*, 12(2), 1992: 215–32.

15 Krewski, D., *et al.* 'Health risk perception in Canada I', *Human and Ecological Risk Assessment* 1(2), 1995: 117–32.

16 Krewski, D., *et al.* 'Health risk perception in Canada II', *Human and Ecological Risk Assessment* 1(3), 1995: 231–48.

17 Flynn, Slovic, Mertz, *op. cit.*, 1994.

18 *Project Green*, report prepared for Ministry for the Environment Manatu Mo Te Taiao, Wellington: Colmar Brunton Research, 1993.

19 Couchman, P.K., Fink-Jensen, K. 'Public attitudes to genetic engineering in New Zealand', DSIR Crop Research Report No. 138, Christchurch, 1990.

20 Govindasamy, R., Italia, J., Adelaja, A. *Predicting Consumer Risk Aversions to Synthetic Pesticide Residues: A Logistics Analysis*, Piscataway, NJ: Rutgers University Press, 1998.

21 Merchant, C., *Earthcare: Women and the Environment*, New York: Routledge, 1996.

22 Sparks, P., Shepherd, R., Frewer, L.J. In *Agriculture and Human Values*, 11(1), 1994: 19–28.

23 Barke, R., Jenkins-Smith, H., Slovic, P. In *Social Science Quarterly*, 78(1), 1997: 167–76.

24 Barke, R., *et al.* cited Nelkin, D. 'Nuclear power as a feminist issue', *Environment*, 23, 1981: 14–39.

25 Examples cited by Merchant, *op. cit.*, 1996.

26 Short, K. 'The Australian Toxics Network: why women do it', In Harding, R. (ed.) *Ecopolitics*, Centre for Liberal and General Studies, Sydney: University of New South Wales, 1992.

27 Flynn *et al. op. cit.*, 1994.

28 Slovic, P., *et al.* In *Risk Analysis*, 15(6), 1995: 661–75.

29 Miller, C.S., Mitzel, H.C. In *Archives of Environmental Health*, 50(2), 1995: 119–29.

30 Davidoff, A.L., Keyl, P.M. In *Archives of Environmental Health*, 51(3), 1996: 201–13.

31 Meggs, W.J., *et al*. In *Archives of Environmental Health*, 51(4), 1996: 275–82.

32 MacPhail, R.C. In *Environmental Health Perspectives*, 105 Suppl. 2, 1997: 455–6.

33 Ashford, N.A., Miller, C.S. *Chemical Exposures: Low Levels and High Stakes,* New York: Van Nostrand Reinhold, 1998.

34 Watts, *op. cit.*, 2001.

35 Ashford, Miller, *op. cit.*, 1998.

36 Cullen, M.R., Redlich, C.A. In *Clinical Chemistry*, 41(12), Pt 2, 1995: 1809–13.

37 Miller, Mitzel, *op. cit.*, 1995.

38 Levy, F. In *Scandinavian Journal of Work, Environment and Health*, 23 Suppl. 3, 1997: 69–73.

39 Interagency Workgroup on MCS. 'A Report on MCS', Atlanta: Agency for Toxic Substances and Disease Registry, August 1998.

40 Interagency Workgroup on MCS, *op. cit.*, p. 24.

41 Bell, I.R., In *Toxicology*, 111(1–3), 1996: 101–17.

42 Bell, I.R., *et al*. In *Environmental Health Perspectives*, 105, Suppl. 2, 1997: 457–66.

43 Black, D.W., Rathe, A., Goldstein, R.B. In *Journal of the American Medical Association*, 264(24), 1990: 3166–70.

44 O'Donnell, J.L. 'MCS Syndrome', Wellington, NZ: Report commissioned by ACC Head Office, 1993.

45 Gots, R.E. *Toxic Risks: Science, Regulation, and Perception*, Florida: Lewis Publishers, 1993.

46 Brod, B.A. In *American Journal of Contact Dermatitis*, 7(4), 1996: 202–11.

47 Lucier, G.W., Schecter, A. In *Environmental Health Perspectives*, 106(10), 1998: 623–7.

48 Carpenter, D.O., *et al*. In *Environmental Health Perspectives*, 106 (S6), 1998: 1263–70.

49 Porter, W.P., *et al*. In *Toxicology and Industrial Health*, 15(1–2), 1999: 133–50.

50 Slovic, P., *et al*., In *Human and Experimental Toxicology*, 16, 1997: 289–304.

51 Barke, Jenkins-Smith, Slovic, *op. cit.*, 1997.

52 Kraus, N., Malmfors, T., Slovic, P. In *Risk Analysis*, 12 (2), 1992: 215–32.

25

Implementing pesticide regulation: gender differences

Andrew Watterson and Jenny Watterson

Pesticide hazards and risks to human health relating to gender have often been presented in two quite different and conflicting ways. Either little research has been done or publicized on the risks to women or there has been a focus on reporting risks to women and the fetus when similar research on men has been absent or downplayed. Current occupational health research demonstrates a growing focus on susceptibility issues especially linked to genetics and to women. Women have been excluded from work because of pesticide reproductive hazards known also to affect males who remain in employment. This chapter explores these themes in two case studies: one on a raspberry pesticide and one on a sugar beet pesticide.

Gender can be downplayed in risk assessments and risk management decisions relating to pesticide usage. 'One-eyed science', described by Karen Messing, examines the lack of or skewing of research and related action on workplace health and safety problems facing women. This applies to research on threshold limit values set for chemical exposures 'where women and women's physiology have been excluded from studies used to set the standard' and where pregnant women's concerns and the nature of some women's work may have been handled inappropriately or neglected [1]. Research to establish acute exposure threshold limit values in the USA and the UK was often based solely on young, relatively fit, white military staff. The position may be further complicated by the double jeopardy of work and home hazards for many women [2]. In fact quadruple jeopardy may apply for those exposed to pesticides at work through additional exposure in the home, in the garden and leisure activities, and in the wider environment including food, water and airborne exposures.

Pesticides present both occupational and environmental health threats that cross gender, ethnicity and age barriers. Effective responses to these threats have proved problematic and varied at farm, regional, national and international regulatory levels. Early threshold limits for chemical exposures, where human data were used, have been based on human responses to selective acute chemicals exposures. Even now relatively few pesticides have any threshold limit values or occupational exposure standards set. Relatively little is known about the toxicity of mixtures including inerts and solvents used in pesticides [3]. The debate about long-term low-level exposures to chemicals, especially pesticides, has still not been resolved. Pesticide approvals and monitoring fail to address these issues in most countries, and economic and political factors rather than public health concerns often drive pesticide regulatory policies.

Policies for 'fetal protection' were developed from UK, American and Soviet concerns identified in previous decades relating to lead hazards to the fetus. The concerns led to regulations that excluded pregnant women, or women of childbearing age, from workplaces, while data available about the detrimental effect of lead on male reproduction were ignored. Policies have now been developed in the USA and elsewhere 'when the employer claims that the work environment poses a particular risk to the foetus. Many employers have adopted [these] plans that are most prominent in historically male industries such as the petrochemical and automotive industries' [4,5]. The result has been to shift the workplace health and safety debate away from making workplaces healthy and safe to selecting or selecting out vulnerable individuals or groups considered susceptible to particular hazards [6]. At the same time, the struggle to get effective methods and measures to assess children's susceptibility to environmental toxicants has been long, and only recently has the subject been adequately addressed [7].

In the 1980s adverse reproductive effects of some pesticides were widely flagged in the USA, where 'the response of government agencies when dealing with the reproductive risk faced by men contrasts strongly with its response to the risk faced by women' [8]. The pesticide DBCP, for example, was identified as a cause of sterility in male pesticide manufacturing workers in 1976 and the USA suspended its use in 1979. Other pesticides found to cause birth defects in animal tests, and subject to Environmental Protection Agency (EPA) warnings that women of childbearing age should not use the pesticide, remained on sale. The EPA information provided 'a handy excuse for a grower to refuse to hire women. Thus while it may seem that women are being more quickly protected, in fact it is a form of protection that only serves to further segregate them into the lower rungs of the agricultural workforce' [9].

Development and ethnicity, as well as gender issues, may be entangled with pesticide regulatory toxicology because DBCP continued to be used in Hawaii and, after 1979, in Costa Rica with serious consequences for male workers. White US males were therefore protected from DBCP in the domestic farm setting by bans, but Central American males were not. Globally this showed the unchecked power of the multinational pesticide manufacturers, who continued to export DBCP [10].

The economics and politics of employment practice led to discrimination: first, against younger women gaining or keeping certain jobs because of potentially teratogenic materials used; second, against men or older women who may be exposed to health risks viewed as unacceptable for women of childbearing age. The precautionary principle offers an alternative approach to such a crude application of scientific findings on pesticides. This principle readily recognizes the limits of risk assessment, including the high levels of uncertainty surrounding many assessments and the poor basis for accurate probability calculations on chemical toxicity. It includes a greater recognition of past failures in toxicology, a requirement to consider and perhaps weight more highly than has hitherto been the case the social and political, as well as narrow economic and scientific, underpinning in assessments.

The following case studies of pesticide risk assessment, standard-setting and monitoring involve scientific, community and trade-union interventions and explore gender issues.

The dinoseb case study

The Scottish raspberry industry in the 1980s reveals how different risk assessments and employment patterns were advocated for male and female workers by the farming industry, regulators and trade unions. Dinoseb, 2-(1-Methylpropyl)-4,6-dinitrophenol, first introduced in 1945, is a contact and soil-acting herbicide used across the world on a wide range of vegetables and fruit.

Dinoseb has a range of adverse reproductive effects associated with it, including damage to sperm, fetus and thyroid; these were not fully reported until the 1970s, although its use was continued into

Table 25.1 Dates of knowledge on the effects of dinoseb on males and females

1973	Evidence of teratogenicity of dinoseb in mice was reported [15].
1975	Evidence of increased maternal mortality, fetal toxicity and teratogenicity when mice were fed dinoseb in high-temperature environments [16].
1981	Dinoseb found to inhibit the rate of rat fetal development *in vitro* [17].
1982	Dinoseb linked to testicular effects in rats [18].
1983	Some sources do not note any adverse reproductive effects linked to the chemical [19].
1984	*Standard Guide* on toxicology for occupational health professionals lists dinoseb as an experimental teratogen [20].
1985	Dinoseb was found to produce extra ribs in fetuses of pregnant mice at low or moderately toxic levels [21].
1987	UK government banned the sale, supply and use of dinoseb as a weedkiller following a US EPA ban after animal tests showed dinoseb caused birth defects and infertility [22].
1990	Canada used a risk–benefit analysis to ban dinoseb on health grounds except for critical need use on early cane control in raspberries [23].
1992	Studies reported on the 'substantial spermatotoxicity' of dinoseb in short-duration animal tests [24].

the 1980s (see Table 25.1). In the UK the suspension of approvals for dinoseb use were announced in December 1986 because of teratogenicity data. However, the inability to set a 'no effect' level of exposure was relaxed in 1987 for 'economic' reasons to allow Glen Clova raspberries in the Tayside region to be treated to control cane vigour. However, no women were allowed to use dinoseb, only male contractors, following advice from the Advisory Committee on Pesticides [11,12]. As the Health and Safety Executive (HSE) noted at the time, 'the decision to relax the ban was made following strong representation by the National Farmers Union of Scotland' [13]. No mention is made in the HSE report itself to the strong opposition by trade unions to any relaxation of a dinoseb ban. The UK unions pressed for a ban on dinoseb on the grounds that it could affect both male and female employees adversely, supported by US data clearly referring to effects on sperm as well as the fetus. US farm workers had done likewise, arguing successfully against industry groups who obtained an order to permit continued use of dinoseb as long as fertile women were excluded from working exposures [14]. Dinoseb was phased out in the USA in 1988/9.

Thus scientific data on dinoseb's health hazards were used in the UK in different ways for females and males at different times by regulators, scientific advisors, the farming industry and trade unions. Only the trade unions argued against gender-specific employment policies for dinoseb users and consistently for a full and permanent ban on dinoseb because of its teratogenicity hazard to women and its fertility hazard to men. The case raises major questions about what research does and doesn't tell us about health risks, how we handle data gaps, and how and why countries adopt or have adopted different responses to the same data.

The lindane case study

This study reveals differential responses to the non-reproductive threats to males and females from one pesticide used on sugar crops in the northern and southern hemispheres. Breast cancer is a major global cause of mortality in women, and in the UK has been the principal cause of mortality in women for several decades. Work environment and wider environmental factors may play a part in breast cancer aetiology in humans, and there is significant experimental evidence that chemicals including pesticides may cause or contribute to breast cancer [25,26,27,28,29,30]. Breast cancer is not a disease solely of women but there are very few cases in males. The lack of urgency in preventing breast cancer in the UK is therefore a very gender-specific issue [31,32].

Organochlorines have been found to feminize male animals and alter the oestrogenic cycle and hormonal levels of female animals [33,34]. Lindane or gamma-HCH is an organochlorine insecticide that is less persistent than DDT but nevertheless is persistent across the globe. Lindane has long been linked with reduced ovulation rates in animals and anti-oestrogenicity. It accumulates in the ovarian follicles, fallopian tubes and uterus of animals and after fetal exposures has been found to change immune system development [35]. From the early 1970s, lindane had been identified as a direct-acting reproductive toxicant [36]. Peer reviewed research in 1979 reported lindane carcinogenicity in animals: including increased rates of ovarian cancer in rats. By 1985, the US EPA was citing lindane as a mouse oncogen – causing an increased incidence of liver tumours in males and females when dosed with levels between 80 ppm and 400 ppm – and a possible human carcinogen [37]. In 1988 US EPA data sheets noted that lindane had been shown to cause not only liver but also lung, endocrine and other types of cancer in animals [38].

By 1988, research suggested that lindane could 'affect female reproductive function by altering multiple processes [39]. Lindane has already been banned or restricted in Finland, Austria, Australia, the Netherlands, New Zealand, Indonesia and Cyprus. Thailand in the 1980s only permitted lindane use on livestock pests. In Japan lindane use as an insecticide was stopped in 1971 [40]. Now the European Union has restricted lindane usage, and all its agricultural uses will be phased out by 2002; the same chemical is under review in Canada and the US.

These dates of knowledge indicate the problems faced by regulators in interpreting limited, fragmented, contradictory or inconclusive data. Some countries decided, by bans and restrictions at an

Table 25.2 Dates of toxicological and epidemiological knowledge linking lindane and other factors with breast cancer

1938	Lacassagne showed oestrogen exposure induced breast cancer in mice.
1962	Oestrogens found to synergize the carcinogenic effects of polynuclear hydrocarbons in the breast.
1971	Oestrogens noted as synergizing the carcinogenic effects of radiation on the breast
1975	An Israeli study found that breast cancer mortality in Israel from 1984 onwards declined following various bans and tighter controls on organochlorine pesticides, including lindane in 1976.
1977	An NCI researcher noted that oestrogens as dietary contaminants in beef, pork, poultry and milk were a risk factor in breast cancer.
1979	Lindane carcinogenicity in animals was reported.
1985	Women working as professional chemists were reported to have a high incidence of breast cancer
1986	Exposure to agricultural pesticides known to cause breast cancer in rodents were linked by US government researchers to high human breast cancer incidence in Nassau and Norfolk counties
1993	Medical hypothesis about xeno-oestrogens as preventable causes of breast cancer [41,42,43,44,45,46] includes organochlorines, HCH, atrazine [47,48].

early date, that the potential risks presented by organochlorines justified a precautionary response to lindane because of possible links with breast cancer through direct or indirect mechanisms [49]. In the UK the HSE looked at the hazards presented to male forestry workers treating sapling roots with lindane. Yet no significant research work was commissioned on the potential health hazards to women from exposure to lindane in either an occupational or an environmental setting. Lincolnshire women working primarily in horticulture or agriculture where lindane was widely used on sugar beet crops found that no detailed occupational epidemiology studies have been conducted on women workers in the rural region, where relatively high rates of breast cancer exist for younger women, although rural areas are generally viewed as a lower risk factor for breast cancer [50].

Policy and action

> Employers have framed the problem of reproductive risk and other health hazards in a way that reinforces, and in fact deepens, the division of labor by sex, race and ethnicity. Susceptibility policies also widen the wage gap between men and women and between blacks and whites. Policies intended to be preventive medicine may actually penalize workers without protecting them at all [51].

Information, education and action are needed to address the occupational health and safety issues often created by poor or limited evidence about women's health hazards generally and about reproductive health hazards specifically. Female and male employees need both more and better information about workplace hazards; so do employers, regulators and politicians [52]. The United Kingdom Trades Union Congress and Danish trade unions, for instance, have begun to campaign on issues surrounding gender and health in the workplace [53]. More powers for trade unions on health and safety – to enable workers to stop work when faced with potentially serious reproductive hazards – would be of significant assistance. So, too, would a shifting of the burden of proof on gender and reproductive hazards from employees, consumers and communities – who currently have to demonstrate that substances are dangerous – to manufacturers of chemicals such as lindane, who should be able to demonstrate the safety of their products. To address reproductive health hazards, toxics use reduction strategies must be developed, and be linked to more comprehensive inventories of chemical use than exist at present. Policies must include the 'sunsetting', or phasing out, of carcinogens, teratogens, and other pesticides linked to chronic health effects [54,55,56].

Participatory research or community and worker epidemiology by women themselves on health hazards and effects should be an important policy strand [57]. Public health funding should support such initiatives. The prospect of litigation, too, has been raised against employers who fail to warn male employees about reproductive health hazards reported in the scientific literature, when warnings are often provided on the same subject to women, 'sometimes on the basis of limited and unverifiable data, establish[ing] a self-imposed duty of care that should logically extend to male workers' [58].

'Precautionary principle' strategies offer the best way to address some of the problems created by a 'gendered' response to pesticide hazards such as those illustrated in the dinoseb and lindane case studies. For 'the Precautionary Principle has a dual trigger: If there is a potential for harm from an activity and if there is uncertainty about the magnitude of impacts or causality, then anticipatory action should be taken to avoid harm' [59]. Instead of ignoring or downplaying pesticide risks to females or males, or trying to exclude females from work when males may also be at risk, the precautionary principle should lead us towards a healthier and safer workplace for both sexes and for the fetus. This type of approach has been used in Sweden and Denmark to some extent, with a toxic use reduction strategy for pesticides. This has meant cutting usage generally and removing the most potentially toxic pesticides altogether where data indicated problems or where there were data gaps.

References

1 Messing, K. *One-Eyed Science: Occupational Health and Women Workers*, Philadelphia: Temple University Press, 1998.

2 Chavkin, W. (ed.) *Double Exposure: Women's Health Hazards on the Job and at Home*, New York: Monthly Review Press, 1984.

3 Zielhuis, R.L., Stijkel, A., *et al. Health Risks to Female Workers in Occupational Exposure to Chemical Agents*, Berlin: Springer Verlag, 1984.

4 Paul, M. (ed.) *Occupational and Environmental Reproductive Hazards: A Guide for Clinicians*, Baltimore: Williams & Wilkins, 1993.

5 Bertin J.A., Werby, E.A. 'Legal and policy issues'. In Paul (ed.) *op. cit.*, 1993, pp. 150–62.

6 Draper, E. *Risky Business: Genetic Testing and Exclusionary Practices in the Hazardous Workplace*, Cambridge: Cambridge University Press, 1991.

7 Faustman, E.M., Silbernagle, S.M., *et al.* In *Environmental Health Perspectives*, 108 Suppl. 1, March 2000: 13–21.

8 Jasso, S., Mazorra, M. 'Following the harvest: the health hazards of migrant and seasonal farmworking women'. In Chavkin (ed.) *op. cit.*, 1984, pp. 86–99.

9 Jasso, Mazorra, *op. cit.*, 1998, p. 96.

10 LaDou, J. In *International Journal of Occupational Environmental Health*, 5(2), 1999: 151–3.

11 Health & Safety Executive (HSE). 'Food & Environmental Protection Act 1985: Addition to Consent 2 (Use) Report on Use of Dinoseb in Scotland on Glen Clova raspberries', HSE ChemAg IP/16. July 1987.

12 Ogilvy, G. 'Battle in raspberry field over herbicide', *Glasgow Herald*, 15 May 1987.

13 HSE, *op. cit.*, 1987.

14 Bertin, Werby, *op. cit.*, 1993.

15 Gibson, J.E. In *Food and Cosmetics Toxicology*, 11, 1973: 45–52.

16 Preache, M.M., Gibson, J.E. In *Teratology* 12, 1975: 147–56.

17 Beaudoin, A.R., Fisher, D.L. In *Teratology* 23(1), 1981: 57–61.

18 Linder, R.E., Scotti, T.M., Svensdsgaard, D.J., McElroy, W.K., Curley, A. In *Archives of Environmental Contamination and Toxicology* 11(4), 1982: 475–85.

19 *The Agrochemical Handbook*, London: Royal Society of Chemistry, A159, October 1983.

20 Sax, N.I. (ed.) *Dangerous Properties of Industrial Materials*, New York: Van Nostrand Reinhold, 1984.

21 Kavlock, R.J., Chernoff, N., Rogers, E.H. In *Teratogenicity Carcinogenicity Mutagenicity*, 5(1), 1985: 3–13.

22 'Dinoseb – immediate ban', *Pesticides Action Bulletin*, 4, 1987.

23 Agriculture Canada. 'CAPCO Note: Dinoseb Regulatory Position', Ottawa: Pesticide Directorate, 1990.

24 Linder, R.E., Strader, L.F., Slott, V.L., Suarez, J.D. In *Reproductive Toxicology*, 6(6), 1992: 491–505.

25 Davis, D.L., Bradlow, H.L., *et al.* In *Environmental Health Perspectives*, 101, 1993: 372–7.

26 Davis, D., Axelrod, D., *et al.* In *Environmental Health Perspectives*, 106, 1998: 523–9.

27 Woolf, M.S., Tomiolo, P.G., Lee, E.W., Rivera, M., Dubin, N. In *Journal of the National Cancer Institute*, 85, 1993: 648–52.

28 Moses, M. 'Pesticides and breast cancer', *Pesticides News* 22, 1993: 3–5.

29 Epstein, S. In *Internal Journal of Health Services*, 1994: 145–50.

30 Watterson A. 'Breast cancer and the links with environmental and occupational carcinogens: public health dilemmas and policies', De Montfort University, Leicester, 1995.

31 Watterson, *op. cit.*, 1995.

32 'Breast cancer and industrial exposures', *Hazards* 62, April–June 1998.

33 Colbourn, T., Myers, J.P., Dumanoski, D. *Our Stolen Future*, Boston: Little, Brown, 1996.

34 Schettler, T., Solomon, G., *et al. Generations at Risk: Reproductive Health and the Environment*, Cambridge, Mass.: MIT Press, 1999.

35 Schettler *et al.*, *op. cit.*, 1999, pp. 184–5.

36 Plowchalk, D., Meadows, J., Mattison, D.R., In Paul, *op. cit.*, 1993, pp. 18–24.

37 US EPA, 'Pesticide Fact Sheet: Lindane No 73', Washington, DC, 1985.

38 US EPA, 'Pesticide Fact Sheet, Lindane', Washington, DC, 1988.

39 Mattison, D.R., Bogumil, R.J., *et al.* In Baker, S.R., Wilkinson, C.F. (eds), *The Effects of Pesticides on Human Health, Advances in Modern Environmental Toxicology*, 18, 1990: 297–389.

40 Watterson, A.E., *The Pesticide Users Health and Safety Handbook: An International Guide*, Basingstoke: Gower Technical Press, 1988, p 262.

41 Reuber, M., In *Environmental Research*, 19, 1979: 460–81.

42 Davis, *op. cit.*, 1993.

43 Woolf *et al.*, *op. cit.*, 1993.

44 Epstein, *op. cit.*, 1994.

45 Watterson, *op. cit.*, 1995.

46 Cadbury, D. *The Feminization of Nature*, Harmondsworth: Penguin, 1997.

47 Davis *et al.*, *op. cit.*, 1998.

48 Schettler, *op. cit.*, 1999.

49 Davis *et al.*, *op. cit.*, 1998.

50 Watterson, *op. cit.*, 1995.

51 Draper, *op. cit.*, 1991.

52 Women's Environment Network, *Mapping the Risks*, London, 1998.

53 Kenen, R.H. with McLeish, J., May, D., *Pregnancy at Work: Health and Safety for Working Women*, London: Pluto Press, 1998.

54 Colbourn, *op. cit.*, 1996.

55 Watterson, *op. cit.*, 1995.

56 Watterson, A.E. In *Journal of Institution of Occupational Safety and Health*, 1, 1997: 31–40.

57 Watterson A. In *Journal of Public Health Medicine*, 16, 1994: 270–74.

58 Bertin, Werby, *op. cit.*, 1993.

59 Raffensberger, C., Tickner, J. (eds) *Protecting the Public Health and the Environment: Implementing the Precautionary Principle*, Washington DC: Island Press, 1999.

26

Double jeopardy:
chemicals in the home and workplace

David Watt

The presence of potential chemical hazards inside buildings is an increasing concern as changing lifestyles dictate a greater time spent inside the home or workplace. In the USA, it is estimated that most Americans spend 90 per cent or more of their day indoors, 'often in tightly constructed buildings with poor air quality' [1]. In the UK, 70 per cent of indoor time is inside the home [2].

Of the many types of indoor air pollutants, the use of chemical treatments, including pesticides, has attracted particular attention. Surveys in the USA have shown that 75 per cent of households used at least one pesticide product indoors during the period of one year, and that measurable levels of up to a dozen pesticides have been found in the air inside homes [3].

In a survey undertaken between 1995 and 1997, 6 per cent of adults in California and 2 per cent of adults in New Mexico indicated that they had been diagnosed with multiple chemical sensitivity (MCS) or 'environmental illness', whereas 16 per cent in both states indicated that they were 'unusually sensitive to everyday chemicals' [4].

As more becomes known about human health and sensitivity to chemical exposures, information from the medical and legal professions indicates the effects that chemical treatments and treatment residues might have on buildings and their occupants [5,6,7,8,9,10,11,12,13]. This is matched by scientific research linking exposure to symptoms [14,15,16,17,18,19,20]. It has been suggested that 20–25 per cent of treated properties receive multiple treatments, and that many treatments are unnecessary [21]. The need for greater comprehension of chemical exposure and chemical sensitivity is clear. This includes research to develop a deeper understanding of the causes and symptoms of MCS, to consider the chronic long-term effects of low doses of chemicals, and to improve the diagnostic and classification procedures applied by the medical and health care professions [22].

Chemical exposure

For exposure to be proven, an identified hazard (pesticidal ingredient), exposure pathway (inhalation of dust, ingestion, absorption through skin contact), and target or receptor (building occupant or user) have to be present, but the degree of risk will depend on various factors, including extent of the hazard, ease of migration, and susceptibility of the target.

In the case of pesticidal treatments as potential contaminants of indoor air, only limited research has been conducted, and there is a lack of data on concentration levels following timber treatment [23]. Adequate evaluations of occupant exposure and health risk are therefore unavailable. The nature and extent of preparation and protection to buildings and their occupants prior to treatment to limit or reduce exposure pathways have been documented [24], although little practical attention has been paid to those to whom exposure to chemical treatments or their residues might cause serious harm.

In considering the risk of exposure, residential use is particularly hazardous as occupancy times are greater than for commercial premises and residents may include children and old and infirm persons. Special precautions – including specialist advice from a medical practitioner before work commences – should be taken in the case of people with respiratory problems, or for the very old or very young. Supervisors are required to check whether other occupants of the building to be treated or those in nearby properties suffer from respiratory conditions or allergies that might be triggered as a result of the remedial work. If, despite all safeguards, a potential health risk remains and evacuation is impossible, the supervisor is required to seek non-pesticidal alternatives.

In spite of such concerns for occupants' health and safety, cases of exposure, both during and after chemical treatment, typically result from a lack of adequate preparation and protection and a disregard of relevant and widely available guidance documentation.

In the context of developing countries, evidence for chemical exposure relates typically to agricultural pesticides and obsolete pesticide stocks. Despite a paucity of specific data relating to chemical treatments in the home and workplace, it is essential to consider implications of exposure, particularly for children, in developing regulatory and advisory procedures, managing the potentially greater risks associated with widespread spraying (control of termites, cockroaches and other insect pests), and improving diagnosis of exposure symptoms [25]. It is necessary to be aware of the implications of health costs associated with treating affected persons and their reduced capacity for work.

Chemical sensitivity and gender

A review of scientific literature on MCS (symptoms in more than one organ system elicited by various unrelated chemicals at very low levels of exposure), commissioned by the UK Health and Safety Executive (HSE) to consider the clinical response of certain individuals to very low doses of chemicals, concluded that, 'there is evidence to suggest that in some people exposure to chemicals can initiate a clinical response to subsequent exposures to very low doses of that chemical and structurally unrelated chemicals' [26].

The health of children (0 to 18 years) has been shown to be at greater risk from exposure to certain chemicals and environmental pollutants [27,28]. The vulnerability relates to immature biological development, behaviour, metabolism, greater exposure relative to body weight, and longer life at risk, and has prompted action to reduce children's exposure by the wider application of the precautionary principle whenever risks are likely to be serious and irreversible. In relation to gender, limited epidemiological evidence on wood preservatives suggests 'that females may be more susceptible to adverse reproductive effects than males' [29]. Clinical evidence would suggest that females are at greater risk than males:

- Referrals to the Biolab Medical Unit (London) for pesticide screening are close to 50 per cent female and 50 per cent male. Medical histories, however, suggest that the more significant clinical effects and longer-term problems are female dominant.
- Biochemical investigations exploring the detoxification pathways demonstrate significantly higher levels of abnormality in females, even when the exposure has been the same or less than that of a male partner. Chemical sensitivities related to, or apparently resulting from, pesticide exposure occur in the ratio of about 75 females to 25 males.

- Reasons for the gender difference in effects, as opposed to exposure levels, probably include the increased fat cell availability and mobilization and the increased proportion of hormonally sensitive tissue in females. Remember that most pesticides are fat soluble and many have been shown to be oestrogenic [30].

In addition to chemical sensitivities, recent research has indicated that the prevalence of occupational asthma in women and in specific occupations (cleaners) has been underestimated [31]. Women working in the home have been found to have a small but significant excess risk of developing asthma, or asthma is exacerbated as a result of exposure to certain irritant substances (cleaning materials, detergents and indoor allergens or air pollutants). For those sensitized to the house dust mite allergen, triggering of asthmatic symptoms may also occur as a result of exposure to such irritant substances, although solvent-related triggering is considered unlikely unless exposure is continuous (at petrol-filling stations and in some industrial works) [32].

Apart from chemical sensitivity, certain commonly reported symptoms (lethargy, loss of concentration, headaches, and eye and nose irritation) may be experienced at work and relate to cases of sick building syndrome (SBS). Such symptoms generally disappear or decline away from work, are more prevalent in clerical staff, occur more in public buildings, are most common in office buildings with air conditioning, and affect people with little individual control over their environment [33].

Although SBS is a concern of international proportions, it is important to be aware that there are differences between the countries in which research has been undertaken. Chemically sensitive subgroups were not found in SBS research in Scandinavian countries [34], but findings in European studies suggest the importance of factors such as the use of wall-to-wall carpeting (common in the USA and relatively infrequent in continental Europe), or the use of certain fragrances, air fresheners, cleaners, and/or extermination practices.

Managing the hazards and risks

Chemical treatments and treatment residues

Within an indoor environment, chemical treatments divide into those that disperse directly in the air and those that are absorbed by surfaces and that might subsequently be released into the air [35].

Chemical residues could exist as reservoirs within the structure and fabric of treated buildings when concentrations have not been reduced by sinks (evaporation, ventilation). Residential pesticide monitoring studies in the USA have demonstrated that measurable, though relatively low-level, residues exist in treated buildings, and that indoor exposures are often higher than outdoor exposures [36,37]. Increases in levels of indoor air pollution and corresponding risks of exposure have been noted as being of greater significance than risks associated with outdoor pollutants [38].

Exposure to the active ingredients and/or solvent carriers of chemical treatments, and the effects that such exposure might have on the health of an individual or group, depend on various factors. It is possible to identify factors that might influence the behaviour of chemical residues in buildings and the effects on occupants [39,40]. Clinical evaluation has shown that acute systemic effects and local reactions may result from pesticide exposure and poisonings [41] while solvents may cause serious long-term neurological damage [42, 43,44]. The possible synergistic effects of active ingredients and carrier solvents need to be considered. A recent UK study identified issues relating to medical information and data sources, reporting and notification procedures, and the need for GP-based surveillance of pesticide-related illness and the determination of a causal link between chronic ill-health and pesticide exposure [45].

Dealing with chemical treatments and treatment residues

Professionals dealing with the built environment must consider health and comfort. Poor working conditions have a significant effect on efficiency and productivity, whilst increases in asthma and respiratory diseases have been linked to building defects and deficiencies. These problems require a combination of actions based on careful planning and implementation and a fundamental shift in current thinking and practice [46,47]. Such an approach might include:

- removing the source of pollution (avoiding chemical treatments);
- avoiding particular pollutants (using alternative products or treatments);
- isolating the source(s) of contamination or pollution (containment, encapsulation, shielding, sealing);
- designing to avoid problems (effective ventilation, improved maintenance);

- removing existing contamination or reservoirs of pollutants (decontamination, regular cleaning of furnishings);
- assessing and monitoring conditions (regular inspections, surveys).

The long-term accommodation design requirements for those suffering from MCS have been considered to a limited extent [48,49], including issues relating to building ecology and sustainable development [50,51]. A growing number of companies offer ecological building materials and products, typically involving low-solvent and solvent-free paints and finishes, natural flooring and insulation materials, and natural timber preservative and treatment products [52].

Containment and decontamination

The containment of chemical treatment residues within treated building fabric may offer a solution to potential problems of long- and short-term emissions of pesticidal ingredients. Use of appropriate paint films, plasters and other coverings, together with improved ventilation (such as the use of mechanical ventilation with heat recovery), may reduce the risk of exposure to acceptable levels. The use of coatings on timbers treated with chlorinated pesticides has been shown to trap gaseous emissions, while retaining the chemicals within the fabric, so prolonging their active life [53]. Emissions may be reduced by up to 74 per cent, even after accelerated ageing equivalent to 18 months [54]. Little information is available on decontamination of treated buildings or building fabric, and is typically restricted to reports of individual cases [55] and work carried out in the USA and Germany [56]. Tests on decontamination of museum objects and treated timbers are yet to be fully published [57,58] although successful alternative treatments for insect pest infestations in museum artefacts, collections and buildings have been reported [59,60].

Non-chemical treatments

Advances in the development and application of alternative treatments for fungal and insect decay in buildings are typically based on research for historic building conservation. There is a fundamental difference between the treatment of fungal and insect decay in domestic and conservation markets, dictated by expectations [61]. The former requires guarantees for no-risk solutions. The latter demands treatment that does not damage or change the appearance of the historic fabric, and relies on primary measures (eliminating sources of moisture and promoting drying of building fabric), monitoring and targeted treatments, and a greater acceptance of risk. The 'quick fix' treatment will no doubt persist until such time as the conservation approach, with its element of risk, is more widely understood and adopted.

Greater regard for holistic approaches to building maintenance and management, particularly for historic buildings and monuments, has led to a growing interest in benign and environmentally friendly methods of managing decay. This has been prevalent in the management of timber decay [62,63,64,65]. Recent developments in the application of environmental (management and monitoring of moisture, humidity, temperature and ventilation) and natural (insect parasitism and predation) control techniques seem to offer viable options for avoiding chemical treatment [66,67]. These practices, and adoption of integrated pest management, are currently restricted to the conservation of historic buildings.

It is increasingly recognized that regular and appropriate levels of repair and maintenance of buildings can reduce dampness and prevent the conditions necessary for fungal and insect decay. A wider holistic approach to building management, both at home and in the workplace, can ensure that such buildings are safer and less likely to cause illness in the future [68,69].

Conclusions and recommendations

It is essential to increase awareness, within the built environment and associated professions, of potential problems of chemical treatments in the home and workplace. This should include a greater understanding of the implications of using chemical treatments against fungal infections and insect infestations in buildings, the potential associated health risks, and the availability of alternative non-chemical treatments.

In particular, there is a fundamental need for those who regulate, specify and implement such work to be aware of these issues, and be prepared to consider alternative approaches on a case-by-case basis. Every effort should be made to adopt a precautionary approach.

To be made habitable for MCS sufferers, buildings already chemically treated for fungal or insect decay need viable practical solutions to contain chemical residues and decontaminate the fabric, fixtures, fittings and personal belongings.

The causes and symptoms of chemical sensitivity and chronic long-term effects of low doses of exposure to pesticides and other chemicals need to be better understood. The diagnostic and classification procedures applied by the medical profession need improvement. Lack of reliable information relating to pesticide exposure and MCS needs to be addressed before appropriate action can be taken to reduce risks from chemical treatments and residues in the home and workplace. Until then, a precautionary approach should be adopted by those responsible for specifying or implementing treatments.

Underpinning all strategies, there must be improved gender-sensitive consideration and reporting of chemical treatment issues in the home and workplace.

References

1 Duehring, C. In *Our Toxic Times*, 7(4), May 1997: 13–15.
2 Donaldson, R., Donaldson, L. *Essential Public Health Medicine*, London: Kluwer Academic, 1993.
3 *The Inside Story: A Guide to Indoor Air Quality*, Washington: EPA/US Consumer Product Safety Commission, 1998.
4 'Multiple chemical sensitivity: a 1999 consensus', *Archives of Environmental Health*, 54(3), 1999: 147–9.
5 Lawson, R. In *General Practitioner*, May 1989: 71.
6 Curwell, S., Marsh, C., Venables, R. *Buildings and Health: The Rosehaugh Guide*, London: RIBA, 1990.
7 Nemeskeri, R., Clare, R., Macor, J. *A Conceptual Facility for Environmentally Sensitive People: Recommendation and Guidelines*, Calgary: University of Calgary Press, 1991.
8 Care, A. 'Compensation for chemical and pesticide victims: the way forward', *Butterworth's Personal Injury Litigation Service*, March 1994: 21.
9 Care, A. In *Occupational Health*, November 1995: 390–91.
10 *Breakspear Guide to Chemical Sensitivity*, Hemel Hempstead: Breakspear Hospital, 1993.
11 Care, A., Day, M. In *Occupational Health*, March 1995: 97–8.
12 Driver, J., Whitmyre, G. In *Pesticide Outlook*, August 1996: 6–10.
13 Hargreaves, P. In *Environmental Liability*, 5(3), 1997: 59–66.
14 Jorens, P., Schepens, P. In *Human and Experimental Toxicology*, 12, 1993: 479–95.
15 Ashford, N., Miller, C. In *International Archives of Occupational and Environmental Health*, 68, 1996: 367–76.
16 Meißner, T., Schweinsberg, F. In *Toxicology Letters*, 88, 1996: 237–42.
17 Baker, H. In *New Scientist*, 154(2087), 21 June 1997: 30–35.
18 O'Malley, M. In *Lancet*, 349(9059), 19 April 1997: 1161–6.
19 White, R., Proctor, S. In *Lancet*, 349(9060), 26 April 1997: 1239–43.
20 Tielemans, E., *et al*. In *Lancet*, 353(9177), 7 August 1999: 454–8.

21 Oxley, R. *Is Timber Treatment Always Necessary? An Introduction for Homeowners*, SPAB Information Sheet 14, London: SPAB, 1999.
22 Graveling, R., Pilkington, A., *et al*. In *Occupational and Environmental Medicine*, 56, 1999: 73–85.
23 Spalding, D. 'Characterisation of treated timber sources of pesticide contaminants using source modelling techniques, unpublished PhD thesis, De Montfort University, Leicester, 1999.
24 *Remedial Timber Treatment in Buildings*, London: HSE/DoE/HMSO, 1991.
25 Dinham, B. pers. comm., London: PAN UK, 2 March 2000.
26 Graveling *et al*., *op. cit*., 1999.
27 Gee, D. *Children in Their Environment: Vulnerable, Valuable and at Risk*, draft report for third ministerial conference 'Environment and Health', London, 16–18 June 1999, WHO Regional Office for Europe/European Environment Agency.
28 Howard, V. 'New findings about chemicals in the home and their effects on the foetus and child', *PEX Newsletter*, September 1999.
29 Arbuckle, T.E., Sever, L.E. In *Critical Review in Toxicology*, 28(3), 1998: 229–70.
30 McLaren Howard, J., Biolab Medical Unit, London, pers. comm., 10 November 1999.
31 Kogevinas, M., Antó, J., *et al*. In *Lancet*, 353(9166), 22 May 1999: 1750–54.
32 Maunder, J. pers. comm, Cambridge: Medical Entomology Centre, 10 November 1999.
33 Rostron, J. In Rostron, J. (ed.) *Sick Building Syndrome: Concepts, Issues and Practice*, London: E&FN Spon, 1997, pp. 151–66.
34 Ashford, N., Miller, C. *Chemical Exposures: Low Levels and High Stakes*, New York: Van Nostrand Reinhold, 1998.
35 Driver, J., Whitmyre, G. In *Pesticide Outlook*, August 1996: 6–10.
36 Fenske, R., Black, K., *et al*. In *American Journal of Public Health*, 80, 1990: 689–93.
37 Whitmore, R., Immerman, F., *et al*., In *Archives of Environmental Contamination and Toxicology*, 26, 1994: 47–59.
38 Wallace, L. In *Risk Analysis*, 13, 1993: 135–9.
39 Watt, D. In *Journal of Nutritional & Environmental Medicine*, 2000.
40 Singh, J. In *Construction Repair*, 40–42, May/June 1996.
41 White, R., Proctor, S. In *The Lancet*, 349(9060), 26 April 1997: 1239–43.
42 Hilditch, E. In Singh, J. (ed.) *Building Mycology: Management of Decay and Health in Buildings*, London: E&FN Spon, 1994, pp. 212–38.
43 Laurance, J. 'Solvents can cause damage to nerves', *The Independent*, 25 April 1997.
44 White, R. *op. cit*., 1997.
45 *Monitoring by Government Departments of the Ill-Health Effects of Pesticide Exposure: A Review of Existing Arrangements*, London: HSE, February 1999.
46 Singh, J. In *Indoor Built Environment*, 5, 1996: 22–33.

47 Shaw, C., *et al*. In *Building and Environment*, 34(1), January 1999: 57–69.
48 Nemeskeri *et al.*, *op. cit.*, 1999.
49 Crowther, D. 'Health considerations in house design', unpublished report, University of Cambridge, 1991.
50 Vale, B., Vale, R. *Green Architecture: Design for a Sustainable Future*, London: Thames & Hudson, 1991.
51 Anink, D., Boonstra, C., Mak, J. *Handbook of Sustainable Building: An Environmental Preference Model for Selection of Materials for Use in Construction and Refurbishment*, London: James & James, 1998.
52 *Boron Salt*, Holzweg Technical Sheet H20 and *Timber Treatment Fluid*, Holzweg Technical Sheet H33, London: Construction Resources, 1999.
53 Huddersman, K. In *Building and Civil Engineering Research Focus*, 23, October 1995: 7.
54 Huddersman, K. *Novel Coatings to Reduce Gaseous Emissions of Chemically Treated Timbers*, Department of Chemistry, De Montfort University, Leicester, 1997.
55 *Toxic Treatments: Wood Preservative Hazards at Work and in the Home*, London: London Hazards Centre, 1988.
56 Howell, J. In *Building Engineer*, 70(4), May 1995: 14–16.
57 von Rotberg, W., Gagelmann, M., *et al*. *First Results of a Pilot Decontamination in a PCP Polluted Building by Means of a Humidity Controlled Thermal Process*, abridged translation from German, Heidelberg, Germany: Thermo Lignum, 1997.
58 Roux, K. Thermo Lignum (UK) Limited, pers. comm., 24 January 2000.
59 Pinniger, D. In *Conservation News*, March 1996: 59.
60 Nicholson, M., von Rotberg, W. In *Proceedings of the 2nd International Conference on Insect Pests in the Urban Environment*, Heriot-Watt University, 7–10 July 1996, pp. 263–5.
61 Coleman, G. *Chemical Control, Treating Dry Rot in Historic Buildings*, English Heritage conference, London, 24 November 1999.
62 Ashurst, J., Ashurst, N. *Practical Building Conservation – Volume 5: Wood, Glass and Resin*, Aldershot: Gower Technical Press, 1988.
63 Weaver, M. *Conserving Buildings: A Guide to Techniques and Materials*, New York: John Wiley, 1993.
64 Lloyd, H., Singh, J. In Singh, J. (ed.) *Building Mycology: Management of Decay and Health in Buildings*, London: E&FN Spon, 1994, 159–86.
65 Pain, S. 'Knock knock, who's there?', *New Scientist*, 156(2113/2114), 20/27 December 1997: 52–4.
66 Ridout, B. *Timber Decay in Buildings: The Conservation Approach to Treatment*, London: E&FN Spon, 2000.
67 Singh, J. In *Journal of Architectural Conservation*, 6(1), March 2000: 17–37.
68 Watt, D. *Building Pathology: Principles and Practice*, Oxford: Blackwell Science, 1999.
69 Watt, D., Colston, B., Spalding, D. *Assessing the Impact of Chemical Treatments on the Health of Buildings and their Occupants*, RICS Research Paper Series, 3(13), London: RICS Foundation, 2000.

Part IV

Taking action

27

Introduction to Part IV

Barbara Dinham

The previous sections have given insight into many of the problems associated with the use of chemical pesticides, particularly in developing countries, but also in industrialized parts of the world – and in both rural and urban areas. Acute pesticide poisoning symptoms can be identified, but under many conditions are unavoidable. The chronic effects resulting from long-term pesticide exposure, or background levels in the environment, are more intractable, and Part II covers the scientific efforts to increase understanding of the different ways women and men may be affected physically. Part III looks at the gap between regulation and reality, the seeming difficulty of developing policies to reduce pesticide use, risk and dependence in the absence of scientific certainty, and a general lack of awareness at the differential impacts on women and men, and of the different routes of exposure. This final section looks at the achievements and strategies for change.

Although pesticides are used in urban settings and for public health purposes, the major use remains in agriculture. Industrial agriculture – with the use of synthetic pesticides, inorganic fertilizers, and, increasingly, genetically engineered crops – remains the dominant model for production of food and fibre [1], and this has critical implications for health, environment and development strategies. Of the total planet's land surface, about 25 per cent is suitable for crop cultivation, around half of which is already in use, and around 30 per cent of which is in developing countries. In the light of pervasive use of pesticides, and the actual and potential adverse impacts, greater priority must be given to high standards and to reduction strategies in both industrial and developing countries.

Governments have recently taken two major initiatives to address some of the most hazardous pesticides. The 1998 Rotterdam Convention on Prior Informed Consent (PIC) acts as an early warning system to share information globally about bans and severe restrictions on pesticides taken by a government, and helps developing countries identify pesticides causing particular problems because of the conditions of use. PIC can be used to prevent the import of unwanted pesticides when they are included in the Convention. The second initiative, the Stockholm Convention on Persistent Organic Pollutants (POPs) of 2000, aims to eliminate the production and use of twelve chemicals, including nine pesticides (see Annex 1 for a list of PIC, POPs and other problem pesticides).

Globally about 800 pesticide active ingredients remain in use in tens of thousands of combinations. The long-term effects of most of these chemicals are unknown, and may only emerge after decades of use – as with the case of endocrine disrupting chemicals. Taking action on a chemical-by-chemical basis is a slow and inadequate response, and more proactive measures need to be introduced, particularly in developing countries. The FAO *International Code of Conduct on the Distribution and Use of Pesticides* was revised in 2001, taking account of fifteen years of experience to introduce more stringent standards. At national levels, governments rely on pesticide registration systems for regulating pesticides, but regulation is a limited response and does not address the different ways women and men are exposed to or affected by pesticides. Registration systems are essential, but cannot be the only means of regulating and reducing pesticide dependence.

Two strategic routes for action are open to reduce pesticide hazards. The first involves campaigns and approaches that eliminate the most hazardous pesticides, and introduce more stringent controls to reduce pesticide use, risk and dependence. The second promotes sustainable alternatives to control pests and increase yields in agriculture – or to manage domestic and public health pests.

Research, studies, documentation and actions underpinning these approaches need to address differential impacts of pesticides on health and physical development, cultural and social systems, and on local and household economies. Research and action need to recognize and respond to the ways that women and men, girls and boys, are affected by dependence on and exposure to pesticide use.

Sarojeni Rengam, Director of PAN Asia and the Pacific Regional Centre, explains the importance of the region's community-based

Women and Pesticides programme, which helps women to monitor their health, and document the real impact of pesticides on their lives and livelihoods. The 'feminization of agriculture' means women are increasingly important in the sector, in spite of owning only 2 per cent of all agricultural land. Women in agriculture play a major, but largely unrecognized, role in food production, and have responsibility for ensuring food is on the table. With responsibility for childcare and household tasks, women's workload is twice that of men. PAN Asia and the Pacific has found that women's occupational health issues have been ignored or downplayed by scientists and legislators, and points out the urgency of increasing the research on women's health, and is working with grassroots organizations to build social movements, campaigning for rural people's rights.

On another continent, Jill Day points out the effectiveness of a campaign to ban a single pesticide active ingredient. Rural women concerned about the long-term health impacts of lindane – particularly a possible link with breast cancer – in a heavily sprayed part of the UK launched a campaign through their trade union, and joined forces with women's and environmental organizations. Topsy Jewel shows how women have launched a local food market to encourage local organic production.

The campaigns to reduce pesticide use may inevitably clash with those who see no alternative to the present industrial agriculture, and with the US$30 billion pesticide industry. Campaigns need to monitor developments in the industry. But there is a limit to the extent and impact of action campaigns, and governments need to play a bigger role in reviewing, evaluating and screening chemicals, and develop ways to operate the precautionary principle for pesticides. In Sweden, for example, the government carries out comparative risk assessments and registers the least risky products as part of a far-reaching pesticide reduction programme.

PAN groups have established a 'Day of No Pesticide Use' and seek recognition of this day by governments and UN agencies to draw attention to public concern about pesticides. The annual day is observed on 3 December, to commemorate the tens of thousands of victims of the leak from the Union Carbide pesticide plant in Bhopal. Satinath Sarangi's chapter provides information on the legacy of the worst industrial accident in history, and on a remarkable community local health and documentation clinic. Workers at the clinic are horrified by the impacts on all sufferers, but particularly on women's reproductive systems. Women are also affected through their responsibility for running the household and as carers, and have largely led the ongoing struggle, refusing to give up on their rights despite having been let down by the government, the legal system and the medical profession.

Too often government policies and the free market promote seeds, fertilizers and pesticides as the only agricultural development strategy. Many farmers, researchers, scientists, communities, NGOs and ordinary women and men believe that the extent of dependence on pesticides is unnecessary. Sustainable strategies are viable and can maintain or increase yields, and help lay the foundation for more sustainable and equitable agricultural systems. Great strides have been made in developing community-based integrated pest management (IPM), organic or other agro-ecological strategies to pest management.

Adrienne Martin and Kerry Albright, on behalf of the UK's Department for International Development, show the role that development agencies and donor organizations can and should take in supporting knowledge-based, sustainable and ecological agricultural strategies in developing countries. In the past, many development projects have made assumptions about decision-making and cultural roles that have undermined women's economic position, or excluded women. Among the most exciting developments have been the Farmer Field School (FFS) and Community IPM activities that have helped to establish farmer-led village IPM programmes across rice production in Asia. The paper from John Pontius and Alifah Sri Lestari of the FAO team in the region discusses how to ensure women benefit fully from the training programmes, and explain the success in reaching women in the region.

The chapters in this section, and throughout the volume, help to establish a basis for moving towards gender-sensitive, equitable and sustainable agricultural systems that pay equal homage to the efforts of women and men producers, and take account of the health, environmental and economic benefits of promoting sustainable strategies for agriculture.

Reference

1 FAO, *Agriculture: Towards 2015/2030*, FAO Report, 2000.

28

Breaking the silence:
women struggle for pesticide elimination

Sarogeni Rengam

The health and environmental problems of pesticides are well documented. It is estimated that 25 million workers suffer pesticide poisoning annually [1]. Farmers and agricultural workers are exposed to pesticides directly when they are mixing and spraying these pesticides. Communities and consumers are insidiously exposed to pesticides through contamination of the soil, air and water.

The chronic effects of pesticides are particularly alarming: new studies indicate certain pesticides and industrial chemicals in the environment mimic natural hormones, possibly causing a wide variety of adverse effects – not only on specific body organs and systems but also on the endocrine system, including reduction in male sperm count and undescended testes, as well as breast cancer [2,3]. Overall, the scientific literature shows a drop in sperm quality and quantity [4]. Other studies have shown that women with relatively high levels of oestrogen-imitators in their blood are far more likely to get breast cancer than women with relatively low levels [5]. Some of these suspect chemicals include pesticides such as alachlor, malathion, maneb, methomyl, heptachlor, benomyl, DDT and endosulfan, most of which are organochlorines. Another report indicates 'substantial grounds for concern about the public health risks from pesticide induced suppression of the immune system' [6].

Today the pressure to increase agricultural production and thus exports has led to a high-yielding, monocultural production that has often meant increasing use of pesticides without addressing their health and environmental effects. Even today we are faced with the challenge of achieving wider acceptance that food security is about access, not about production. Meanwhile, however, the pesticide industry continues to promote the view that increasing production can eliminate hunger and continues to market pesticides aggressively in the South. This is not surprising when there are profits to be made, regardless of health and environmental concerns. Six transnational corporations control 80 per cent of the global agrochemical market, a US$30 billion a year industry.

As their use increased, the problems of pesticides mounted, including the adverse health and environmental impacts. Pesticides are poisons and they kill off natural enemies and beneficial insects, thus causing the emergence of secondary pests. For example, the use of pesticides in the rice ecosystem killed off the natural enemies of a pest, the brown plant hopper, which emerged as a major problem. Brown plant hopper outbreaks in Asia decimated a large hectarage of rice fields, creating a crisis in rice production in the 1980s. Only with the introduction of, and training in, integrated pest management (IPM) – which emphasized participatory farmer training, now known as Farmer Field Schools, and pesticide reduction in rice – was the problem of the brown plant hopper kept in check.

Such recurring pest outbreaks caused by pesticide-induced resurgence have resulted in other serious crop losses. Examples include the early use of wide-spectrum insecticides in the Malaysian oil palm and cocoa plantations [7].

Resistance to pesticides is also increasing. Today, more than 504 species of insects and mites are conservatively estimated to have developed insecticide resistance. Over half of these resistant pests are agriculturally important and only 3 per cent are beneficial predators, parasites and pollinators. Most of these species exhibit resistance to more than one group of chemicals [8].

Women are exposed

Women farmers and workers are frequently exposed to dangerous pesticides directly when working as pesticide applicators, or indirectly during harvesting, planting and soil preparation. However, information about women's exposure to pesticides is often unavailable or is a non-issue in many research and formal institutions.

In response to the high incidence of pesticide misuse and dangerous pesticide practices that have direct, adverse effects on women in agriculture and on plantations in Asia, and due to the lack of information, PAN Asia and the Pacific (PAN AP) embarked on a Women and Pesticides Programme in 1991. Since its inception, the programme has been providing information, training and resources to women about the dangers of and alternatives to pesticides. The programme involves national training workshops, case studies on the impact of pesticides on women, and a wide distribution of informational materials in several local Asian languages on the hazards of pesticides and the alternatives.

Strategies for action

Community-based pesticide monitoring

In the years 1991–95, more than 2,500 farmers and agricultural workers, mostly women, were interviewed to look at the impact of pesticides on women. The studies undertaken by network partners in Indonesia, Malaysia, Korea, Sri Lanka, Pakistan, the Philippines and India revealed the extent of the problem, and the invisibility and marginalization of women's problems with pesticide use. While interviews with farmers formed the primary research, analysis of published papers and statistics was also included. The studies will hopefully prompt more studies, specifically epidemiological ones, to show the direct correlation of pesticide use and poisonings, and the adverse impact on women. These studies are a powerful tool for awareness building and training among farmers as well as garnering support for alternatives – in particular the move towards sustainable agriculture. In general, the results of these case studies (see Box 28.1) show that

- Most women farmers and workers spray pesticides or come into direct contact with pesticides in their work. In Malaysia, all the plantation workers interviewed were pesticide sprayers.
- Most pesticide users are unaware of the adverse effects of pesticide use. In many cases, pesticide applicators cannot read labels or do not follow instructions.
- Most users do not use protective clothing because it is unsuitable for the climate, unavailable or too expensive. Korea was the exception, where 53 per cent of the farmers surveyed said that they used protective clothing.
- Farmers and agricultural workers in the region use highly toxic pesticides including methyl parathion, monocrotophos, as well as phorate and phosphamidon (in India) – all of which are listed as WHO Class 1 (extremely hazardous).
- Most of those surveyed stated that they have been poisoned and cited acute effects such as dizziness, muscular pain, sneezing,

itching, skin burns, blisters, difficulty breathing, nausea, nails changing colour and sore eyes.

• Women spray pesticides while they are pregnant, even in early pregnancy, and while breastfeeding. This may endanger the unborn fetus as well as their young children.

To follow up this programme, PAN AP has produced a community-based pesticide monitoring kit, called the Community Pesticide Action Kit (C-PAK). The Women and Pesticide project indicates that community participation in pesticides monitoring is a tremendous asset – and a matter of social justice.

PAN AP has worked with partners in three countries in Asia (Indonesia, Malaysia and the Philippines) to develop C-PAK. Modules have been field-tested. The kit will be published in English and three regional languages (Indonesian, Visayan and Tamil). C-PAK is designed to guide community groups in investigating problems caused by pesticides in their communities and to assist them in recording information in a systematic and reliable way.

The aim of the kits is to make people realize the potential impacts of pesticides use. They provide a guide to what data should be collected to document impacts in a systematic way. The actual design of the monitoring programmes will need to evolve as they are implemented and are likely to vary in each country.

Box 28.1   Case study: Malaysia

'I have been spraying pesticides for the last twenty years. I spray paraquat all the time. It is so strong that the odour makes me sick most of the time. In the beginning, I used to cry (tearing in my eyes from the strong fumes). Now my only main problem is nosebleed and chest pain. I also have a bad stomach pain.' Woman plantation worker in Malaysia [9].

An estimated 30,000 women workers spray pesticides almost daily in the plantations in Malaysia. These women suffer poor health, have no alternate skills, often are the breadwinners and are in terror of losing their meagre incomes and their homes in the plantations. They are constantly exposed to pesticides such as paraquat, methamidophos, monocrotophos and carbofuran (most classified as highly hazardous under Malaysian law).

Annually in Malaysia, about RM 293 million is spent on pesticides: 78 per cent on herbicides, 14 per cent on insecticides and 4 per cent on fungicides. Some 60 per cent of the herbicide use is in the rubber and oil palm plantations, and 10 per cent in cocoa plantations. With such amounts of pesticides used, the problems have mounted, including adverse health and environmental impacts.

In Malaysia, fifty women plantation workers who spray pesticides participated in in-depth interviews between January and June 1991 by Tenaganita, a local women's organization. All reported suffering skin rash due to the use of paraquat. About half the women said they suffered sore, red eyes and 60 per cent said that they had discoloured, irregular nails. The survey revealed that there are no washing facilities in the field where workers spray pesticides, and no access to washing facilities even when pesticides spill onto their skin. After four hours of spraying the women were only able to wash when they returned home. None had received training on how to properly mix and spray pesticides. The survey results were published in *Victims Without Voice* [10], which also reports on the struggles of Malaysian women plantation workers for better working conditions.

Following the survey, Tenaganita embarked on a programme to monitor the health of the women workers. The first C-PAK module for monitoring pesticide use in plantations was produced, and participation in community monitoring of pesticide hazards began. A second survey was initiated, and regular meetings and workshops provided training and information to the workers on the health impacts of pesticides. The survey and training were supplemented by sampling for blood cholinesterase levels. A university involved in the monitoring compiled the results and performed the blood analysis using a calorimetric procedure based on the Eliman reaction. Subjects who showed severe cholinesterase depression were given follow-up examinations. Some samples were tested for paraquat exposure.

The survey is being undertaken in plantations in three areas of peninsular Malaysia, with a hundred women pesticide sprayers taking part. In a few cases, women were found to spray while pregnant. Preliminary results showed that the women had significant depression in their levels of cholinesterase. This level returned to normal in women who stopped spraying. Further medical checkup showed some workers suffering from severe skin itching; two suffered prolapsed wombs; one had cervical cancer. Results are shared with the sprayers. The sprayers are now participating in a longer-term self-monitoring of health symptoms where they are asked to record each day what pesticide they spray and to indicate if they experience any of a set of symptoms. The preliminary sharing shows that there is correlation between the type of pesticides used and the workers' symptoms being recorded.

Training and strategy workshops for advocacy

From the beginning, the Women and Pesticides workshops were designed to be action-oriented and to examine local pesticide use and its impact on women. The studies provided baseline information for strategizing and were crucial in the workshop discussions. In designing the sessions, PAN AP worked closely with its network partners, who were national or local grassroots organizations working on problems of pesticides use and able to identify related training needs and information gaps.

The first workshop in Malaysia in June 1991 resulted in the 'Serdang Declaration', which analysed the exploitation of women plantation workers and the pesticide problems they face, and presented several strategies for action. As a result, a women's organization has been conscientizing women workers to say no to pesticides. In two plantations as a result of workers' refusal to work as pesticide sprayers, they have been reassigned other duties that do not expose them to pesticides.

A series of workshops followed in Thailand, East Malaysia, Korea, Indonesia, the Philippines, South India, Pakistan and Sri Lanka. In 1998, workshops were conducted in Nepal and in Tamil Nadu, India, and in Bangladesh. Such workshops aim to build and mobilize people's organizations and local groups to create awareness, to pressure governments for pesticide reduction policies, and to create the impetus to move towards agricultural systems not dependent on pesticide use.

Outcome

Community and pesticide monitoring

One of the major achievements of the project in Malaysia is the increased self-worth of the plantation sprayers. For many of them, this is the first time that others have shown a serious concern over their health and well-being. This is providing them with the courage to improve their living and work situations. In addition, a national consultation is being planned to launch the results of the study, and a strategy for action is being discussed. It is hoped that the publication of the data will encourage government action to address the health impact of pesticide use in plantations.

In the past, government response to the issue of pesticides poisoning in the plantation sector has been very slow. Malaysia has a pesticide registration scheme and regulations on labelling and advertising; however, it took more than ten years for the Highly Toxic Pesticides Act, which provides some safeguards to pesticide sprayers, to come into force. In fact, the final regulation was a watered-down version of earlier drafts, which had stipulated shorter hours for spraying and requirements for medical examination.

The plantation management would not support this survey. In several cases, workers lost their jobs because of their involvement. The risk of job loss was also a hindrance to the giving of blood samples. Tenaganita sought the support of local doctors and clinics to help in the blood sampling and medical checkup. Even the National Union of Plantation Workers has not treated pesticide poisoning as a priority. Women are not well represented within the leadership of the union and thus their problems are not taken up.

It is hoped that in the future a more open process will be initiated to deal with the problems of pesticide use and the problems that women workers face in the plantation sector.

The importance and usefulness of community-based surveys is highlighted by the addition in 1997 to the Prior Informed Consent (PIC) procedure of five pesticides (methamidophos, methyl parathion, monocrotophos, parathion and phosphamidon) causing problems under conditions of use in developing countries. PIC was then part of the FAO International Code of Conduct on the Distribution and Use of Pesticides, and in 1998 governments finally completed negotiations for PIC to become an international treaty, known as the Rotterdam Convention. The initial documentation, which led to the nomination of these pesticides as candidates for PIC, was collected by NGOs and published by PAN as 'The Missing Ingredients'. With the development of an international agreement on persistent organic pollutants (POPs), experience at the grassroots will be able to provide data to help select chemicals for consideration for international control.

Training and strategy workshops for advocacy

The training and strategy workshops organized from 1991 to 1998 helped to initiate advocacy plans. At the 1993 workshop in the Philippines, there was a call for a people's ban of four pesticides as a follow-up to the national Consultation on the Effects of Pesticides and Women's Health, which focused on the problem of women's invisibility in spite of their extensive roles in agriculture. Dr Romy

Quijano, one of the resource persons at the conference, stated there that endosulfan (Hoechst product: Thiodan) may cause cancer. Hoechst slapped a lawsuit on Dr Quijano, as well as on the Philippines News Service for publishing this statement. PAN AP launched an international campaign against Hoechst and endosulfan. SIBAT, the alternative technology network, launched a people's ban on endosulfan. Eventually both suits were dismissed, in June 1994.

In August 1997 in Sri Lanka thirty women village leaders came together for a training workshop to discuss the problems of pesticide use, regulation, the international market, and promotion and sale. The women have initiated street theatre, songs and drama to highlight the problems at the community level. Women working with children have incorporated the issues into the school curriculum. Women have initiated organic agriculture exchange and training programmes to help their communities move away from pesticide use.

In June 1998 a hundred women leaders from Tamil Nadu discussed the problems of globalization, chemical-based agriculture and women's invisibility and loss of control over resources since its introduction. They called for a ban on the production and sale of hazardous pesticides that pollute the environment and damage human health. They demanded the protection of traditional seeds and the promotion of sustainable agriculture systems, and organized exchange visits and training workshops on the conservation of biodiversity and sustainable agriculture. They are also planning participatory action research and the systematic monitoring of the pesticides used, the companies marketing them and pesticide practices in several villages.

In Bangladesh, workshops and surveys to monitor pesticide problems in villages have given an added impetus to community leaders to strive for pesticide-free villages where all residents commit to not using pesticides in their farming and home activities. To date, three villages have signed on.

In Korea, Citizens Alliance for Consumer Protection (CACPK) participated in the Women and Pesticides surveys and research studies on the impact of pesticides and has used these studies to advocate the reduction of pesticide use in Korea. Due to pressure from CACPK and other citizens' organization the Seoul city government is working with farmers along the Plang Dang river to convert them into organic producers. Their pesticides were contaminating the river, which supplies the city with its drinking water. With the help of the Korean Organic Farmers Association, CACPK has played a pivotal role in moving the government towards reducing pesticides use and the contamination of Seoul's drinking water.

Consumers can also take action. An example of women organizing in the UK to encourage organic agriculture, and build a responsive outlet, is shown in Box 28.2.

Box 28.2 Local produce farmers' markets and local activism: methods that are working in the UK

Topsy Jewel

Common Cause Co-operative is a community development organization in Lewes whose initiatives span a wide range of environmental and social equity issues. As part of these activities, a group of young women and mothers have developed a number of projects aiming to promote and support ecologically and socially sustainable food production and consumption.

One of the initiatives is the Lewes Farmers' Market. Common Cause runs the market once a month on a non-profitmaking basis. Local producers sell directly to customers. They meet strict environmental and animal welfare conditions. The market increases opportunities in the town for consumers to purchase locally produced organic food. In response to demand, the small independent food shops in the town are increasingly supplying and promoting local organic produce. We are currently looking at ways to forge better links between local producers and small town and village shops, including an online ordering scheme.

Farmers' markets can enable people on a low income to benefit from the advantages of fresh local produce. We worked with a group of mothers on low income to explore whether the Lewes market could improve their access to organic produce. The women were keen to support local producers and had a high awareness of fresh produce being an essential, though expensive, component of a healthy diet. We found that organic fruit and vegetables sold at the Farmers' Market were cheaper than organic produce in the supermarket and often the same price as conventionally produced items. But the busy Saturday market presented difficulties for mothers with young children. In Arundel, another town in Sussex, the market manager, herself a producer, runs the Farmers' Market twice a month on a Saturday and a Thursday. Thursday is pension day, and she has found that there are many more older people and mothers shopping on this day.

Another Common Cause initiative is the OATES project. This is a partnership programme with the local authority and agriculture college. It provides training in organic horticulture for local unemployed people, with funding support for travel and childcare. The project aims to give participants an opportunity to gain the practical skills and confidence to find employment in the organic farming industry or establish their own organic plot. Five local organic enterprises also benefit from the programme. They provide work experience placements for the trainees in return for labour at one of the busiest times of their growing season.

In the UK, women have pioneered the organic farming and retailing businesses. The demand for fresh organic food is increasing by 40 per cent per year – in large part due to mothers wanting chemical-free, antibiotic-free, and non-genetically modified food for their children. This demand is being met by farmers selling through local delivery schemes, by leading branded foods such as Baby Organix or Simply Organic, and by retail outlets such as Planet Organic, a national chain of organic shops. It is women farmers and businesswomen who have tended to initiate these ventures. More recently, the large supermarket chains have registered the demand for organic food and are now major retail outlets.

In Sussex a number of local initiatives to promote more sustainable food production and consumption are being developed and run by women. These include farmers' markets, organic vegetable box schemes and a training scheme for unemployed people in organic horticulture. Both the larger independent organic business ventures and the smaller-scale local initiatives share a common ethos. They embody the principle that the growing of vegetables, the rearing of animals, and the making and selling of food should be a caring and community-based activity.

The IPM approach

The IPM approach to rice cultivation adopted by IPM-trained farmers in nine countries in Asia reduced pesticide use with no drop in yields, demonstrating success not only in pest control but also in economic management through savings in expenditure on pesticides. Unlike the response of plantation owners to pesticide poisoning in Malaysia, the government has responded to the brown plant hopper threat to rice by initiating an IPM programme, showing a positive lead in the reduction of pesticide use.

The Education and Research Association for Consumers (ERA) initiated a project on IPM in rice to reduce farmers' exposure to pesticides. The project was undertaken with the Department of Agriculture in the area and PAN AP. ERA worked closely with the department to conduct a successful series of training workshops and field training on IPM. Farmers reduced insecticide use by 90 per cent and herbicide by about 60 per cent. More importantly, the women rice farmers involved in the project were seen to be the best IPM farmers in the community and able to articulate their concerns and needs. Some of those who participated in the training assumed leadership positions in the local community.

In Indonesia, the government was planning to withdraw the 1986 restriction on the use of pesticides that had created the resurgence and resistance of pests in rice such as the brown plant hopper. Citizens' groups involved in PAN AP's Women and Pesticides and C-PAK programmes such as PAN Indonesia and Gita Pertiwi and its networks of citizens' groups protested strongly against the move. The government has cancelled the order to withdraw the restriction.

The combination of a national pesticide reduction plan with a farmer-first IPM programme would create the opportunities for crop protection that could be both economically viable and ecologically sound.

Lessons learned and recommendations

Surveys and community health monitoring document the real situation of how pesticides are used by agricultural workers and farmers in Asia and the impact of pesticides on them. It has helped women maintain records of health problems and give them exposure information. The information has initiated further discussion, and workshops on women's health have been established. With these inputs, and support from local groups such as Tenaganita, women plantation workers are articulating the problems they face and exploring ways to stop their daily exposure to pesticides. Such programmes are necessary to facilitate women to use research and monitoring results to improve their working conditions and prevent their exposure to hazardous pesticides.

The Malaysian IPM rice programme has been more positively pursued than have pesticide reduction strategies in the plantations. The reasons for this are apparent: plantation crops are for export and the sector comes under the purview of the Ministry of Primary

Industry; rice cultivation is under the aegis of the Ministry of Agriculture. Rice is grown by thousands of small farmers, whereas large corporations generally own the plantations. Economic interests far outweigh the health and safety of workers and consumers.

The occupational health issues which women face have been ignored or downplayed by scientists and legislators. This reflects a lack of, or selective, research on women's health. Information and research on the impact of pesticides on women's health are needed. Community monitoring and campaigning are essential to help women record the health impact of pesticides they use and to look at ways to address these issues. Community or plantation worker groups need to be directly involved in pesticides monitoring, and it is important that this is undertaken at the local level. Technical and financial support must be made available for women to plan and implement community-based pesticide monitoring, and programmes to implement IPM and sustainable agriculture. Governments need to implement pesticide reduction policies, support IPM approaches, and ultimately implement sustainable agriculture programmes.

Governments need to review, evaluate and screen chemicals for acute and chronic toxicity under the prevalent conditions of use. Chemicals must be screened for reproductive and endocrine disruptive effects, with bans and severe restrictions imposed on the use of these chemicals. But in reality it will be impossible to screen everything, and governments need to adopt the precautionary principle when dealing with pesticides where toxicological hazards have been established and risks not fully understood, or where there are toxicological gaps in knowledge on the precise effects of the pesticides or on the mechanisms of toxicity. Even when governments have evaluated and restricted pesticides, companies have challenged them in court to overturn the decisions.

Women's organizations have often been urban biased in the issues they have tackled. Food production, pesticide poisoning, access to land and resources, and issues concerning the livelihood of women in rural areas have never been among the priorities of women's organizations. This needs to change, as women farmers and agricultural workers are becoming the most marginalized sector of our societies. FAO calls it the feminization of poverty, which is apparent in the rural sector of many Asian countries. We all have a responsibility to ensure safe and secure food for our families, and women farmers and workers are the most crucial in the chain of food production.

References

1 Jeyaratnam, J. In *World Health Statistic Quarterly*, 43, 1990.
2 Hileman, B. In *Chemical and Engineering News*, 31 January 1994.
3 Soto, A.M. Testimony before the Subcommittee on Health and the Environment, US House of Representatives, 21 October 1993.
4 Danish EPA. 'Male reproductive health and environmental chemicals with estrogenic effects', Denmark: Ministry of Environment and Energy, 1995.
5 Soto, *op. cit.*, 1993.
6 Repetto, R., Baliga, S.S. *Pesticides and the Immune System: The Public Health Risks*, Washington, DC: World Resources Institute, 1996.
7 Lim, G.S. In Lim, P.A.C., *et al.* (eds) *Proceedings of the Conference on IPM in the Asia-Pacific Region*, Kuala Lumpur, 23–27 September, 1991, CAB International/Asian Development Bank, 1991.
8 Davies, W.P. In Aziz, A., Kadir, A.S., Barlow, H.S. (eds) *Pest Management and the Environment in 2000*, Wallingford: CAB International, 1992.
9 Arumugam, V. *Vicims without Voice: A Study of Women Pesticide Workers in Malaysia*, Malaysia: Tenaganita/PAN Asia and the Pacific, 1992.
10 Arumugam, *op. cit.*, 1992.

29

The Bhopal aftermath: generations of women affected

Satinath Sarangi

Midnight in Bhopal: 2–3 December 1984

Late on Sunday evening, 2 December 1984, during routine maintenance of the methyl isocyanate (MIC) tanks at the Union Carbide pesticide plant, a large quantity of water entered one of the 60 tonne storage tanks. This triggered a runaway reaction, resulting in a tremendous increase of temperature and pressure. None of the safety systems was operating. Just before midnight, a deadly cocktail of MIC, hydrogen cyanide, mono methyl amine and other chemicals was carried by a northerly wind to the neighbouring communities. Over the next couple of hours close to 40 tonnes of the chemicals spread over the city of about one million people. People woke up surrounded by a poison cloud so dense and searing that they could hardly see. As they gasped for breath, the effects of the gas grew even more suffocating.

The death toll

Official figures estimated that over 500,000 people were exposed to the gas within several hours. This number was arrived at by totalling the population of residential districts where any fatalities occurred. An estimated 8,000 people died in the three days following the disaster due to respiratory failure, pulmonary oedema, brain damage and other acute complications of gas exposure. According to official figures, exposure-related deaths in the years subsequent to the disaster were higher than in the immediate aftermath. According to data from the Centre for Rehabilitation Studies (a medical research agency of the state government), in 1997 the difference of mortality rates in exposed and non-exposed communities was 4.33 per thousand. Data for the subsequent years remain to be published but unofficial estimates range from 10 to 15 exposure-related deaths per month, even today. Survivors' organizations and independent health care organizations estimate that the current death toll has exceeded 20,000.

The continuing tragedy

Research by the Indian Council of Medical Research (ICMR), a government agency, showed that the toxins crossed the lung barrier and circulated in the bloodstream, causing multi-systemic damage. The ICMR carried out twenty-four research projects that documented respiratory, ocular, reproductive, neurological, immunological, gastro-intestinal, muscular, genetic and psychological damages caused by Union Carbide's gases. In 1994 ICMR abandoned all research in Bhopal without publishing its final report.

Meanwhile, Union Carbide (now Dow Chemical, following its February 2001 merger) continues to claim as a 'trade secret' over sixty years of research (including research on human 'volunteers') on methyl isocyanate. These denials of information have resulted in a situation where there are no treatment protocols specific to the multi-systemic chronic health effects. As a consequence, drugs for temporary symptomatic relief have been the mainstay of medical care ever since the morning of the disaster. The indiscriminate prescription of steroids, antibiotics and psychotropic drugs is compounding the damage caused by the gas exposure. Tens of thousands of victims are not able to earn a livelihood due to loss of their capacity to do physical labour; hence ill health is compounded by the impoverishment of families.

Over five thousand people living in the neighbourhood of Union Carbide's closed and abandoned factory are routinely being poisoned with carcinogenic and persistent toxins in their drinking water. Several official and independent reports show that this groundwater contamination is a result of reckless dumping of chemical wastes by Union Carbide during its fourteen years of operation.

Today in Bhopal

Currently well above 120,000 people are chronically ill with exposure-related diseases and their complications. Several latent effects are now glaringly manifest. In 1993, ICMR reported that pulmonary tuberculosis among the affected was over three times higher than the national average. The situation has worsened drastically since then. MIC is classified as a known animal carcinogen and a potential human carcinogen. This appears to explain the sharp rise in cancers among the exposed population in the last three years. Survivors who were exposed *in utero*, and even those born to exposed women, show marked retardation in physical growth. Increasingly large numbers of young women are found to experience menstrual irregularities, sterility and early menopause. Anecdotal information suggests that the number of children born with deformities such as cleft lip and missing palate is a matter of concern.

The impact on women's health

Though ICMR recorded elevated menstrual irregularities and excessive bleeding among gas-exposed women, none among the twenty-four research projects it carried out was directed towards identifying, assessing or treating female reproductive health consequences of the disaster. In the context of official neglect, non-government agencies and individual researchers have generated critical, albeit sporadic, information on short- and long-term reproductive consequences of the disaster.

In March 1985 Drs Rani Bang and Mira Sadgopal examined 224 women from severely and mildly affected communities. Their report, 'An epidemic of gynaecological diseases', based on a study of 218 women, indicated high rates of leucorrhoea, pelvic inflammatory disease, cervical erosion and excessive menstrual bleeding.

Dr Daya R. Varma of McGill University, Canada, studied the pregnancy outcome of women who were pregnant at the time of the disaster. Results of this community-based study show that 43 per cent of 865 pregnant women experienced spontaneous abortion.

In March 1985, 104–109 days after exposure, a study was initiated by the Citizens' Committee for Relief and Rehabilitation, Bhopal. This cross-sectional community-based study, with random sampling of both seriously exposed and mildly exposed populations, showed that out of 198 women clinically examined, 100 (50.5 per cent) had persistent symptoms relating to the reproductive system.

In the same month, a survey carried out by another non-government organization, Medico Friend Circle (MFC), showed that among women in the age group of 15–45 years there was a significant alteration in the menstrual cycle in the severely exposed as compared to the less exposed. Differences included shortening of the cycle length, excessive bleeding during menstruation, change in the colour of blood, dysmenorrhoea and leucorrhoea.

A study carried out five years after the gas leak, on 136 women from the seriously affected area and 139 from mildly affected area (aged 20–44 years) who had borne at least one child in the previous five years, showed that the rate of spontaneous abortion in pregnancies exposed *in utero* was 26.7 per cent in the seriously exposed group, compared to 10 per cent in the mildly affected population. In the subsequent period, rates of spontaneous abortion were 26.3 per cent and 7.8 per cent respectively in the two populations.

In January 1994, Dr Ingrid Eckerman, the Swedish member of the International Medical Commission on Bhopal, an independent group of fifteen medical specialists from eleven countries, reported menstrual disturbances and excessive vaginal secretion (as well as respiratory, neurological and other symptoms) among a majority of the gas-affected women she interviewed.

The personal and social impact on women

In many senses women in Bhopal are bearing the brunt of the disaster. Women survivors in the family largely provide care for the sick at home or in hospital. The lowering of family income has had its maximum impact on the food that is available to the women in the family. There is also social discrimination against exposed women, particularly owing to the effects on the reproductive system. Parents find it difficult to marry their daughters and many women are deserted by their husbands. However, the tragedy has also produced a welcome change in the traditional roles and status of women in the family and in society at large. Muslim women, who prior to the disaster were not allowed out of their houses without a chaperone, constitute today the overwhelming majority of the membership of survivors' organizations.

Health care of women survivors at the Sambhavna Clinic, Bhopal

A clinic set up in 1996 by the Sambhavna Trust – an independent group of medical and other professional staff situated close to the severely affected communities – provides free medical care to survivors. In view of the exposure-induced injuries to women and gross official neglect regarding the health and care of women survivors, the clinic pays special attention to these women, who form the majority of those reporting to the clinic.

The commonest symptoms presented at the Gyn-care unit are dysmenorrhoea, amenorrhoea, menorrhagia, metrorrhagia, poly-menorrhagia, scanty menses, irregular menses, infrequent menses, spotting, premature menopause, excessive vaginal secretions, lumps and pain in breasts, and pain during sexual intercourse. Backache, joint pains, and pain, numbness and tingling in the limbs are the most common associated symptoms. The main diagnoses offered have been pelvic inflammatory disease, vaginitis, cervicitis, bacterial vaginosis, vulvitis, dysfunctional uterine bleeding and pre-menstrual syndrome.

Preliminary findings of a gynaecology screening programme at the Sambhavna Clinic indicate a likely high prevalence of cervical cancer among the survivors of the Union Carbide disaster. Un-fortunately, facilities for screening, diagnosis and treatment of cervical cancers are unavailable at the hospitals designated for survivors, including the 150-bed Indira Gandhi Hospital built espe-cially for women survivors.

The Sambhavna Clinic carries out routine pelvic examinations and Pap's smear test facilities for colposcopy and LLETZ (Large Loop Excision of Transformation Zone). LLETZ is a state-of-the-art surgical procedure that allows excision of abnormal tissue, thus sparing the rest of the reproductive organs.

Community health workers at Sambhavna carry out health educa-tion in five severely affected communities to make survivors aware of the benefits of pelvic examinations and cervical screening and help them receive these facilities at the clinic.

Along with modern medical care, Sambhavna Clinic also offers care through Ayurveda – an Indian indigenous system of medicine based on herbs and minerals and yoga. This has been found to be remarkably effective in the treatment of a number of gynaecological and reproductive system symptoms, including menstrual cycle dis-turbances, premature menopause and excessive vaginal secretions. Many of the herbal preparations are manufactured at the clinic with locally collected or purchased herbs. A research study on the efficacy of yoga in the treatment of menstrual problems among young women is currently under way.

Recording of subjective accounts of teenage women with regard to their menstrual problems is part of a monitoring exercise at the clinic. Among the teenage women who were interviewed at the clinic 75 per cent presented symptoms of dysmenorrhoea; 43 per cent reported lengthened, shortened and irregular cycles; 53 per cent reported heavy, scanty or irregular menstrual flow; and 51 per cent reported excessive vaginal secretions. Fever, giddiness, various pains in the body, loss of appetite, tingling and numbness, and irritability were six main symptoms that were found to appear or get worse during menstruation (see Box 29.1).

To a significant extent the work of the Sambhavna Clinic demonstrates that it is possible to evolve simple, safe, effective and ethical ways of carrying out research, monitoring and treatment within the realities of Bhopal. However, Sambhavna is small compared to the magnitude and complexity of the disaster. The clinic run by this trust has provided direct treatment to about 11,000 people while severalfold more survivors desperately await proper medical attention.

Box 29.1 Typical accounts of young women presented at the Sambhavna Clinic

Young woman one (age 17 years; age at exposure 2 years; menarche at 12 years)

When I started menstruating it was quite bearable but I have been having terrible problems for the last three years. I have periods once in four months. I become irritable, have abdominal pain and cannot concentrate on anything. There is pain all over my body. For days before my periods I writhe in agony like a fish out of water. My eyes are weak. I am sad most of the time. I do not know how but I feel that my health problems are my fault and I have to bear them. I do not know how long. I am told not to mention my problems to anybody but it is the truth. I used to feel I would rather die than have a life like this. At last I know I can do something about it.

Young woman two (age 17 years; age at exposure 2 years; menarche at 12 years)

When I started my periods, they were regular for three to four months but then they stopped for four months. So I took some pills and got my periods. For the last one year my problems with irregular cycle are getting worse. I had my periods once in five months. For the last seven months I have not had my periods at all. I have been taking medicines but there is no improvement. I hope you can help me.

Young woman three (age 19 years; age at exposure 4 years; menarche at 15 years)

For the first five to six months my periods were irregular and without much discomfort. Then I stared getting terrible abdominal cramps. I get nauseous, giddy and my head aches. I take allopathic medicines to get relief from pain. My cycles are irregular and there is a delay of 5–7 days. There have been times when I did not get my periods for two months. Also there is excessive bleeding, in the form of clots. During my periods I cannot do any work.

Young woman four (age 21 years; age at exposure 6 years; menarche at 15 years)

At first my periods seemed OK but after four months there was excessive bleeding. My periods are very irregular and I have severe pain before I get them. The pain lasts for two to three days. I get fever and a severe headache. I cannot work or sleep. I cannot eat and just take tea or milk. When I have excessive bleeding there are clots. Currently I am taking treatment at the Sambhavna Clinic and I have got much relief from pain. I have seven sisters and all of them have similar menstrual problems. Several of my friends at school too.

The need for health care, monitoring and research initiatives in Bhopal women's health

The utter neglect of the health of women survivors by official agencies is not only evident in ICMR's oversight with regard to research studies of the gynaecological health impact. Official attention towards medical treatment of gynaecological problems is marked by its absence. Facilities for routine pelvic examinations are non-existent in the government-built hospitals, let alone cervical screening and diagnosis. The situation is worse with respect to the Union Carbide-sponsored Bhopal Memorial Hospital Trust that runs community clinics.

In the face of an epidemic of reproductive health problems among women survivors, government officials continue to deny exposure-related consequences. This is only part of the Indian government's policy of downplaying the health consequences of the disaster to help Union Carbide evade its liabilities. In the current wave of globalization this collusion between the Indian government and multinationals such as Union Carbide is likely to grow stronger. The reality is that the deteriorating health status of women survivors is unlikely to be addressed by concerned officials.

In the context of these harsh realities there is an urgent need for the international community to respond to the situation in Bhopal. An encouraging beginning has recently been made in this direction, with financial support extended by the French bestselling author Dominique Lapierre and technical cooperation being given by Gynecologie sans Frontières towards improving the health of the women survivors.

30

The campaign against lindane: the lessons of women's action

Jill Day

In late 1994, some women members of the trade union UNISON brought their concerns about the use of the pesticide lindane (gamma-HCH) and its links with breast cancer to a meeting of the Regional Women's Committee. They related what they had seen on a recent television programme; several other women present confirmed that they had also seen it. A discussion started.

The *Dispatches* programme [1] suggested that the heavy use of pesticides on the intensive prairie-style cultivation of potatoes and sugar beet in Eastern England might be linked to clusters of breast cancers in South Lincolnshire. These clusters were 40 per cent higher than the national average. The pesticide used was lindane and it was applied to the crops by aerial spraying. The Lincolnshire women interviewed in the programme confirmed that there was no family history of breast cancer and that they were suffering from it at an unusually early age.

The UNISON women who lived in Lincolnshire described how impossible it was to avoid the spray, and that the whole area was thick with a choking chemical mist. The programme also highlighted the persistence of this pesticide. It continued to pollute the environment long after its application and bio-accumulated up the food chain. The waste tops of the root crops were also fed to cattle – another reason for the presence of lindane in samples of milk tested by *Dispatches*.

As the discussion at the Committee meeting continued, it became clear to the women that it was impossible for them to avoid this chemical, even if they had not been caught by the spray. They felt that their whole environment in Lincolnshire was contaminated and, worse, they were feeding lindane-contaminated food to their children and families.

Breast cancer: time for action

It was the link between the use of lindane and the presence of clusters of breast cancers in Lincolnshire that really motivated the UNISON women towards taking action. The UK has the highest incidence of breast cancer in the world: it is the most common cause of death in women between the ages of 35 and 54 years. Most of the women present had been directly touched by experience of breast cancer, having mothers, friends or relatives who had suffered or died. Every woman fears that she will be next, yet has no knowledge of how to protect herself. A feeling of indignation grew amongst the women – how dare people continue to use this chemical if there were *any* chance that it was implicated in breast cancer? Could we try and stop its use and so take back some control over our own health? Or avenge the helplessness and anger felt at the loss of those dear to us from breast cancer? These are naive sentiments, of course, but we felt so strongly that we wanted to do something and, with the optimism of inexperience, thought that change could be achieved.

Where to start?

Our combined knowledge of farming methods, chemistry, pesticide regulation and control, or the politics of cancer were practically zero. We represented a small part of the structure of the UK's largest trade union, which organises within the public sector of the economy. However, UNISON has over a million members and more than 700,000 of them are women. Breast cancer and its causes would be an issue for them too.

Raising awareness locally

Our first aim was to raise awareness within our own region of UNISON's organization, the East Midlands, of which Lincolnshire forms part. The Regional Women's Committee was already affiliated to the Women's Environmental Network (WEN), a national non-profit organization whose purpose is to educate, inform and empower women who care about the environment. We discovered that WEN knew about the possible links between lindane and breast cancers, and had been campaigning for a ban on lindane for some time. Using their information and that provided by the *Dispatches* programme producers, we began to inform ourselves.

Raising awareness nationally

Lindane became a standing item on the agenda of the Committee. At each meeting, women would share what more they had learned. Some of the women were conducting a parallel exercise at meetings of their local branch committees. But to increase awareness within the wider union, we needed to use its democratic processes.

The structures of any trade union are complex, as they attempt to ensure the widest possible democratic involvement. In UNISON, women members are encouraged to 'self-organize' because it is recognized that power is still held and exercised by men. Trade unions are a product of their history, and traditional values still hold sway. Unless women are given their own space and structures to develop their own perspectives and agendas, change will not happen despite women's numerical majority. Women can therefore use their own self-organized structures at local, regional and national levels, within UNISON, or attempt to use the mainstream, mixed agenda, structures. The Regional Women's Committee formed part of the self-organized structure, with links to women at branch level and women at national level with whom it could communicate fairly easily. However, our objective – banning lindane's use – required the commitment of UNISON's mainstream structures to unleash resources and actions which were not available to women's self-organization.

We decided to go straight to the top and submitted a motion to UNISON's National Delegate Conference in 1995 which set out our concerns about lindane and called for the union to publicize the facts about this pesticide's use and campaign for its ban. The motion reached the final agenda with the stated support of the Union's National Executive Committee. We were, however, stunned that they had placed the motion last in the list of priorities, so it was never debated. Angered by this turn of events, we decided to concentrate our activities within the East Midlands Region, where we were better placed to influence outcomes. Our aim was to build support locally for the union to conduct a national campaign, and also to develop some good practice within the region for the form the campaign could take.

Raising awareness regionally

The democratic process was reignited by another motion early in 1996, but this time to the East Midlands Regional Council of UNISON. This time, though, we had prepared more carefully. The motion had an angry tone, seeking to associate the region with the view that the union nationally should have a better sense of priorities, and demanding action be taken. The women had lobbied key people and ensured that they were briefed and ready to speak at the meeting. The motion was passed overwhelmingly and marked the start of the campaign locally.

The original women activists and their allies now sought to move the resolution between the relevant committees of the region within the mainstream structure and each was challenged to identify appropriate action. The women also ensured that the action was taken.

In this way, lindane also became a 'health and safety' as well as a 'women's' issue within UNISON, even though it was not a work-related risk for our members. The Regional Health and Safety Committee undertook to raise awareness and distribute materials to their network of safety representatives. The Publicity Committee gave money to support a leaflet campaign. The Local Government Committee took the issue to the Midlands Provincial Council and sought to stop local authorities using lindane on public parks and gardens. The Political Committee took the issue to UNISON's sponsored Members of Parliament (MPs) and into the Regional Conference of Labour (Party) Women. The Regional Committee took motions into the Regional TUC and Women's Committees.

UNISON motion: 'Ban lindane'

With the region now on board and active in support of our aims, it was time to get the union committed at national level. Our motion, calling for a campaign for a ban on lindane to be conducted throughout the Union, and outside UNISON through our political contacts and allies, and the TUC with other unions, was debated and carried in June 1996. At last, the banning of lindane had become national UNISON policy. We had great expectations of the campaign that would now be launched by National Office and what would be achieved. In the meantime, continued support was needed at the local level. There was still a level of active interest within the East Midlands Region among members and representatives who wanted to do something themselves. Having stimulated these concerns we now needed to encourage people into activism. We produced a folder on lindane, its uses, production and health risks. This contained information about breast cancer and how to work within UNISON and with the local community to highlight lindane's association with it; how to call for better resources for breast cancer services; details of campaign groups and lobbies and how UNISON could link up with them; and how lindane *had* been banned in other countries, to show that our campaign was winnable. The folder was distributed within East Midlands UNISON, and throughout UNISON's women's self-organization structure across the country.

At national level, UNISON's Health and Safety Department commissioned the Pesticides Trust (now PAN UK) to produce a briefing that provided a technical underpinning and confirmation of the dangers of lindane. The document clarified the UNISON position and encouraged branches to take action by ensuring employers were not using lindane, advising members to check domestic use, and lobbying their own MPs for a ban.

Union complacency

We awaited further news of campaign actions and successes from national level, but none came. We put suggestions to staff at National Office regarding what they might do. We had, for example, a local MP who was willing to raise an Early Day Motion in Parliament for a ban on lindane – could the UNISON machine organize the support of UNISON-sponsored MPs?

It seemed that UNISON nationally felt they had done what was required by the conference resolution. There was no time available to staff to take other actions; an added difficulty seemed to be that the issue fell between departments and responsibilities – women, health, health and safety, environment, politics. Lindane was not yet banned; nor was there any early prospect of it.

The East Midlands women took stock. We were still fired up and wanted to win: how could we instil this sense of priority into the national machine? After much discussion, we decided to 'take back' the national campaign and run it from the region. Having done so much groundwork, and brought kudos to the East Midlands Region, winning the support of key players at national and regional levels, we were able to win this argument and responsibility for UNISON's national campaign was transferred to us.

Common goals: strength in unity

We believed that achieving a ban would require a great deal of public pressure, which could only come from much greater awareness. We looked to ourselves and what had made us angry and motivated to do something – it was those same features that we needed to replicate in an appeal to a wider public. We also felt that we needed to target the pesticide regulatory process and particularly the associated politics. We needed a bigger campaign group with more expertise, but which remained focused on the lindane ban.

We started by asking the Pesticides Trust and WEN to work with us. They suggested others. We eventually brought together a campaign group which included those two organizations, the Green Network, Friends of the Earth, the Soil Association and Breast UK. Then things really started to take off.

The benefits of the coalition were immediately apparent. Together there was a wealth of knowledge, expertise, ideas, resources and impetus that was not available to one organization on its own. UNISON could not call on any of its own expertise to campaign in the field of pesticide regulation – it had none. But it did have a large constituency of members, access to power brokers, some resources and campaigning experience. It was unusual to see a very large trade union in such a coalition with environmental groups.

The one drawback of this approach for the UNISON women was that it excluded them from direct involvement. The campaign group met regularly for half a day, usually in London. They had to be represented by their Women's Officer, a full-time paid official, since their own jobs would not permit that amount of time away. Despite briefings and feedbacks, they, perhaps inevitably, lost direct control of the campaign.

Conscious of this aspect, and of the need to involve each of the constituencies of the coalition groups for maximum effect, some of the activities organized by the Campaign Group were aimed at our respective memberships. Since most of the members of the group were women, this was anyway our style of working – provide information, support and empower women to take their own action.

During 1998, for example, WEN undertook their project 'Putting Breast Cancer on the Map'. They worked with women to gather evidence about their health and the environments in which they lived, in an attempt to identify any breast cancer clusters which may be linked to environmental pollution. The East Midlands UNISON women ensured that not only were they involved in this project but that women's self-organization throughout the union took part. The lindane message was thus taken to more women within UNISON by another organization, in a different context and in a way that encouraged women to ask their own questions and take action.

Early in 1999, Austria circulated to member states the results of its evaluation of lindane under the European Council Directive 91/414/EEC. This recommended that lindane should be removed from the market but left member states to make their own decisions. The Campaign Group had submitted evidence to the Austrian review and the resulting decision provided hope that success was in sight. Every avenue we could think of to influence and publicize public opinion was considered to pressurize the political system into following the Austrian lead. We worked collaboratively, setting up opportunities for others to exploit, each using our own organization's particular qualities to best effect. Friends of the Earth were best placed to produce press releases, which they did in all of our names. Green Network had a good contact with the *Daily Express* newspaper and we asked UNISON's general secretary to go to the meeting with the editor to discuss a joint campaign. The Pesticides Trust took the lead on lobbying the pesticides regulatory process, briefing the rest of us to take part. Those with skills in organising demonstrations did just that, and members from all groups joined. Groups had their own political contacts; we used these to achieve three Early Day Motions, presentations to the All Party Groups on Breast Cancer and Cancer, several presentations to MPs and the media in the House of Commons, as well as direct lobbying of the relevant ministers.

The Austrian decision allowed us to target continuing lindane use and lobby for its withdrawal. We knew which products containing lindane were still licensed and simply asked the public to tell us where they were on sale. This took people into supermarkets, garden centres and DIY shops, looking along shelves and reading labels. It raised awareness in a very effective way, and gave us data on which outlets were selling lindane products. We then wrote asking shops to withdraw them, which many did, so generating another media story – and one which the public itself had initiated.

Victory

Such actions also put pressure on the British government's regulatory process, which decided initially not to support the Austrian view but to continue to sanction lindane. However, in July 2000 the European Union Standing Committee on Plant Health voted for the non-inclusion of lindane under Directive 91/414. This meant that lindane would be removed from agricultural and amateur gardening use throughout Europe. The UK government voted in favour of this action. UNISON women were delighted. The union was so delighted that it paid for a campaign victory leaflet to be produced.

Women taking trade unions into new societal concerns

When the women reviewed the campaign, a number of interesting factors emerged. Perhaps most important was the women's pride in successfully running a campaign which had 'altruistic' aims within the trade-union movement. They admitted feeling uneasy about the 'self-interest' nature of trade-union activity. They felt they had achieved something valuable in the lindane campaign for all women, rather than just themselves. Second, we had all learnt an extraordinary amount about subjects and processes totally new to us, and we had done this through our union. We had changed the union's agenda and pushed it to incorporate our concerns. Eventually, it had responded flexibly. Near the start of the campaign, whenever any of us introduced ourselves as coming from UNISON, we were asked which of our members used lindane. When we replied none, as far as we knew, we were asked what our interest was, then, in breast cancer. Now, perhaps, people would be less surprised that trade unions can be a force for societal changes wider than terms and conditions of employment.

Certainly, East Midlands UNISON women realize this. Now our work on lindane has led us into the issue of food safety and quality. But we have our own contacts and information/expertise streams. We have skills that were developed through the campaign. We have new knowledge and lines of inquiry that we want to follow up. We have learnt lessons about our union and its members. We are growing.

Reference

1 *Dispatches*, Channel Four, November 1994.

31

Integrated pest management:
gender-sensitive and participatory approaches

Adrienne Martin and Kerry Albright

The UK government Department for International Development (DFID) is committed to the international development target of halving the proportion of people living in extreme poverty by 2015. Its development and policy work is aimed at improving livelihoods (including the removal of gender discrimination), securing better education, health and opportunities for poor people, and protection and better management of the natural and physical environment [1]. DFID funds a range of natural resources research and development activities through the bilateral aid programme, through the eleven Renewable Natural Resources Research Programmes, and through funding to NGOs and multilateral organizations.

DFID works within a livelihoods perspective that helps to focus on the priorities of the poor by putting people at the centre of analysis and the formulation of development strategies [2]. Women are amongst those most affected by the problems of poverty and are crucial to its reduction. Whilst special efforts to enhance the role of women in development remain necessary, the focus has widened to ensure that promotion of gender equality is seen not purely as a 'women's concern', but as encompassing both women's and men's roles, their responsibilities, needs, and access to and control of resources.

The emphasis of DFID-funded crop protection research is on reducing reliance on pesticides by developing integrated pest management strategies (IPM) and socially acceptable alternatives to pesticides. IPM technologies contribute to livelihoods, food security and income, through reducing health hazards and developing sustainable approaches to managing crop pests, combining the use of biological, cultural, physical and chemical tactics to minimize health and environmental risks. Most DFID-funded crop protection projects are carried out in partnership with national agricultural research or extension organizations, international research centres or NGOs. Project proposers are encouraged to undertake social, economic and gender analysis to identify the potential benefits or negative impacts of improved crop protection strategies, particularly for women and the poor. Without this analysis, projects risk perpetuating inequalities and disadvantaging women.

The following discussion draws on a range of projects to raise issues and give examples of gender concerns in the development and implementation of integrated pest management technologies.

Understanding gender and pesticide use

Gender analysis is necessary to understand roles and responsibilities in relation to crop and pest management technologies. However, mainstream methods of data collection have tended either to omit information about female farmers or to provide distorted and cursory accounts which belittle their significance [3]. Gender analysis and stakeholder analysis are vital complements to participatory rural appraisals. Women and men farmers' perceptions of their needs and priorities are a good foundation for developing crop protection strategies that are viable and sustainable. Group discussions and household interviews should not only specifically incorporate the views of women but also disaggregate by gender the data collected, wherever possible. These can reveal very different perspectives and attitudes towards pesticide use, health and agricultural practice.

Men and women traditionally have differing roles in food security, agricultural production and storage and pesticide use, which imply different technology needs. For example, women tend to perform the majority of weeding, harvesting and post-harvest processing and storage tasks, and in some areas marketing, whilst men are more involved in pesticide spraying, ploughing, clearing land and planning. However, gender responsibilities also tend to be crop specific, with women contributing most to subsistence food crops and men concentrating activities more in cash crops. Women's subsistence crop plots tend to be small-scale and non-uniform, and even in female-headed households plots tend to be smaller, more scattered and less fertile than those of their male counterparts.

Gender roles are dynamic and change over time, hence it is important to recognize the degree of flexibility in gender roles and the distinctions between cultural norms and actual practice. For example, the increase of out-migration from rural to urban areas by men seeking work intensifies the burden of work falling on the shoulders of women. Whilst men have traditionally undertaken pesticide spraying in many counties, in some areas women are increasingly carrying out this task themselves. Researchers in Embu, Kenya, found that female cowpea farmers were generally not involved in pesticide spraying for safety reasons, but in practice increasing numbers of women were having to undertake this and other additional tasks as their husbands migrate looking for work elsewhere [4].

Explanations for the gender division of labour for spraying are rather conjectural. The physical weight of sprayers is often mentioned, but is comparable with the weight of a toddler or water containers regularly carried by women. Other influences are perceptions of the health hazards for women and access to and responsibility for finance. The cultural meanings attached to pest control and the associated gender roles may also be significant.

It is also vital to understand how gender influences control over resources and the distribution of benefits from different enterprises. Men and women often have different opportunities to access the resources they need to secure their livelihoods. These include natural resources (land and water), social linkages, financial resources, education and health care, and physical structures (housing, roads). An understanding of these patterns of access can guide the development of crop protection technologies to fit with the needs and resources of specific groups.

Work on pest control in cowpea in Kenya found that lack of finance and information were huge constraints on farmers' access to pesticides [5]. It was very difficult for both men and women to get access to credit in dry and risk-prone areas of Kenya. Many people preferred not to borrow, as the banks could repossess their only asset (their land) if times became hard. Such problems of access have led to some interesting initiatives: for example, women formed groups to produce baskets, using the proceeds from sales to buy pesticides for group members.

Decision-making processes within households, with respect to control of the budget, pesticide purchase and application, may have an impact on IPM technology adoption. In the Philippines, women, as managers of the family purse, control purchase of pesticides and fertilizers for rice farming and carry out the marketing of produce.

The wider policy and institutional context relating to crop protection – for example, decisions on the importation, marketing, pricing and packaging of agricultural chemicals, investment in extension services, staffing and training – has an important influence on the uptake of pest control technologies and their outcomes for men and women.

Gender and knowledge of pests

Men and women grow different crops, perform different tasks and engage in different communication networks, and as a result they may possess different knowledge about crop varieties, indigenous

---

Box 31.1 Farmers' perceptions of pests in peri-urban agriculture, Kumasi, Ghana

An investigation of farmers' perceptions of pests, diseases, organic composts and inorganic fertilizers within their farming systems was carried out in four villages. Separate discussions were held with groups of women and men on the pest and disease problems with vegetables and their control measures, and differences were noted. Male farmers were more likely to specialize in vegetable production, particularly tomato, and therefore had larger monocropped plots. Most of the women grew vegetables – tomato, eggplant, pepper and okra – on a smaller scale within a mixed farming system. Women's main cash crops were staples such as maize, cassava, plantain and cocoyam, and their main concern was the pest and disease problems with these crops. Although they were aware of and sometimes used chemicals, it was on a limited scale due to the cost. Men's focus was on pest and disease problems with their major cash crop, tomatoes; and most were using purchased inputs of chemicals and fertilizer.

Farmers appeared to have very little access to information on pests and diseases or associated problems such as health hazards or destruction of natural enemies. The men who specialized in vegetable farming were able to list details of pests and diseases more easily than others, and had more knowledge of insect life cycles (specifically the relationship between caterpillars and butterflies). In two of the women's groups, most had never heard of this and did not think the information was useful for pest control. This pattern may well reflect the greater contact male specialist vegetable producers have with extension staff and agrochemical dealers, as well as years of schooling.

Source: Reference 6.

methods of pest control, awareness of pest life cycles and natural predators and sources of genetic resistance to diseases (Box 31.1).

An understanding of men's and women's knowledge of pests is important as the basis for developing alternatives and in order to maximize chances of eventual uptake. Non-chemical pest control often implies knowledge and attitude changes. The technologies are often more location-specific and knowledge-intensive than chemical-based control methods and changes in practice and collective action may be needed to apply new strategies.

Gender, IPM and participatory research

Women's participation throughout the research and development process, particularly in IPM field trials and participatory technology evaluation, is usually recognized as vital to ensure the development of appropriate technology and its eventual uptake by the community. This is especially important, as the technology needs of women farmers are in many ways distinct from those of men. Women farmers often require low external input, time-saving technologies adapted to small-scale, non-uniform subsistence crop production [7]. Many IPM technologies are labour-intensive and time-consuming – for example, pest scouting or manual removal of eggs. Women may reject such technologies because of the implied increase in workload. The example in Box 31.2 illustrates the complexity of the issues surrounding the participation of women in IPM technology testing.

Communication, extension and technology uptake

There is often an informal assumption in many development projects that information given to men through training will automatically 'trickle across' to women. Unfortunately, this is often not the case, as illustrated in Box 31.2. This example also shows how new pest-control technologies developed outside the local setting are often targeted directly at men. The new alternatives to conventional pesticides risk being limited in their benefit to women if they are transmitted and controlled through the same channels and fit into the same gender roles as conventional pesticides.

Women's exclusion from extension services both as extension agents and as farmers is striking, yet there are several well-recognized reasons for this. Access to information by women tends to be limited by their lower educational levels, which may entirely exclude them

Box 31.2 Pheromone technology to control yellow stem borer in rice, Andhra Pradesh, India

This project investigated smallholders' responses to management practices for control of yellow stem borer in rice, including the use of pheromones to disrupt insect mating behaviour. Analysing the respective roles of men and women in rice cultivation, it emerged that some tasks were conventionally gender-specific, but the division was not clear-cut. Men and women seemed to share responsibility for decision-making in the selection of seeds and agricultural inputs, while men were entirely responsible for applying pesticides.

Project staff were conscious of involving both women and men in the validation process. Group discussions were held with men and women separately to encourage full participation, although independent consultation with women was sometimes difficult, possibly associated with the lack of female project staff. The objectives of the research were explained to both men and women, but the NGO intermediary trained only male farmers in placing the pheromone dispensers. In separate discussions, some women described how they had sought more clarification on the project from their husbands, but had been told that the new technology was 'men's business'.

The trial evaluation process was probably the most effective activity in ensuring equal participation of women and men. Their perceptions of pest prevalence and pest management practices were remarkably similar, although women had less information than men on the purpose of the technology. Their criteria for assessing the new technology differed: men cited positively the convenience of application, whilst women pointed out that, when bending to harvest the crop, they had to take care to avoid the pheromone dispenser sticks damaging their eyes.

The project raises questions as to why only men took responsibility for the practical application of the technology. If men are conventionally responsible for applying pesticides because of the health risks these may pose to women, then pheromone technology, which poses no such risk, offers an opportunity for increasing women's involvement in pest management strategies. If other social and cultural factors, such as husbands' unwillingness for their wives to participate, or the gender-related assumptions of researchers and facilitators, are defining men's control over pest management technologies, then involving women becomes a more complex task.

Source: Reference 8.

Box 31.3 Cotton IPM in India

Cotton is a very important source of income for food, medicines, education and shelter for smallholder farmers, yet cotton production is becoming less viable because of the increasing cost of pest control. Without chemicals farmers face devastating attacks by pests such as the cotton bollworm caterpillar. The threat of this pest is increasing, due to poor pesticide application practices, badly targeted applications and development of resistance to insecticides. Growers are applying ever-higher doses of pesticides, with very serious consequences for health, environmental safety and sustainability. Building on previous DFID-funded research, the project developed and tested an IPM package of methods which reduced the need for insecticides, by encouraging the build-up of natural predators and spraying only when absolutely necessary. Technically the project was a resounding success, with a dramatic reduction in the quantity of pesticides used, a substantial increase in yield, and reduction in health hazard, and with the net profit per farmer rising between three- and tenfold.

In terms of gender roles, all aspects of chemical control of cotton were carried out by men. However, although men were the only ones to mix and apply pesticides, women were responsible for monitoring tasks and for weeding. Project staff attempted to hold separate training sessions for men and women, but there were not enough female researchers to make this possible on a regular basis. Furthermore, when these sessions were held, only men seemed to apply the knowledge learned. On-farm trials to evaluate technologies were a central component of the project, but only male farmers attended. Women only began to participate fully towards the end of the three-year project.

Specific attempts were made to recruit female extension agents; it was difficult to integrate them fully into the project. The project also had a policy of placing extension agents in trial villages, but to place a young single woman in such a position would have been culturally unacceptable. Male farmers appeared to find it extremely difficult to take questions from female extensionists seriously, although were happy to be interviewed by Western women.

The Indian Ministry of Agriculture is funding promotion of the successful technology. Longer-term monitoring of the level of women's involvement will be necessary to gauge the effect that gender-related constraints will have on the impact and sustainability of the interventions.

Source: Reference 10.

from training programmes if literacy is a criterion. Constraints on women's time may make it impossible for them to attend extension sessions or to participate in research projects, and there may also be social constraints on women's mobility. Socio-cultural or religious barriers may prevent women from being in direct contact with a male extension worker or from speaking out or asking questions in a public context. In Blantyre State Highlands in Malawi, men rated local extension services more highly than did women, despite assertions by both that there was no discrimination by gender when it came to access to the extension officer [9]. Men were more likely to have access because of the type of crops they grow and through membership of (predominantly male) specialist crop clubs. Men also rated written extension material more highly than did women – unsurprising given women's lower literacy rates.

The experience outlined in Box 31.3 of an IPM cotton programme in India highlights the difficulties of fully incorporating gender concerns into projects in certain cultural environments, even where projects are fully committed to gender-sensitive approaches and necessary interventions have been identified. Box 31.4, on the other hand, demonstrates the benefits.

Box 31.4 Women benefit from cotton IPM in India

Stephanie Williamson

Increasing pesticide use by smallholder cotton farmers and its consequences for farm family health and economic welfare is a critical issue in India, particularly given the much-publicized suicides by farmers faced with bankruptcy when chemically based pest management strategies spiralled out of control. A study of farmer decision-making in pest management in cotton systems looked at differences between trained and untrained men and women farmers in training projects aiming to reduce or rationalize pesticide use.

The Farmer Field School (FFS) IPM training project is run by the local Voice Trust NGO in Tamil Nadu, in collaboration with a regional NGO: Agriculture, Man, Ecology. The FFS training helps farmers learn about the agro-ecology of their crops and promotes a wide variety of physical, cultural and biological methods of pest management, with synthetic pesticides used only when all else fails. While the FFS-trained farmers produced lower yields than those reliant on pesticides, their net income was similar or slightly higher due to the massive savings on pesticide purchase. Their pest management costs only amounted to 23–28 per cent of total costs, compared with 50 per cent for untrained farmers. The savings on pesticides were, to some extent, invested in labour (their own or hired), up to 55 per cent of total costs, compared with under 18 per cent for pesticide users. In Tamil Nadu, as in Maharashtra, women carry out the vast bulk of cotton labour, 93 per cent in the case of FFS families.

FFS farmers tended to share decision-making in pest management with their spouse, and both women and men would carry out scouting for pests and natural enemies, release parasitic wasps, and install and monitor pheromone and light traps. FFS farmers interviewed stressed that they or members of their family had suffered mild symptoms (dizziness) of pesticide poisoning after mixing and applying pesticides. One farmer said that his health had improved markedly since the training, due to reduced pesticide use. The women, who carry the water for knapsack spraying from wells, sometimes up to 2 km away, also benefited from reduced workloads, as many hours of time and drudgery were saved.

These findings reveal particular benefits for women of IPM programmes that bring significant reductions in pesticide applications. Women spend far more time working in cotton fields than men, and are at much higher risk of chronic exposure to pesticides, regardless of whether they carry out spraying themselves. Cutting back drastically on pesticide spraying therefore helps safeguard women's health in many ways.

Source: References 11,12,13.

The examples in Box 31.5 highlight projects that have considered gender differentiation in crop decision-making, labour division, workload and time constraints, knowledge, skills and confidence. Gender analysis, and incorporation into project activities, help to encourage change in crop and pest management practice, and address the needs of both women and men farmers.

Lessons learned from pest management work and gender

DFID has a clear underlying policy commitment to removing gender inequality. Experience has shown that it is crucial for projects to invest in approaches which ensure direct consultation with women in the early stages, if the whole community is to understand and participate fully in project activities.

Box 31.5 Understanding women's needs in Nicaraguan coffee production

Stephanie Williamson

A gender analysis approach has been incorporated into the training of farmers and extension staff since 1995 in the Tropical Agronomy Center for Research and Teaching's IPM programme in Nicaragua, funded by Norwegian aid. The programme uses farmer-centred learning methods based on agro-ecological understanding, field observation and group discussion and experimentation, working with over seventy different government, NGO and private sector collaborators. Programme staff soon realized that women's participation in training was low despite their involvement in many agricultural tasks, and the significant proportion of households headed by single women. From the outset, the programme set up an inter-institutional working group to understand and address gender issues related to IPM.

Studies by Gender and Agriculture Working Group members have revealed critical issues for incorporation of women farmers into training. For instance, a key reason women's participation in farmer group training had been so low was that they had not been specifically invited to attend, rather than the commonly held perception that their husbands were unwilling to let them attend. Extension staff are encouraged to consider gender aspects in their work with farmer groups and focus activities on farm families to give greater prominence to women and children. Extensionists have looked at the division of labour among family members and hired workers for different crops.

In smallholder coffee production, women play an important role in most tasks. The issue of weeding raised interesting differences between men and women's choice of control method. The programme aims to persuade farmers to reduce their use of herbicides in coffee as far as possible, for health, environmental and economic reasons. Some women coffee farmers were reluctant to move away from herbicide use because they felt it was less hard work than manual control with a machete, or cheaper than hiring a male farm hand to do manual weeding. However, women in the farmer IPM group facilitated by an NGO at Las Sabanas near Somoto explained that they decided to adapt to manual control for weeding and there was no particular reason why, with practice, they could not do this as well as men. Two women described how they did an hour or so slashing weeds each day, after sending the children to school, and this way did not exhaust themselves. After all, they added, women are used to doing lots of heavy work around the house, chopping firewood and hauling water.

Source: References 14,15,16.

The approach is inclusive, but more rigour is needed in monitoring the gender dimensions of participation in farm testing and evaluation, response, uptake and consequences – both within the research process, and in considering the pathways by which the research results will reach women and how they will be affected by changes. The need for more effective approaches and tools for monitoring changes in gender relations throughout the process of technology development has been recognized [17], and recent work has focused on this aspect [18].

When monitoring inclusion, it is important to look not just at quantitative indicators but also at the quality of inclusion, as, for example, women may attend planning sessions, but not effectively participate in them for a variety of reasons. Gender monitoring is not generally a high priority for collaborating institutions, which raises the question of incentives.

There is an important need for innovative communication and extension strategies for new alternatives to conventional pesticides, informed by an understanding of gender roles. Given lower education levels among women than men, it is very important to recruit extension staff fluent in regional languages and familiar with local practices. Projects must bear in mind the cultural constraints to incorporating women fully in projects, and consider ways to overcome this. If it really proves impossible to recruit more female extension workers, then male extension workers should receive regularly updated gender-sensitivity training. This is vital if uptake is to be maximized and knowledge gained socially embedded within the community. Some aspects, however, such as transformation in the attitudes of many male farmers to female extension workers, will necessarily have to remain a longer-term objective.

There is a danger of overgeneralization, for, although gender-specific trends and disparities clearly exist, the situation and expectations of women across the developing world are highly diverse. Nevertheless, for any DFID intervention in the area of IPM, gender sensitive and participatory approaches must remain at the core.

References

1 Department for International Development (DFID). *Eliminating World Poverty: A Challenge for the 21st Century*, White Paper, London: DFID, 1997.

2 Ashley, C., Carney, D. *Sustainable Livelihoods: Lessons from Early Experience*, London: DFID, London, 1999.

3 Malena, C. 'Gender issues in IPM in African Agriculture', NRI Socio-Economic Series 5, Natural Resources Institute (NRI), 1994.
4 DFID project, Natural Resources Systems Programme, Dryland Applied Research and Extension Project, Kenya, 1993–97.
5 DFID Project, 'Dryland research and extension project'. In Kang'ara, J.N., Sutherland, A.J., Gethi, M. (eds) *Proceedings of the Conference, Participatory Dryland Agricultural Research East of Mount Kenya*, KARI, Kitale, Kenya, 21–24 January 1997.
6 DFID project, 'The use of composted urban wastes in IPM systems to control pests and pathogens in peri-urban agriculture', DFID, Renewable Natural Resources Research, Crop Protection Programme (CPP). Case study: Warburton, H., Sarfo-Mensah, P. 1998.
7 Malena, C. *op. cit.* 1994.
8 DFID project. 'Application of mating disruption to control yellow stem borer in India'. Renewable Natural Resources Research, CPP. Case study information from Joanna White, NRI.
9 DFID project, 'The farming systems IPM project'. Blantyre State Highlands Malawi.
10 DFID project. 'Development of an area-wide strategy for the management of insecticide resistant pests of cotton in Southern India'. Renewable Natural Resources Research CPP. Case study, Russell, D., Overfield, D., NRI.
11 DFID/CPP Project. 'Analysis of farmers' decision making in pest management'. ZA0352 (R7500).
12 Little, T., Ali, M., Kimani, M., Oruko L., Williamson, S. 'A report on fieldwork carried out in Kenya and India'. CABI Bioscience for DFID CPP, December 1999–February 2000.
13 'Learning to cut the cost of chemicals in cotton: Case studies and exercises in farmer focused cotton IPM from around the world'. UK: CABI Bioscience and PAN UK, 2001.
14 CATIE-INTA IPM Project, Managua, Nicaragua, funded by Norad 1995–98, Final report, 1999.
15 First Extensionists' meeting on technical and methodological updating in vegetable and basic food crops in the Matagalpa/Jinotega region, Nicaragua, Report (Spanish), 1998.
16 Guharay, F. pers. comm. and interviews with women coffee farmers, October 2000.
17 Goldey, P., Le Breton, S., Martin, A., Marcus, R. In *Agricultural Systems*, 55(2), 1997: 155–72.
18 Locke, C., Okali, C. In *Development in Practice*, 9(39), 1999: 274–86.

32

Integrated pest management: training women to take control

John Pontius and Alifah Sri Lestari

Farmers Field Schools and Community IPM

This chapter focuses on the challenge of involving farming women in integrated pest management (IPM) educational activities through Farmer Field Schools and Community IPM activities in rice production. The goal of the programme strategy is to establish farmer-led village IPM programmes.

The Food and Agriculture Organization of the United Nations (FAO) has been providing training in IPM for farmers in irrigated tropical rice for nearly two decades [1]. The goal of the FAO programme is to help farmers establish a more ecologically balanced agro-ecosystem. To accomplish this requires that farmers learn about the impact of insecticide use in the rice agro-ecosystem.

A new departure for farmer IPM education was developed and first used in Indonesia in 1990. This training approach, known as the IPM Farmer Field School (FFS), has been successfully applied throughout Asia. The FFS is a '"learner-centred" discovery process. It seeks to empower people to solve living problems actively by fostering participation, self-confidence, dialogue, joint decision-making and self-determination' [2]. Results of FFS training include reduced pesticide use and stable yields. The FFS helps 'farmers regain the competence to make rationally based decisions concerning the management of their crops (in contrast to the instructions which were part and parcel of the Green Revolution packages). Secondly the participants gain social competence and confidence to speak and argue in the public' [3].

In 1998 the FAO programme was given a new name: the FAO Programme for Community IPM in Asia. This reflected a change in the programme's strategic approach to farmer IPM education. The term 'Community IPM' describes a strategy in which the FFS is a first step in developing sustainable management by a community of its shared agricultural and ecological resources. The goal is to institutionalize IPM at the village or local level. In a successfully institutionalized community IPM programme, farmers would be:

- acting upon their own initiative and analysis;
- identifying and resolving relevant problems;
- conducting their own local IPM programmes that include research and educational activities;
- establishing or adapting local organizations that enhance the influence of farmers in local decision-making;
- promoting a sustainable agricultural system.

An important element in the institutionalization of IPM by farmers at the village level has been Farmer IPM Trainers. Over 30,000 women and men in the Asia region have participated in post-FFS Training of Trainer (TOT) courses to learn how to facilitate the FFS approach [4]. The TOTs for Farmer IPM Trainers focus on technical issues, facilitation and leadership skills, planning, field studies and organising. These people have provided the leadership in organising local IPM programmes across the region. Box 32.1 profiles an Indonesian Farmer IPM Trainer and her efforts to help institutionalize IPM in her village.

Box 32.1 Mrs Sudaryanti, Indonesian Farmer IPM Trainer

Mrs Sudaryanti is 45 years old and a mother of four children. Her husband is an official in their village, Ngalang. She is one of sixty-seven women in the district of Gunung Kidul, Jogjakarta, Indonesia, who have been trained as Farmer IPM Trainers. Sudaryanti and her husband farm about 0.4 hectares, a fairly average farm size for their area. Her husband does the land preparation and fertilizing; she takes care of the rest, including making field observations and decisions regarding pest control.

'It's been three years since I have used any insecticides. There have been pests, but I haven't sprayed. Our yields have been as good as our neighbours'. I continue to do field observations because I want to know what is happening in the field and what actions I need to take. My farming work helps my work as a Farmer IPM Trainer. Other farmers know that I too am a farmer.'

Mrs Sudaryanti participated in an FFS in 1992. Her FFS group formed an IPM alumni group. Sudaryanti has been a leading voice in the group. 'Our alumni meetings help attendees to increase their technical understanding of IPM. The meetings also help to maintain our motivation to spread IPM to other farmers.'

In June 1994, Sudaryanti attended a TOT for Farmer IPM Trainers. In October of the same year she conducted her first FFS. Since 1994, Sudaryanti and the three other Farmer IPM Trainers in her village have organized six FFSs.

'The participants have really been highly motivated. It is important for me to maintain their trust. For example, in recent FFSs participants haven't received any compensation for attending. But I receive an honorarium as the facilitator. The participants know this. So I contribute a part of my honorarium to the group. It isn't much, but it helps to maintain our relationship. Participants know that I am serious about the FFS.'

In 1996 the village IPM alumni group decided to establish their own IPM programme. The goals of the group included: ridding their village of agricultural poisons, helping all farmers to understand and apply IPM, and empowering farmers. Sudaryanti explained empowerment in the following way.

'Before following an FFS, farmers are dependent on insecticides and government officials. If there are a few pests in the field, farmers spray insecticide and run to officials for help. After an FFS, these same farmers are able to think for themselves. This is what an FFS does: farmers learn to stand on their own and think for themselves. IPM farmers can make their own field observations, discoveries and decisions, and take action for themselves.'

The village of Ngalang now has 175 FFS alumni. The village IPM alumni group has divided itself up into seven subgroups by neighbourhood. Each subgroup has identified representatives who meet monthly to discuss field issues and the field studies of each subgroup (for example, balanced fertilizer use, urea tablet trials, and the use of organic fertilizer). These representatives then meet with their own subgroups to tell them what other subgroups are doing and what is happening in their field studies.

Women in the alumni group are trying different approaches to attract the farmers of Ngalang to IPM. Sudaryanti and several other women have been writing poems and songs about IPM. They then sing their songs or read their poetry at village festivals. 'We try to warn other farmers of the danger in using poisons and describe the role of natural enemies in the field.'

Source: Reference 5.

The countries conducting IPM farmer educational programmes using the FFS approach with support of the FAO Community IPM programme are Bangladesh, Cambodia, China, India, Indonesia, Laos, Nepal, Philippines, Sri Lanka, Thailand and Vietnam.

The role of women in rice production

Gender analyses can illustrate the division of labour between men and women in farming. Throughout Asia and Southeast Asia these analyses show high levels of involvement of women in agricultural activities, as the following highlights show.

- In Bangladesh, the commonly held view is that women do not take part in fieldwork. The reality is that women, especially in poorer households, share rice production. The Grameen Krishi Foundation found that in the northwest women equally share all tasks [6].
- Women in Cambodia are playing an increasingly large role in rice production due to the lack of male labour. Traditionally men were responsible for the initial stages of rice production and women the later stages. Women are now taking over tasks such as land preparation, irrigation and threshing [7].
- Men play the larger role in rice production in China, making decisions about what to grow, how much to grow, and where to sell. However, women are highly active in agricultural tasks, and with men migrating to cities to seek wage labour, their role is increasing [8].
- Rural women in India are extensively involved in farming activities. One study found that on a 1 hectare farm in the Indian Himalayas, a pair of bullocks work 1,064 hours, a man 1,212 hours, and a woman 3,485 hours. Typically women contribute 55–66 per cent of the labour in farm production [9].
- In Indonesia, depending on the area and the family, women's involvement might be as high as 80 per cent of the workload and 100 per cent of the decision-making, including the application of pesticides. Typically the workload is fairly balanced, with women doing more work in planting and weeding and men having a greater role in ploughing and the purchasing of inputs. Decision-making is also balanced among women and men with men taking a larger role in deciding about irrigation issues and women being more involved in determining when to weed [10]. Women head 17

per cent of farming households in Indonesia, and manage their farms alone [11].

- Lao women, due to a lack of male labour, are increasingly involved in land preparation, irrigation, preparing bunds, and seedbed preparation. Traditionally women were active only in transplanting, weeding, harvesting, threshing and post-harvest work [12].
- In Nepal, women play a large if not predominant role in agricultural production. Women both take part in and make decisions about planting, transplanting, weeding, harvesting, and post-harvest activities [13].

Box 32.2 Ms Wu Guiying: 1998 IPM alumna, China

Ms Wu Guiying lives in Xindian Village, Wangdian Town, Hubei Province. She is 32 and has a son at elementary school. She talks about how IPM has influenced her farming activities.

'My husband works in a factory far from the village. He is rarely at home, so I take care of the farm work. The area of our rice field is 0.5 hectare. I used to put pesticides on my field every time I saw a bug. I averaged ten applications of pesticides per rice season until I attended an IPM Farmers Field School in 1998.

'I observe our rice field at least once a week and often more than that. I don't take any decisions until I have had an opportunity to examine my field and analyse the conditions there. Last year we had a major outbreak of the striped stemborer. Other farmers lost as much as 30 per cent of their plants. I had a good harvest while at the same time reducing my pesticide applications from ten times the year before to only two applications. In spite of the outbreak I increased the yield on my half hectare to 4,103 kg.

'This past season I worked with three other farmers to help them learn about IPM. I visited them in their fields once a week. I helped them to learn IPM principles and how to apply them in their fields. The four of us planted rape. I learned about IPM in a rice FFS so rape was a bit new. We simply applied the same process. We observed our fields, discussed and analysed our observations, and took what we felt to be the appropriate decisions. We then applied the decisions in our fields and went through the cycle again. My half hectare yielded 1,050 kg. Not too bad; the other farmers also did pretty well.

'I am now the leader of the village Women's Union. In this position I try to remember what I learned in the FFS about group dynamics and leadership.'

Source: Reference 14.

- Women in Vietnam have traditionally been perceived as performing the 'light work' associated with rice production. In a study in the Mekong delta, it was found that ploughing was in fact the only task that women were seldom involved in, as labour for this task was generally hired [15].

The Asia region has seen an increasing feminization of agriculture. Box 32.2 presents a profile of Ms Wu Guiying from Hubei Province in China. Her husband's off-farm job means that he is rarely at home and that she must take on the major share of farm labour and management activities. This story is repeated across the region as households seek to achieve a standard of living that guarantees children's education and family well-being [16]. This seemingly basic aspiration has become increasingly difficult to achieve by relying solely on rice production for income. Thus farming families find it necessary to seek off-farm income. Usually the man takes on this role. The wages for men are generally higher than those for women, and it is thought to be easier and safer for men to journey to cities where wage labour is available. Thus it is not just coincidental that three of the four profiles of women FFS alumni presented in this article are of women whose husbands are away from home and unable to contribute to their farming enterprise. Community IPM activities, especially FFS's, need to be accessible to women in order that they become more skilled managers of their farming operations.

Insecticides and women working in agriculture

During the last ten years two major studies concerning the impact of insecticide use on the health of farmers have been conducted in Indonesia. The first study was conducted among farmers who grew rice and vegetables in Central Java. The second study was conducted among women growing vegetables in the highlands of West Sumatra. Both studies demonstrated that these farmers were at considerable risk of acute pesticide poisoning when spraying their crops. A total of 21 per cent of the respondents in the Central Java study had three or more neurological, intestinal or respiratory signs or symptoms of pesticide toxicity per spray operation [17].

Visits to respondents' homes showed that 84 per cent stored agricultural chemicals there, 75 per cent within the living or kitchen area and 82 per cent easily within the reach of children. Twenty-two per cent of the containers were partially or completely unsealed, and 50 per cent were leaking their contents. Over half of the respondents said that they used the agricultural pesticides for home and garden spraying. In 76 per cent of the households, the wife or children washed the farmer's field clothing mixed in with family laundry [18].

The West Sumatra study demonstrated that women who apply insecticides are heavily exposed to multiple hazardous insecticides and experience and exhibit acute signs and symptoms commonly associated with pesticide poisoning. Specifically, 75 per cent of the 161 farmers were using a neurotoxic substance. Most (68 per cent) experienced two to five new symptoms following the spraying operation, while 19 per cent had six or more symptoms. A household survey showed that all farmers stored pesticides in their homes and that 24 per cent of homes contained at least one leaking pesticide container; 30 per cent of the households stored pesticides within easy reach of children; 50 per cent of these women admitted to spraying during pregnancy. Fortunately, these women did not demonstrate higher rates of poor reproductive outcomes compared to age-matched rice farmer controls, although there was a statistically insignificant greater rate of congenital defects [19].

A study of pesticide use in Bangladesh found that women prepare and mix pesticides – often with their bare hands – into pots for application in the fields by men [20]. Women wash these pots after the pesticide has been applied. Additionally, women are responsible for applying pesticide to home gardens, where they often apply the pesticide directly to vegetables using a broom without wearing protective clothing.

The Pesticide Action Network Asia and the Pacific (PAN AP) interviewed over 2,500 farmers, mostly women. Their studies [21] found that:

- most women farmers and workers sprayed pesticides or came in direct contact with pesticides as part of their work;
- farmers used highly toxic pesticides including methyl parathion and monocrotophos;
- most pesticide users were not aware of the adverse effects of pesticides;
- most users did not wear protective clothing, finding it either unsuitable for the climate or too expensive;
- most of those surveyed had experienced pesticide poisoning and identified specific signs and symptoms associated with it.

All these studies demonstrate that those who apply insecticides put their health at risk. The chemicals are generally improperly stored in the home, putting all members of the household at risk. Whether farm women are applying insecticides or not (and frequently they are), if the household's farming operation includes the use of insecticides, women are likely to come into contact with them. Providing women the opportunity to participate in an FFS and in Community IPM makes sense, not only because of the feminization of agriculture but also because of the need to reduce their and their families' exposure to insecticides.

Challenges to involving women in Community IPM activities

There are many challenges to overcome in involving women in Community IPM activities. Some challenges are real; some are imagined. The most difficult to overcome have been structural challenges. Religious or cultural attitudes are not so intractable, but structural challenges usually are a result of two cultures coming together: the culture of the society reinforced or formalized by the culture of the organization providing the context for activities, usually a government organization. Some examples are:

The selection process Often the selection of FFS participants by facilitators relies on selection from farmers groups or co-operatives previously organized by the government for the purpose of extending information. Often membership in these organizations is open only to the 'head of household', generally excluding women. However, especially in Training and Visit extension systems, they offer the government field worker trained to facilitate Field Schools the easiest access to potential participants.

Lack of women field workers in the system In many countries, the government agriculture systems implementing Community IPM activities have failed to recruit significant numbers of women field workers. This limits the ability of the system to have face-to-face contact with women, especially in countries where cultural or religious barriers exist.

Structural attitudes that discourage women's participation The most common of these attitudes is that male farmers are considered the appropriate recipients of agricultural training. In Vietnam, for example, the role of women in agriculture, especially in the South, is not visible [22]. Vietnamese men hold that women 'cannot understand quickly, women are not active, and women have a low educational level' [23]. In essence, women have neither the education nor the experience needed to be able to learn and apply any agricultural training that they happen to receive. This attitude, which is not limited to Vietnam, can result in little attention being given to recruiting women farmers as FFS participants.

Non-structural issues that present challenges include:

Prevailing attitudes and habits In many parts of the region it is considered inappropriate for men and women to participate together in training activities.

The heavy workload of women It is often assumed that women's workload makes it more difficult for them to spend several hours in the morning attending a Field School. Women in Asia undertake a heavy workload inside and outside the household. In coastal central Vietnam,

> Women are the major labour force in their families. They not only take care of their husband and children, do domestic work such as cooking, washing, shopping ... but also take on other hard work, for example picking fire wood from the forest. They also take on petty trading and other jobs to earn money. Finally, they have to work in the field. They do everything from soil preparation, to sowing and transplanting, weeding, and harvesting [24].

The work is especially heavy in the early morning for rural women. There have been objections to including women in FFS because, it is argued, women cannot get food preparation, washing, and other chores completed and arrive at an FFS at the usual 8 a.m. starting time. This can be an excuse for not recruiting women. When women are involved in an FFS they manage their work such that they can attend and arrive on time.

> Often it is suggested that women, due to their many household tasks, their small trading activities, and their social obligations, present a scheduling problem for a Field School. Indeed, in the Field Schools observed, women did have obligations that drew them away from the school. In no case was a Field School meeting cancelled because too many women were unable to attend the meeting. All Field Schools were conducted at the usual time of 8:00 a.m. to 12:00 noon. Household tasks were usually completed by women before they went to the Field School. Food for the day was cooked before school, cleaning and washing was done before the Field School,

field chores, if any, were completed before the Field School. Several husbands of Field School participants were interviewed. No husband felt that the Field School disrupted the routine of their household [25].

Results of women's participation in FFSs

Boxes 32.3, 32.4 and 32.5 describe some of the benefits women have enjoyed because of their participation in FFS and Community IPM activities.

Box 32.3   Ms Romini, 1996 FFS graduate, Indonesia

This is the story of Ms Romini who lives in the village of Sempor Lor, Purbalingga District, Central Java, Indonesia. Ms Romini, 45 years old with four children, farms her family's rice fields and is the primary decision-maker regarding purchase of farm inputs and their use. Ms Romini's husband works as a trishaw driver; his farming activities are limited to field preparation and harvesting. She has been growing rice since she was a child.

'My husband's income is not enough for us to live on. The area I farm is only 750 m². I have always been interested in finding ways to farm more effectively so that I might have yields that are as high as possible. I was happy when I was asked to be one of ten women to participate in a Field School in the rainy season of 1995–96.

'Before I took part in the Field School I farmed the way my parents had taught me. I used Urea and TSP and applied diazinon three times a season. I usually made applications just after transplanting to control brown plant hoppers. Later, when rice seed bugs would appear, I sprayed again. Finally, at a point just before harvest, I would put on a final application to insure against damage before harvest. Yields from my plot averaged between 200 and 300 kg.

'After attending the Field School I changed my approach to farming. I learned that by applying pesticides I was increasing my costs as well as increasing my risks. Pesticides kill both pests and natural enemies. If I don't spray, the natural enemies do my pest control work for me. The Field School also helped me to learn about balanced fertilization and planting distances. I first started to apply IPM principles without telling anybody. My yield for the first season went up to 350 kg. Since then I have averaged around 400 kg.

'I now meet with women's groups and tell them about IPM principles and the dangers of pesticides. I tell the farmers in the fields around me to watch what I am doing and learn from me; don't stick with outmoded ways. No one near me is applying any pesticides.'

Source: Reference 26.

Box 32.4   Changes

Interview with six women farmers from Dong Phi Village in Ha Tay Province, Vietnam, who have completed IPM Field Schools.

Why did you attend Field Schools rather than your husbands?

'Our husbands work in construction and as day labourers outside of the village. This brings in cash to our households and is important. Because they are often away from home we take on the responsibility for farming. Our husbands usually are present for land preparation and harvesting, but we make the day to day decisions regarding the management of our fields.'

Did you teach them about IPM? How did you teach them?

'Our husbands needed to know about IPM. This was all new information and we learned new ways of doing things. If we were to change our ways, our husbands had to know what we were doing and why.'

'I would take my husband out to the field and show him different insects and talk to him about their functions.'

'I tried out different fertilizer practices and showed my husband what I was doing and then we weighed the results from each of our different trials.'

'Yes, I had to make sure that my husband would not be afraid because I wasn't applying pesticides. This meant I had to take him into the field and show him how the ecosystem worked.'

'Because I was buying more fertilizer my husband wanted to know what I was doing. So I talked to him about fertilizer and balanced fertilization. Then, after harvest, the first season after I attended the Field School, my husband could see the results of better fertilization. Our yield was 50 per cent higher than before.'

In general how have your yields been since attending Field Schools? Why do you think that this is true?

'Perhaps each of us has experienced different levels of increase in our harvests, but we have all seen better harvests since attending Field Schools.'

In what other ways has attending a Field School changed your lives?

'I think that we women work better together as a group. Our discussions are more open and we make sure that everybody gets to say what she is seeing in the field and give her opinion about her observations.'

'I think my husband and I are a little more careful in our decision-making, more analytical. For example, my husband thinks that we need a motorcycle. I agree that it would be useful. But rather than buying the motorcycle right away, we have analysed how we would benefit because of a motorcycle and what we would have to give up because of buying a motorcycle. Also we are examining how to purchase the motorcycle, credit or cash.'

'I go to sleep easier at night. Before my husband and I didn't know much about what was going on in our field. Now we make better, more informed decisions. We know about different factors in the field such as pests, natural enemies, fertilization, and we know how to care for our crop. We can actually take control of many things to ensure better yields. This makes me sleep easier.'

Source: Reference 27.

Box 32.5 Returns to field decisions of alumnae, Quang Binh Province, Vietnam

Having recruited women into IPM FFS, the IPM team in Quang Binh Province conducted a study to determine whether there was any financial advantage for women. They analysed economic benefits accruing to thirty women who participated in a 1998 FFS focuses on changes made in their farming practices and how these affected their crop budgets. Changes made were in seeding rate, fertilizer use, and pesticide use. The women enjoyed, on average, increased yield and incomes. When the changes in costs (in this case an overall decrease) are included, it is possible to see whether there is a positive benefit from the changes and management decisions. In this case, changes in farming practices resulted in an increased return of US$160.13.

	Seed (kg)	Fertilizer (kg) use			Pesticide apps	Cost ($/ha)	Yield (kg/ha)	Income
		Urea	P	K				
Pre-FFS	186	176	400	66	2.4		4700	752.00
Cost	59.52	31.68	24.00	13.86	34.65	163.71		
Post-FFS	156	170	454	114	1.1		5600	896.00
Cost	49.92	30.60	27.24	23.94	15.88	147.58		
Cost change	−9.60	−1.08	3.24	10.08	−18.77	−16.13		144.00
Returns to management								**$160.13**

Source: Reference 28.

Increasing women's participation in Community IPM

Several approaches have been employed to increase the participation of women in Community IPM programmes in the region. Steps have included:

Setting targets for women farmers' participation in IPM FFS The purpose of a target is simple. The national programme is attempting to achieve some designated level of rate of participation of women in FFSs. The target set in Indonesia was 30 per cent. Other countries have set similar targets.

Instituting a participatory preparation process for planning IPM Field Schools and participant selection The process includes an analysis of roles and decision-making of women and men farmers in the village where the FFS will be conducted. The goal of the gender analysis is to help people at the village level to determine locally acceptable rates of participation for women and men. The representation of men and women FFS participants is based on the degree to which each is active in rice production activities and decision-making. Since this division of labour can vary widely from one location to another, it is important that the gender analysis be 'on site'.

Training in gender awareness for IPM field trainers and field managers FFS facilitators and field managers need to understand the importance of providing opportunities for women to participate in Community IPM activities. They, too, should have the opportunity to analyse the roles of men and women in agriculture and examine the structural barriers that constrain the recruitment of women. Workshops and other activities have been used to provide this gender training.

Preparation meetings with village leaders related to the purpose of the FFS and the importance of including women as well as men Village leaders and officials in various organizations can have a major influence on who participates in an FFS. They need to be allowed to think through the role of women in rice-based agricultural systems. Meetings for these people are generally preliminary to the village gender analysis activity.

Training FFS alumnae to be IPM Farmer Trainers Increasing the number of female FFS facilitators boosts the opportunities for women to play leadership roles in Community IPM. Women FFS facilitators may have greater access to other women. It is often more acceptable for women to be training women. In general, Farmer IPM Trainers, because of their leadership skills and training, have become leaders of farmer-organized IPM programmes. The influence of women Farmer IPM Trainers in post-FFS activities helps to ensure the participation of women in Community IPM activities.

Conducting FFS in which all participants are women   Conducting FFSs that are exclusively for women is an effective option in achieving national targets for participation of women. This becomes very viable in those areas where for one reason or another it is difficult for men and women to meet together in the same group.

Using existing women's organizations or groups for basis of organising FFS   Women's unions, literacy learning groups, and other women's organizations have been used to approach women and involve them in IPM activities. China and Vietnam have had good results in working through women's unions. Nepal is undertaking an FFS within the context of women's literacy groups.

Lessons learned for gender-sensitive Community IPM activities

Generally, the steps above have been successful in drawing more women into FFS and Community IPM activities. Some of the lessons learned in trying to conduct gender-sensitive Community IPM activities include:

Target and process   The combination of applying both a target and a process provides a dual incentive for field staff. Those eager to increase women's participation have a process that can help them. Those who are less enthusiastic about involving women tend to find a target an important motivational tool. On the other hand, reliance on a target rather than employing a gender analysis process can bring about some unwanted effects and misunderstandings. For example, a target of 30 per cent for women participants in an FFS might lead to having only eight women participants in a village when there should actually be many more because of their role in agriculture in that village. Or you may get women participating when women don't play a role at all in farming in that area. Or using a target may miss the point of the gender analysis.

Farmer IPM trainers involve more women participants Data from Indonesia suggest that Farmer IPM Trainers are more successful in involving women in FFS [29]. Farmer IPM Trainers tend to be active in their own villages and are better able to involve neighbours. At least some of the structural barriers are absent. Farmer IPM Trainers become more effective in involving women when their TOTs conduct gender analyses and they become sensitized to the importance of the role of women in agriculture in their area. Farmer IPM Trainers need to know that the national programme supports and encourages the participation of women in FFS and Community IPM activities. Such knowledge will further encourage them to recruit women as FFS participants.

Female Farmer IPM Trainers improve women's participation IPM Field Trainers and male Farmer IPM Trainers have said that the quality of women's participation improves when women Farmer IPM Trainers are facilitating an FFS. Women trainers seem better able to draw other women into presenting their ideas on topics than male trainers. Women Farmer IPM Trainers have been able to affect the perceptions of local leaders, participants, farmers and other trainers regarding the capabilities of women.

Constraints to women's participation in post-FFS activities Potential constraints to women's participation in routine meetings may arise from the timing of meetings, local convention, or the media used for spreading the word about upcoming meetings. If local IPM programmes evolve with leadership that is preponderantly male, these constraints will go unheeded and limit women's participation. All villages should have women Farmer IPM Trainers. These women will be involved in organizing farmer-led IPM programmes. This will help to secure a voice for women farmers in the village.

To mix or not to mix The option of organizing FFSs that are exclusive to one gender or the other has mixed blessings. Exclusive FFSs crop up when there are national targets or dynamic women's organizations that want to organize FFSs. These might not be the best option for every village. The downside is that a mixed-gender FFS offers positive aspects that are lost in gender-exclusive FFSs [30]. Men and women bring their own different interests, experience and viewpoints. Sharing these in the FFS helps learners expand their agroecological understanding and enhance their awareness of diverse experiences, which could lead to a more collaborative atmosphere for post-FFS farmer-led activities.

Conclusion

Women can and should be participating in FFS and Community IPM activities. The profiles presented here demonstrate how women who participate in an FFS can benefit, and how communities can benefit through women's participation in FFS and Community IPM activities. The FAO Programme for Community IPM is committed to continuing to increase the participation of women in IPM field activities. This commitment arises from the desire to see rural women in Asia not only reducing their exposure to pesticides but also enjoying increased opportunities to contribute to the sustainable development of their communities.

References

1   For current information, see www.communityipm.org.
2   Roling, N., van de Fliert, E., In Roling, N, Wagemakers, M. (eds) *Facilitating Sustainable Agriculture*, Cambridge: Cambridge University Press, 1998.
3   Schmidt, P., Stiefel, J., Hurlmann, M. 'Extension of Complex Issues: Success Factors in IPM', SKAT, St Gallen Switzerland: Swiss Center for Development Cooperation in Technology and Management, 1997.
4   Programme Advisory Committee Meeting, Jakarta, FAO Programme for Community IPM in Asia, July 1999.
5   Simon, H.T. Consultant Report, FAO Technical Assistance Team, Jakarta: Indonesian National IPM Programme, 1996.
6   FAO Regional Office for Asia and the Pacific, 'Women in Agriculture, Environment, and Rural Production, Fact Sheet Series for Bangladesh, Cambodia, China, India, Lao, Nepal, Vietnam', FAO, Bangkok, n.d.
7   FAO Regional Office for Asia and the Pacific, *op. cit.*, n.d.
8   FAO Regional Office for Asia and the Pacific, *op. cit.*, n.d.
9   FAO Regional Office for Asia and the Pacific, *op. cit.*, n.d.
10 Kingsley, M.A., Suharn Siwi, Sri. 'Gender Study II: Gender Analysis, Agricultural Analysis, and Strengthening Women's Leadership Development', FAO Technical Assistance Team Report to Indonesian National IPM Program, Jakarta, 1997.
11 van de Fliert, E. In van de Fliert, E., Proost, J. (eds) *Women and IPM: Crop Protection Practices and Strategies*, Amsterdam: Royal Tropical Institute, 1999.
12 FAO Regional Office for Asia and the Pacific, *op. cit.*, n.d.
13 FAO Regional Office for Asia and the Pacific, *op. cit.*, n.d.

14 Zhang, Qiudong, 'Hubei, China PR: a case study of impact of IPM program', Indonesia: Asian Trainers Team Regional Meeting, 7–18 July, 1999.

15 Nguyen Nhat, T. In van de Fliert, Proost, *op. cit.*, 1999.

16 Saywell, T. 'Hit the road', *Far Eastern Economic Review*, 25 May 2000, pp. 78–81.

17 Kishi, M., Hirschorn N., Djajadisastra, M. *et al.* In *Scandinavian Journal of Work, Environment and Health*, 21, 1995: 124-33.

18 Kishi *et al.*, *op. cit.*, 1995.

19 Murphy *et al.*, 1997, reviewed by Watterson, A., 'Pesticides and reproduction – women farmers in Indonesia', *Pesticides News*, 44, June 1999: 12.

20 Rengam, S.V. In van de Fliert, Proost, *op. cit.*, 1999.

21 Rengam, *op. cit.*, 1999.

22 Nguyen Nhat, *op. cit.*, 1999.

23 'Women and IPM', Center of Family and Women's Studies, Hanoi, 1994.

24 Vien, Le Hong, Women in IPM Programme – Quang Binh Province, Asian Trainers Team Regional Meeting, Vietnam, 1999.

25 Sri Lestari, A. 'Women and IPM Field Schools, in Farmer IPM Training: the Indonesian case', Indonesian National IPM Programme, Yogyakarta, 1993.

26 Susianto, A., Purwadi, D., Pontius, J. 'Kaligondang Sub-district: a case history of an IPM sub-district, Community IPM: six cases from Indonesia', FAO Technical Assistance, Indonesian National IPM Program, Jakarta, 1998.

27 Pontius, J. Consultant Report, FAO Programme for Community IPM in Asia, March 1999.

28 Vien, *op. cit.*, 1999.

29 FAO Technical Assistance Team, Final Report on FAO Technical Assistance Under UTF/INS/072/INS for the IPM Training Project of the Indonesian National IPM Program (Final Draft), Jakarta, June, 1998

30 Sri Lestari, *op. cit.*, 1993.

Technical annex

Pesticides included in international conventions and the PAN Dirty Dozen

Active ingredient	PIC	POPs	LRTAP	Dirty Dozen
2,4,5-T	•	•		•
Aldicarb				•
Aldrin	•	•	•	•
Binapacryl	•			
Captafol	•			
Chlordane	•	•	•	•
Chlordecone			•	
Chlordimeform	•			•
Chlorobenzilate	•			
DBCP				•
DDT	•	•	•	•
Dieldrin	•	•	•	•
Dinoseb and Dinoseb salts	•			
1,2-Dibromoethane (EDB, or Ethylene dibromide)	•			•
Endrin		•	•	•
Ethylene dichloride	•			
Ethylene oxide	•			
Fluoroacetamide	•			
HCH, mixed isomers	•		•	•
Heptachlor	•	•		•
Hexachlorobenzene	•		•	
Lindane	•		•	•

Active ingredient	PIC	POPs	LRTAP	Dirty Dozen
Mercury compounds, including: mercuric oxide, Mercurous chloride, Calomel, other inorganic mercury compounds, Alkyl mercury compounds, Alkoxyalkyl/ Aryl mercury compounds	•			
Methyl bromide*	–	–		–
Mirex		•	•	
Paraquat				•
Pentachlorophenol	•	•		•
Toxaphene (camphechlor)	•	•	•	•

The following severely hazardous formulations are in PIC

Monocrotophos 600 g/l (SL) formulation and higher	•			
Methamidophos 600 g/l (SL) formulation and higher	•			
Phosphamidon 1000 g/l (SL) formulation and higher	•			
Methyl parathion emulsifiable concentrates (EC) with 19.5%, 50%, 50%, 60% active ingredients and dusts containing 1.5%, 2% and 3% active ingredient)	•			•
Parathion all formulations: aerosols, dustable powder (DP), emulsifiable concentrate (EC), granules (GR) and wettable powders (WP) of this substance are included, except capsule suspensions (CS)	•			•

Industrial chemicals in PIC

Crocidolite	•			
Polybrominated biphenyls (PBB)	•			
Polychlorinated biphenyls (PCB), except mono- and dichlorinated	•			
Polychlorinated terphenyls (PCT)	•			
tris (2,• Dibromopropyl) phosphate	•			

* Ozone-depleting pesticide (Montreal Protocol). The Montreal Protocol on ozone-depleting substances requires industrialized countries to phase out use of methyl bromide by 2005, with a period of grace for developing countries to 2015. The pesticide is still widely used as a fumigant and soil sterilant.

Prior Informed Consent (PIC) (the Rotterdam Convention)

The PIC procedure was established by the UN Food and Agriculture Organization (FAO) and UN Environment Programme (UNEP) as a voluntary initiative in 1989, and governments signed a Convention in September 1998. It will enter into force when 50 governments have ratified, but is operating voluntarily. PIC informs governments of bans and severe restrictions taken in other countries, and registers government decisions on whether to allow or prohibit import of these pesticides. Exporting countries must ensure compliance.

Persistent Organic Pollutants (POPs) (the Stockholm Convention)

The POPs Convention was signed in May 2001, and 50 governments must ratify before it enters into force. It will phase out the production and use, or otherwise eliminate, 12 POPs (nine are pesticides) and it established criteria to identify new POPs. Although some of the pesticides are obsolete, many obsolete stocks require disposal. The main pesticide still in use is DDT, used in many countries for indoor control of mosquitoes as malaria vectors.

LRTAP

The Convention on Long-range Transboundary Air Pollution (LRTAP) of the UN Economic Commission for Europe covers chemicals which travel long distances before deposition where they cause damage. The Convention was signed in 1979. A Protocol on Persistent Organic Pollutants (POPs) adopted in 1998 formed the basis of the Stockholm Convention. LRTAP focuses on 16 substances, which include 11 pesticides (grouping HCH and lindane as one), two industrial chemicals and three byproducts/contaminants.

PAN Dirty Dozen

The Dirty Dozen (now 18) is a PAN initiative. Its aim was to bring attention to and stop the use of these particularly harmful chemicals. Although partly successful – most of the Dirty Dozen have now been included in the PIC and/or POPs conventions, three pesticides (aldicarb, DBCP and paraquat) are not yet subject to international regulation.

World Health Organization classifications

The WHO classification measures acute toxicity. FAO recommends that WHO Ia and Ib pesticides should not be used in developing countries, and if possible class II should also be avoided. Note that a 'weaker' formulation will move these active ingredients into a lower hazard classification.

WHO Ia: extremely hazardous

Aldicarb
Brodifacoum
Bromadiolone
Bromethalin
Calcium cyanide
Captafol
Chlorethoxyfos
Chlormephos
Chlorophacinone
Difenacoum
Difethialone
Diphacinone
Disulfoton
EPN
Ethoprophos

Flocoumafen
Fonofos
Hexachlorobenzene
Mercuric chloride
Mevinphos
Parathion
Parathion, methyl
Phenylmercury acetate
Phorate
Phosphamidon
Sodium fluoroacetate
Sulfotep
Tebupirimfos
Terbufos

WHO Ib: highly hazardous

3–chloro-1,2-propanediol
Acrolein
Allyl alcohol
Azinphos ethyl
Azinphos methyl
Blasticidin-S
Butocarboxim
Butoxycarboxim
Cadusafos
Calcium arsenate
Carbofuran
Chlorfenvinphos
Coumaphos
Coumatetralyl
Demeton-s-methyl
Dichlorvos
Dicrotophos
Dinoterb
DNOC
Edifenphos

Ethiofencarb
Famphur
Fenamiphos
Flucythrinate
Fluoroacetamide
Formetanate
Furathiocarb
Heptenophos
Isazofos
Isofenphos
Isoxathion
Lead arsenate
Mecarbam
Mercuric oxide
Methamidophos
Methidathion
Methiocarb
Methomyl
Monocrotophos
Nicotine

Omethoate
Oxamyl
Oxydemeton methyl
Paris green
Pentachlorophenol
Pindone
Pirimiphos ethyl
Propaphos
Propetamphos
Sodium arsenite
Sodium cyanide

Strychnine
Tefluthrin
Thallium sulfate
Thiofanox
Thiometon
Triazophos
Vamidothion
Warfarin
Zeta cypermethrin
Zinc phosphide

Gaseous or volatile fumigants*

Aluminium phosphide
Chloropicrin
1,2-Dibromoethane
1,3-Dichloropropene
Ethylene dichloride
Ethylene oxide

Formaldehyde
Hydrogen cyanide
Magnesium phosphide
Methyl bromide
Phosphine
Sulfuryl fluoride

---

* The WHO classification does not set out any criteria for air concentrations on which classification could be based. Most of these compounds are of high hazard, and recommended exposure limits for occupational exposure have been adopted by national authorities in many countries. [The WHO Recommended Classification of Pesticides by Hazard and Guidelines to Classification 2000–01. UNEP/ILO/WHO. WHO/PCS01.4. www.who.int/pcs/docs/Classification%20of%20Pesticides%202000–01.pdf]

WHo classification of pesticides: LD50 for rat (mg/kg body weight)

Class	Oral		Dermal	
	solids	liquids	solids	liquids
Ia Extremely hazardous	5	20	10	40
Ib Highly hazardous	5–50	20–200	10–100	40–400
II Moderately hazardous	50–500	200–2000	100–1000	400–4000
III Slightly hazardous	>500	>2000	>1000	>4000

The terms 'solid' and 'liquids' refer to the physical state of the active ingredient.

The LD50 value is a statistical estimate of the amount in mg of toxicant per kg of bodyweight required to kill 50% of a large population of test animals.

Organophosphate pesticides

Organophosphates (OPs) are the most widely used group of insecticides in the world and many of these do not appear on restricted lists. They are among the most acutely toxic of all pesticides to both insect pests and to vertebrate animals and humans. OPs are hazardous both to professional and amateur users. They are regularly detected in food items such as fruit and vegetables, and occasionally occur above a safety level known as the acute reference dose (an estimate of a daily oral exposure to the human population, including sensitive subgroups, that is likely to be without an appreciable risk of deleterious effects during a lifetime).

Active ingredient	WHO class		
Acephate	III	Dicrotophos	Ib
Azamethiphos	III	Dimefox	O
Azinphos ethyl	Ib	Dimethoate	II
Azinphos methyl	Ib	Dimethylvinphos	–
Bromophos	O	Dioxabenzofos	O
Bromophos ethyl	O	Dioxathion	O
Cadusafos	Ib	Disulfoton	Ia
Carbophenothion	O	Ditalimfos	O
Chlorethoxyfos	Ia	Edifenphos	Ib
Chlorfenvinphos	Ib	Endothion	O
Chlormephos	Ia	EPN	Ia
Chlorphoxim	O	ESP	O
Chlorpyrifos	II	Ethion	II
Chlorpyrifos methyl	U	Ethoprophos	Ia
Chlorthiophos	O	Etrimfos	II
CI 26691	–	Famphur	Ib
Coumaphos	Ib	Fenamiphos	Ib
Crotoxyphos	O	Fenchlorphos	O
Crufomate	O	Fenitrothion	II
Cyanofenphos	O	Fensulfothion	O
Cyanophos	II	Fenthion	II
Demephion-O	O	Fonofos	Ia
Demephion-S	O	Formothion	II
Demeton-O	O	Fosmethilan	O
Demeton-S	O	Fosthiazate	–
Demeton-S methylsulphon	O	Fosthietan	O
Demeton-s-methyl	Ib	Heptenophos	Ib
Dialifos	O	Iodofenphos (Jodfenphos)	O
Diazinon	II	Isazofos	Ib
Dichlofenthion	O	Isofenphos	Ib
Dichlorvos	Ib	Isothioate	O

Isoxathion	Ib	Profenofos	II
Leptophos	O	Propaphos	Ib
Malathion	III	Propetamphos	Ib
Menazon	O	Prothiofos	II
Mephosfolan	O	Prothoate	O
Methacrifos	II	Pyraclofos	II
Methamidophos	Ib	Pyridaphenthion	III
Methidathion	Ib	Quinalphos	II
Mevinphos	Ia	Salithion	O
Monocrotophos	Ib	Schradan	O
Naled	II	Sulfotep	Ia
Omethoate	Ib	Sulprofos	II
Oxydemeton methyl	Ib	Tebupirimfos	Ia
Parathion	Ia	Temephos	U
Parathion, methyl	Ia	TEPP	O
Phenthoate	II	Terbufos	Ia
Phorate	Ia	Tetrachlorvinphos	U
Phosalone	II	Thiometon	Ib
Phosfolan	O	Thionazin	O
Phosmet	II	Triazophos	Ib
Phosphamidon	Ia	Trichlorfon	II
Phoxim	II	Trichloronat	O
Pirimiphos ethyl	Ib	Vamidothion	Ib
Pirimiphos methyl	III		

U Unlikely to present acute hazard in normal use.
O Active ingredients believed to be obsolete or discontinued for use as pesticides.

Source: This list is taken from PAN UK's active ingredient database and referenced against WHO classification of active pesticide ingredients.

Pesticides that cause cancer

This list cites potential pesticide carcinogens from the International Agency for Research on Cancer (IARC), US Environmental Protection Agency (EPA) and the European Union (EU) found in public documents.

In 1993, Pesticides News listed 70 possible carcinogens – now the list has grown to over 160. Many of the pesticides included are obsolete chemicals but may be found in stockpiles. Other pesticides are still in use, especially those cited by the US EPA. For some pesticides, like DDT, there is agreement about carcinogenic potential, but with many others authorities do not have similar positions.

The information supplied is taken from a range of sources, and it has not been easy to locate the relevant information. Indeed there are some inconsistencies and inaccuracies between and within the source documents. We invite comment, and hope that this information helps to stimulate international debate on how regulators deal with potentially carcinogenic pesticides.

Active ingredient	US EPA	EU	IARC
Acephate	C		
Acetaldehyde	B2		2B
Acetochlor	B2		
Acifluorfen	B2		
Acrolein	C		
Acrylonitrile	B1		2B
AD 67(MON 4660)	L2		
Alachlor	L1	3	
Aldrin	B2		
Amitraz	C		
Amitrole	B2	3	2B
Aramite	B2		2B
Asulam	C		
Atrazine	C		
Azobenzene	B2	2	
Benomyl	C		
Benoxacor	S		
Bifenthrin	C		
Bis(chloroethyl)ether (BCEE)	B2		
Bromacil	C		
Bromoxynil	C		
Buprofezin	S		
Butachlor	L2		
Cacodylic acid	B2		
Captafol	B2	2	2A
Captan	B2	3	
Carbaryl	C	3	

Active ingredient	US EPA	EU	IARC
Carbendazim	C		
Carbon tetrachloride	B2	3	2B
Chlordane	B2	3	2B
Chlordecone		3	2B
Chlordimeform and its hydrochloride	B2	3	
Chlorfenapyr	S		
Chlorothalonil	L2	3	2B
Chlozolinate		3	
Clodinafop-propargyl	L2		
Clofencet (MON 21200)	C		
Clofentezine	C		
Creosote	B1		2A
Cyanazine	C		
Cypermethrin	C		
Cyproconazole (SAN 619F)	B2		
Daminozide	B2	3	
DCPA	C		
DDT	B2	3	2B
Diallate		3	
Dibromochloropropane (DBCP)	B2	2	2B
Dichlobenil	C		
Dichloroethane, 1,2-	B2		2B
Dichloropropene, 1,3-	B2		2B
Dichlorvos	S		2B
Diclofop-methyl	L2		
Dicofol	C		
Dicrotophos	S		
Dieldrin	B2		
Difenoconazole	C		
Dimethenamid	C		
Dimethipin	C		
Dimethoate	C		
Dinoseb	C		
Diuron	Known	3	
Ethalfluralin	C		
Ethiozin	Tentative C		
Ethofenprox	C		
Ethoprop	L2		
Ethylene dibromide	B2	2	2A
Etridiazole		3	
Fenbuconazole	C		
Fenoxycarb	L2		
Fentin acetate		3	
Fentin hydroxide		3	
Fipronil	C		
Fluometuron	C		

Active ingredient	US EPA	EU	IARC
Flusilazole		3	
Fluthiacet-methyl	L2		
Folpet	B2	3	
Fomesafen	C		
Formaldehyde	B1	3	2A
Furilazole	L2		
Furmecyclox	B2	3	
Haloxyfop-methyl	B2		
Heptachlor	B2	3	2B
Heptachlor epoxide	B2		
Hexachlorobenzene	B2	2	2B
Hexaconazole	C		
Hexythiazox	C		
Hydramethylnon	C		
Hydrogen cyanamide	C		
Imazalil	L2		
Iprodione	L2	3	
Isoproturon		3	
Isoxaben	C		
Isoxaflutole	L2		
Kresoxim-methyl	L2		
Lactofen	B2		
Lindane	B2	3	2B
Linuron	C	3	
Malathion	S		
Mancozeb	B2		
Maneb	B2		
Metam sodium and its dihydrate	B2		
Methidathion	C		
Metolachlor	C		
MGK-264	C		
Mirex			2B
Molinate	C		
Monuron		3	
Monuron-TCA		3	
Nitrapyrin	L2		
Nitrofen		2	2B
Norflurazon	C		
Orthophenylphenol and Na salt	B2		
Oryzalin	C		
Oxadiazon	C		
Oxadixyl	C		
Oxyfluorfen	C		
Oxythioquinox	B2		
Parathion, Ethyl	C		
Pendimethalin	C		

Active ingredient	US EPA	EU	IARC
Pentachloronitrobenzene	C		
Pentachlorophenol	B2	3	
Permethrin	C		
Phosmet	C		
Phosphamidon	C		
Piperonyl butoxide	C		
Prochloraz	C		
Procymidone	B2		
Prodiamine	C		
Pronamide (Propyzamide)	B2		
Propachlor	L2		
Propargite	B2		
Propazine	C	3	
Propiconazole	C		
Propoxur	B2		
Propyzamide		3	
Pymetrozine	L2		
Pyrethrins	L2		
Pyrimethanil	C		
Pyrithiobac-sodium	C		
Quintozene (Pentachloronitrobenzene)	C		
Simazine	C	3	
Sulfallate		2	2B
Sulfosulfuron	L2		
Tebuconazole	C		
Terbutryn	C		
Terrazole	B2		
Tetrachloroethane, 1,1,2,2-	C		
Tetrachlorvinphos	C		
Tetraconazole	L2		
Tetramethrin	C		
Thiabendazole	L2		
Thiamethoxam	L2		
Thiazopyr	C		
Thiodicarb	B2		
Thiopanate-methyl	L2		
Toxaphene	B2	3	2B
Tralkoxydim	L2		
Triadimefon	C		
Triadimenol	C		
Triallate	C		
Tribenuron methyl	C		
Trichlorfon	L1		
Tridiphane	C		
Trifluralin	C		
Triflusulfuron-methyl	C		

Active ingredient	US EPA	EU	IARC
Triphenyltin hydroxide	B2		
Uniconazole	C		
Vinclozolin	C	3	
Ziram	L2		
Pesticide groups			
Arsenic and its compounds (herbicides and wood preservatives)			1
Cadmium and its compounds (fungicides)			1
Chlorophenoxy herbicides			2B
Chromium VI compounds (insecticides, fungicides and wood preservatives)			1
Hexachlorocyclohexanes (insecticides)			2B
Methylmercury compounds (fungicides)			2B
Nickel and its compounds (fungicides)			1
Non-arsenical insecticides (occupational exposures)			2A
Polychlorophenols and sodium salts (mixed exposures) (wood preservatives and microbiocides)			2B

Definitions of cancer categories:

US Environmental Protection Agency (EPA)

The US EPA has changed its classification systems in recent years. Some categories have similar definitions.

Weight-of-evidence categories developed during the 1980s:

Group B = Probable Human Carcinogen
    B1 indicates limited human evidence
    B2 indicates sufficient evidence in animals and inadequate or no evidence in humans.
Group C = Possible Human Carcinogen.

Weight-of-evidence categories developed during the 1990s:

Known/Likely = Available tumour effects and other key data are adequate to demonstrate convincingly a carcinogenic potential for humans.
L1 = Likely at high doses but Not Likely at low doses

L2 = Likely to be carcinogenic to humans, available tumour effects and other key data are adequate to demonstrate carcinogenic potential for humans.

S = Cannot be Determined. Suggestive evidence from human or animal data is suggestive of carcinogenicity, but is not sufficient to conclude as to human carcinogenic potential.

Source: Office of Pesticide Programs List of Chemicals Evaluated for Carcinogenic Potential, US EPA. See details at www.epa.gov/pesticides/carlist/ although list not available on website, August 2000.

European Union (EU)

There is no single EU list available denoting carcinogenic pesticides. EC Directive 67/548 and subsequent amendments provide the classification of dangerous substances, including pesticides. The cancer classifications are:

Category 2 (denoted as R45 on the pesticide label) = May Cause Cancer.

Category 3 (denoted as R40 on label) = Possible Risk of Irreversible Effects (Cancer, as cited in table).

Sources: EC Directive 67/548 EEC and subsequent amendments; Chemicals (Hazard Information and Packaging for Supply) [CHIP2] Regulations 1994, Health and Safety Executive, UK.

International Agency for Research on Cancer

Group 1 = Carcinogenic to Humans

Group 2A = Probably Carcinogenic to Humans (limited evidence of carcinogenicity in humans and sufficient evidence in experimental animals).

Group 2B = Possibly Carcinogenic to Humans (limited evidence of carcinogenicity in humans and less than sufficient evidence in experimental animals).

Source: 193.51.164.11/monoeval/grlist.html [Note: lists cited include many non-pesticides].

Endocrine disrupting pesticides

Some pesticides are now suspected of being endocrine disruptors. These chemicals affect parts of the body's hormone systems and can lead to an increase in birth defects, sexual abnormalities and reproductive failure. As yet, there are still many aspects of these substances that we do not understand. Regulators cannot even agree on what is, and what is not, an endocrine disrupting chemical (EDC), and from the lists cited below there are few pesticides that all the authorities agree on as an EDC. The nearest they come to it is with DDT.

Active ingredient	UK EA	DEFRA	Ger. EA	EU	OSPAR	WWF
Acetochlor				3		3
Alachlor				3		3
Aldrin	3					3
Amitraz			3P			
Atrazine	3			3	3P	3
Benomyl			3P			3
Beta-HCH					3P	3
Carbendazim			3P			
Carbofuran			3P			3
Chlordane				3	3P	3
Chlordecone				3	3P	3
Chlorpyrifos			3P			
DDT	3	3		3	3P	3
Deltamethrin			3P			3
Demeton-s-methyl	3					
Dichlorvos	3					
Dicofol					3P	3
Dieldrin	3				3P	3
Dimethoate	3		3P			3
Endosulfan	3				3P	3
Endrin	3					3
Epoxyconazole			33			
Fentin acetate				3		
Glyphosate			3P			
HCB				3	3P	3
Lindane	3	3		3	3P	3
Linuron	3			3		3
Maneb				3		3
Metam				3		
Metiram			33			3
Methoxychlor		3			3P	3

Active ingredient	UK EA	DEFRA	Ger. EA	EU	OSPAR	WWF
Mirex				3		3
Oxydemeton-methyl			3P			
Penconazole			3P			
Permethrin	3					3
Prochloraz			3P			
Procymidone			33			
Prometryn					3P	
Propiconazole			3P			
Simazine	3					3
Thiram				3		
Toxaphene				3	3P	3
Tributyltin	3			3	3P	3
Triphenyltin				3		
Trichlorfon			3P			
Tridemorph			3P			
Trifluralin	3					3
Vinclozolin		3	33	3	3P	3
Zineb				3		3

Key

33 = confirmed EDC

3P = identified as potential EDC

3 = identified according to definitions below

UK EA   On the UK Environment Agency's list of target EDCs, Strategy for Endocrine disrupting chemicals, www.environment-agency.gov.uk/commondata/105385/139909

DEFRA   Identified as associated with endocrine disruption by the UK Department for Environment, Food and Rural Affairs, website: Hormone Disrupting Substances in the Environment www.defra.gov.uk/environment/hormone/index.htm

Ger. EA   Potential and confirmed EDCs by the German Federal Environment Agency column, Pesticides suspected of endocrine disrupting effects by Germany's Federal Environment Agency, ENDS Report 290, March 1999.

EU   Considered as high concern EDC by the European Union, Commission moots priority list of endocrine chemicals, BKH/TNO report, June 2000.

OSPAR   Identified as a potential EDC under Oslo and Paris Commission, Endocrine disrupting pesticide: Gwynne Lyons. Pesticides News 46, December 1999.

WWF   World Wide Fund for Nature list of pesticides reported to have reproductive and/or endocrine disrupting effects. There are a number of other pesticides WWF suspect of being EDCs, but they are not listed if no other authority above cited them (for the full list see below).

WWF list of pesticides in the environment reported to have reproductive and/or endocrine disrupting effects

Herbicides

2,4-D, 2,4,5-T, acetochlor, alachlor, amitrole, atrazine, bromacil, bromoxynil, cyanazine, DCPA (dacthal), ethiozin, glufosinate-ammonium, ioxynil, linuron, metribuzin, molinate, nitrofen, oryzalin, oxyacetmide/fluthamide (FOE 5043), paraquat, pendimethalin, picloram, prodiamine, pronamide, simazine, terbutryn, thiazopyr, triclorobenzene, trifluralin

Fungicides

benomyl, etridiazole, fenarimol, fenbuconazole, hexachlorobenzene, mancozeb, maneb, metiram, nabam, penachloronitrobenzene, pentachlorophenol, triadimefon, tributyltin, vinclozolin, zineb, ziram

Insecticides

aldicarb, aldrin, bifenthrin, carbaryl, carbofuran, chlordane, chlordecone, chlorfentezine, 8-cyhalothrin, DDT and metabolites DDE, DDD, deltamethrin, dicofol, dieldrin, dimethoate, dinitrophenol, endosulfan (a and b), endrin, ethofenprox, fenitrothion, fenvalerate, fipronil, a-HCH, heptachlor and H-epoxide, lindane (g-HCH), malathion, methomyl, methoxychlor, mirex, oxychlordane, parathion (methyl parathion), photomirex, pyrethrins, synthetic pyrethroids, ronnel (fenchlorfos), toxaphene, transnonachlor

Nematicide

DBCP

Rodenticide

n-2-fluorenylacetamide

Sources: Colborn, T. 'Endocrine disruption from environmental toxicants'. In: Rom, W.N. (ed.) *Environmental and Occupational Medicine*, 3rd edn, Lippincott-Raven, Philadelphia 1998. Brucker-Davis. F., 'Effects of environmental synthetic chemicals on thyroid function'. In *Thyroid* 8(9) 1998: 827–56. Short,. P., Colborn. T., 'Pesticide use in the US and policy implications: a focus on herbicides'. In *Toxicol Ind Health* 15(1/2), 1999: 240–75. See also WWF Canada's site on the internet for list and references: www.wwf.ca/satellite/hormone-disruptors/

Web resources

The information in this document was accurate at the time of printing. However for the most up-to-date data it is best to visit the sites of those organizations responsible for the various classifications.

International organizations

Food and Agriculture Organization of the UN (FAO) www.fao.org/
International Agency for Research on Cancer (IARC) www.iarc.fr/
Intergovernmental Forum on Chemical Safety (IFCS) www.who.int/ifcs/index.html
International Programme on Chemical Safety (IPCS) www.who.int/pcs/
United Nations Environmental Programme (UNEP) www.unep.ch/
World Health Organization www.who.int/

United Kingdom

Pesticides Safety Directorate www.pesticides.gov.uk/
Pesticide Residues Committee www.pesticides.gov.uk/committees/PRC/prc.htm

United States

Environmental Protection Agency (EPA) www.epa.gov
Recognition and Management of Pesticide Poisonings www.epa.gov/oppfod01/
safety/healthcare/handbook/handbook.htm

Academic

Pesticide Management Education Program (Cornell University) www. pmep.
cce.cornell.edu/
Program on Breast Cancer and Environmental Risk Factors (Cornell University)
www.cfe.cornell.edu/bcerf/

Persistent Organochlorine Pollutants (POPs)

United Nations Environment Programme on POPs www.chem.unep.ch/pops/
International POPs Elimination Network www.ipen.ecn.c2
Stockholm Convention on POPs www.pops.int/

PAN Pesticide Database

The PAN Pesticide Database (www.pesticideinfo.org/), developed by PAN North America, contains information on pesticides from a collection of sources, providing data on human toxicity (chronic and acute), ecotoxicity and regulatory information for about 5,400 pesticide active ingredients and their transformation products, as well as adjuvants and solvents used in pesticide products. The database has been integrated with the US EPA product databases for information on formulated products containing the active ingredients. The information is most complete for pesticides registered for use in the United States

Pesticide information

EXTOXNET – EXtension TOXicology NETwork www.ace.ace.orst.edu/info/extoxnet/
ghindex.html

Abbreviations and glossary

Units of measurement

g	gram
mg	milligram: 10^{-3} grams, 1 thousandth of a gram
μg	microgram: 10^{-6} grams, 1 millionth of a gram
ng	nanogram: 10^{-9} grams, 1 billionth of a gram
pg	picogram: 10^{-12} grams, 1 trillionth of a gram
ppm	parts per million: mg/kg, μg/g, mg/l, μg/ml
ppb	parts per billion: μg/kg, ng/g, μg/l, ng/ml
ppt	parts per trillion: ng/kg, pg/g, ng/l, pg/ml

Abbreviations

AChE	Acetylcholinesterase
AR	Androgen Receptor
CI	Confidence interval
DBD	DNA binding domain
DPV	Crop Protection Service (French)
EDC	Endocrine disrupting chemical
EPA	Environmental Protection Agency (USA)
ER	Oestrogen receptor
FAO	Food and Agriculture Organization of the United Nations
FFS	Farmer Field School
FSH	Follicle-stimulating hormone
hCG	Human chorionic gonadotropin
HRE	Hormone response elements
HSE	Health and Safety Executive (UK)
IARC	International Agency for Research into Cancer
ICD	International Classification of Disease

ILO	International Labour Organization
IPCS	International Programme on Chemical Safety
IPM	Integrated pest management
I-TEQ	International Toxic Equivalencies
IUPAC	International Union of Pure and Applied Chemistry
LBD	Ligand-binding domain
LH	Luteinizing hormone
MCS	Multiple chemical sensitivity
NGO	Non-governmental organization
PAHO	Pan American Health Organization
PAN	Pesticide Action Network
PIC	Prior informed consent
POPs	Persistent organic pollutant
PXR	Pregnane X receptor
QSAR	Quantitative structure–activity relationship
RXR	Retinoid X receptor
SHR	Steroid Hormone Receptor
SIR	Standard Incidence Ratio
UNITAR	United Nations Institute for Training and Research
UNEP	United Nations Environment Programme
US EPA	Environmental Progection Agency (USA)
WHO	World Health Organization

Pesticides/chemicals

BHC	γ-benzene hexachloride
DBCP	1,2-dibromocholoropropane
DDT	dichlorodiphenyltrichloroethane
DDE	a metabolite of DDT
DNOC	dinitrocresol
EBDC	ethylene bis-dithiocarbamate (e.g. maneb and mancozeb)
HCB	hexachlorobenzene
HCH	hexachlorocyclohexane (of which lindane is a derivative)
OC	organochlorine pesticide
OCDD	octachlorodibenzo-p-dioxin
OP	organophosphorus pesticide
PCB	polychlorinated biphenyls
PCP	pentachlorophenol
TCDD	2,3,7,8-tetrachlorodibenzo-p-dioxin
PCDD	polychlorinated dibenzo-p-dioxins
PCDF	polychlorinated dibenzo-p-furans

Glossary

Note: many of the papers in Part II contain specialized vocabulary. For reasons of length it has not been possible to include all these in the glossary; definitions can be found in a science or medical dictionary.

Acceptable Daily Intake (ADI) The dose of a substance that is anticipated to be without appreciable health risk to humans when taken daily over the course of a lifetime.

Acute toxicity An effect observed within a short period (several days – usually less than two weeks) of a single exposure or multiple exposures of an organism to a pesticide.

Additive effect Combined effect of two or more chemicals equal to the sum of their individual effects.

Aetiology Study or science of the causes of disease; cause of a specific disease

Carcinogen Any substance capable of producing cancer or a chemical that causes or induces cancer.

Chi-square (χ^2) test A statistical test to compare characteristics of more than two groups. It involves comparison of observed differences and those that may be expected to arise by chance. It is useful for testing the presence or absence of association between characteristics that cannot be expressed quantitatively, e.g. eye colour.

Cholinesterase/acetylcholinesterase An enzyme found in nerve junctions which rapidly destroys the acetylcholine released during the transmission of a nerve impulse so that subsequent impulses may pass. Organophosphate pesticides inhibit the production of cholinesterase.

Chronic Occurring over a long period of time, either continuously or intermittently: used to describe ongoing exposures and effects that develop only after a long exposure.

Confidence interval A measure of the estimated results from repeated sampling of a similar size population to the study group. A confidence interval of 1 (equal to or less than one) is not considered significant. Statistical significance tests indicate whether the increased risk could have occurred by chance. See also 'p' value.

Dermal Of the skin/through or by the skin.

Endogenous Naturally originating from within the human body.

Endocrine gland   Manufactures one or more hormones and secretes them directly into the bloodstream: includes the pituitary, thyroid, parathyroid, and adrenal glands, the ovary and testis, the placenta, and part of the pancreas.

Epidemiology   The study of the distribution and determinants of health-related states or events in populations.

Exogenous   Originating outside the body.

Exposure   Contact with a chemical. The main routes of exposure for humans are dermal absorption (skin), ingestion (by mouth) and inhalation (breathing).

Genotype   The genetic constitution of an individual or group, as determined by the particular set of genes it possesses.

Half-life   The period of time necessary for one half of a substance to disappear or be transformed into another substance, which may have different toxicity.

Hormone   A chemical substance secreted by a gland and which exerts control on other body systems.

International Toxic Equivalent Factors (I-TEF)   A summary measure for all PCDD/F and dioxin-like PCBs, which expresses the toxicity of the other PCDD/F-congeners relative to the toxicity of TCDD as a TEQ value.

Isomer   A chemical compound that has the same molecular formula as another compound but different molecular structures or different arrangements of atoms in space.

LD$_{50}$ Lethal dose: the lowest dose causing death in 50 per cent of test animals.

Mutagen   An agent that causes a permanent genetic change in a cell other than that which occurs during normal genetic recombination.

Oestrogen   Steroid hormone that controls female sexual development, promoting the growth and function of the female sex organs and female secondary sexual characteristics.

'p' value   A statistical significance test where 'p' values 0.05 (5%) are considered significant; the smaller the 'p' the more significant the findings. See also Confidence Interval.

Prior informed consent (PIC)   An international convention covering banned and severely restricted pesticides, meeting certain criteria, which cannot be exported without prior agreement of the importing country.

Quantitative structure–activity relationship (QSAR)   A statistically valid mathematical expression describing the variation in biological potency within a series of chemicals in terms of some combination of their structural properties.

Risk The probability of the occurrence of an unwanted adverse effect.

Risk ratios The number of cases observed versus the number expected in a control or the standard population. A ratio greater than one indicates increased risk; two or more indicates greater epidemiological importance.

Synergistic/synergism An interaction of two or more chemicals that results in an effect that is greater than the sum of their effects taken independently.

Teratogen Any substance capable of producing non-heritable structural abnormalities of prenatal origin.

Tertile Value used to divide a set of data into three equal parts each having the same number of observations.

Vector An animal, usually an insect or tick, that transmits parasitic micro-organisms and therefore the diseases they cause, from person to person or from infected animals to humans. For example, mosquitos are vectors for malaria, filariasis and yellow fever.

Authors and contributors

Editors

Miriam N. Jacobs, anthropologist, nutritionist and toxicologist. School of Biomedical and Life Sciences, University of Surrey, Guildford, Surrey; and Royal Veterinary College, University of London. (mjacobs@rvc.ac.uk)

Barbara Dinham, director, Pesticide Action Network, UK. (barbaradinham@pan-uk.org)

Introduction

Marion Moses, MD, founder of the Pesticide Education Center, San Francisco.

Part I

Daisy Dharmaraj, physician and director of PREPARE, Madras. India. (prepare@md2.vsnl.net.in)

Nasira Habib, founder of Khoj Research and Publication Centre, working with rural women since 1991, Lahore, Pakistan. (nasira@brain.net.pk)

Marian J.H. Hulshof, agronomist, freelance journalist, the Netherlands, previously associate expert on agricultural extension, AGRHYMET Regional Centre, Niamey, Niger (rolamari@wanadoo.nl)

Sheila Jayaprakash, lawyer and activist working on domestic violence, board member of PREPARE, India. (sheilajayaprakash@yahoo.com)

Sam L.J. Page, Senior Advisor, African Farmers' Organic Research and Training (AfFOResT), Zimbabwe and UK.

(sampage_zim@yahoo.co.uk)

Margaret Reeves, Staff Scientist, Pesticide Action Network North America, San Francisco. (mreeves@igc.apc.org)

Lucy Rosas, when preparing this paper, staff attorney and program director, Líderes Campesinas, now a trial attorney, Equal Employment Opportunities Commission.

Sankung B. Sagnia, entomologist, Head of the Training Major Programme, AGRHYMET Regional Centre, Niamey, Niger. (sankung@sahel.agrhymet.ne)

Seynabou Sissoko, Information Specialist, PAN Africa Regional Centre, Dakar, Senegal. (seynabousissoko@pan-africa.sn)

Abou Thiam, Co-ordinator of PAN Africa Regional Centre and Doctor in Environmental Science at Cheikh Anta Diop University of Dakar, Senegal. (abouthiam@pan-africa.sn)

Simplice Davo Vodouhe, Coordinator, Organisation Béninoise pour le Promotion d'Agriculture Biologique, and Rural Extension Lecturer at the Université d'Abomey, Calavi, Benin. (obepab@intnet.bj)

Catharina Wesseling, Professor, Central American Institute for Studies on Toxic Substances (IRET), Universidad Nacional, Heredia, Costa Rica. (ineke_wesseling@yahoo.com)

Part II

Zarema Amirova, Environmental Research Centre of the Republic Bashkortostan (BREC), Russia. (ecocnt@diaspro.com)

Nida Besbelli, Project Leader of the Epidemiology of Pesticide Poisoning, Harmonized Collection of Data on Human Pesticide Exposures, International Programme on Chemical Safety, WHO, Geneva. (besbellin@who.ch)

Ordias Chikuni, Medical School, Department of Clinical Pharmacology, Harare, Zimbabwe.

Carissa Diaquino, National Poison Control and Information Service, Philippines. (carissa@pacific.net.ph)

L. Wayne Dwernychuk, PhD, RP Bio, Vice-President and Principal, Hatfield Consultants (environmental investigators), West Vancouver, Canada. (wdwernychuk@hatfieldgroup.com)

Ravindra Fernando, Professor of Forensic Medicine and Toxicology, University of Colombo, and Head, National Poisons Information Centre, National Hospital of Sri Lanka.

(ravindrafernando@hotmail.com)

Dieter Flesch-Janys, Epidemiology Working Group, Ministry of Work, Health and Social Affairs and Institute for Mathematics and Computer Science in Medicine, University Hospital Eppendorf, Hamburg. (flesch@uke.uni-hamburg.de)

Ana M. García, Department of Public Health, University of Valencia. (anagar@uv.es)

Lennart Hardell, MD, PhD, Professor, Department of Oncology, University Hospital, Orebro, Sweden. (lennart.hardell@orebroll.se)

David F.V. Lewis, Reader in Molecular Toxicology, School of Biomedical and Life Sciences, University of Surrey. (d.lewis@surrey.ac.uk)

John McLaren Howard, Laboratory Director, Biolab Medical Unit, London.

Lucia Miligi, DSc., Environmental and Occupational Epidemiology Unit, Center for Study and Prevention of Cancer, Istituto Scientifico della Regione Toscana, Florence. (l.miligi@cspo.it)

Anuschka Polder, Norwegian School of Veterinary Science, Department of Pharmacology, Microbiology and Food Hygiene, Oslo. (anuschka.polder@veths.no)

Jenny Pronczuk de Garbino, clinical toxicologist and Medical Officer at the World Health Organisation, leading Task Force on the Protection of Children's Environmental Health, Geneva.

(pronczukj@who.ch)

Mike Ruse, previously responsible for International Programme on Chemical Safety INTOX Programme, World Health Organization, now at Warwick and Leicester Universities.

Laura Settimi, DSc, Laboratorio di Igiene Ambientale, Istituto Superiore di Sanita, Rome. (settimi@iss.it)

Sung-Il Cho, MD, ScD, Department of Epidemiology, Seoul National University School of Public Health, Korea. (scho@snu.ac.kr)

Xiping Xu, MD, PhD, Department of Environmental Health, Harvard School of Public Health, USA. (xu@hsph.harvard.edu)

Part III

Leslie London, Associate Professor, Department of Public Health and Primary Health Care and Associate Director of the Occupational and Environmental Health Research Unit, University of Cape Town. (LL@anat.uct.ac.za)

Hanna-Andrea Rother, Chief Scientific Officer, Occupational and Environmental Health Research Unit, Department of Public Health and Primary Health Care, University of Cape Town Medical School.

David Watt, chartered building surveyor, Senior Research Fellow, Centre for Conservation Studies, Leicester School of Architecture, De Montfort University, Leicester. (dswatt@dmu.ac.uk)

Andrew Watterson, Professor and Co-ordinator of the Occupational and Environmental Health Research Group, University of Stirling. (a.e.watterson@stir.ac.uk)

Jenny Watterson, health professional in the National Health Service researching mother and children issues, Scotland.

Meriel A. Watts, PhD, when preparing this paper, Director of the Soil & Health Association of NZ Inc, New Zealand. (m.watts@organicnz.pl.net)

Part IV

Kerry Albright, Natural Resources Institute, University of Greenwich, Kent, UK.

Jill Day, Regional Women's Officer, UNISON public service trade union, UK. (j.day@unison.co.uk)

Topsy Jewel, project co-ordinator, Common Cause Cooperative, Lewes, UK. (comcause@element.u-net.com)

Adrienne Martin, Leader, Livelihoods and Institutions Group, Natural Resources Institute, University of Greenwich, Kent, UK. (A.M.Martin@gre.ac.uk)

John Pontius, Consultant to the FAO Community IPM Programme, Indonesia. (www.communityipm.org)

Sarogeni Rengam, Executive Director, Pesticide Action Network Asia and the Pacific Region, Malaysia. (panap@panap.po.my)

Satinath Sarangi, Bhopal activist, and Coordinator, Sambhavna Trust and Bhopal People's Health and Documentation Centre, Bhopal. (sambavna@bom6.vsnl.net.in)

Alifah Sri Lestari, Consultant to the FAO Community IPM Programme, Indonesia. (www.communityipm.org)

Stephanie Williamson, International Project Officer, Pesticide Action Network UK. (stephaniewilliamson@pan-uk.org)

Index